Communism

2nd Edition

Communism
The Story of the Idea and Its Implementation

James R. Ozinga
Oakland University

PRENTICE HALL, Englewood Cliffs, N.J. 07632

Library of Congress Cataloging-in-Publication Data

Ozinga, James R.
   Communism : the story of the idea and its implementation / James
R. Ozinga.—2nd ed.
      p.   cm.
   Includes bibliographical references and index.
   ISBN 0-13-171125-3
   1. Communism—History.   I. Title.
HX36.O94   1991   90-44781
335.43′ 09—dc20   CIP

Editorial/production supervision and
   interior design: Barbara Reilly
Cover design: L. Manley
Prepress buyer: Debra Kesar
Manufacturing buyer: Mary Ann Gloriande
Maps and drawings: Kurt S. Ozinga

Drawings on pp. 111, 166, and 194 based on photos courtesy of Wide
World Photos, Inc.

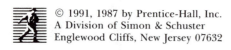

© 1991, 1987 by Prentice-Hall, Inc.
A Division of Simon & Schuster
Englewood Cliffs, New Jersey 07632

Printed in the United States of America
10 9 8 7 6 5 4 3 2 1

ISBN 0-13-171125-3

Prentice-Hall International (UK) Limited, *London*
Prentice-Hall of Australia Pty. Limited, *Sydney*
Prentice-Hall Canada Inc., *Toronto*
Prentice-Hall Hispanoamericana, S.A., *Mexico*
Prentice-Hall of India Private Limited, *New Delhi*
Prentice-Hall of Japan, Inc., *Tokyo*
Simon & Schuster Asia Pte. Ltd., *Singapore*
Editora Prentice-Hall do Brasil, Ltda., *Rio de Janeiro*

For Heidi Lisette Ziegenmeyer

Contents

Maps

Preface

Communism is a complicated subject, involving many different academic fields and geographical areas. A book that covers the whole range of material from philosophy, history, comparative political systems, economics, international relations, futurism, and even theology runs the risk of oversimplification as well as leaving out what specialists feel are significant items.

Alternatives to the one-author, total-coverage approach are many books on narrow subjects, or collections of essays written by many different authors from the perspectives of their specialties. What is gained by the multi-authored book or by several books, however, is diminished considerably by overlaps, gaps, and differences in the authors' styles and emphases. In a single-author book such as this one, despite the risks, all of the presented material is filtered through only one mind and written in a single style so that the entire recent history of communism emerges as a single, unfolding story with many different dimensions.

Moreover, the book is written in such a way that anyone with an interest in learning about communism should be able to do so without extensive earlier preparation. The book is intended for college-age men and women with no specific background in the subject and seeks to communicate a story to those who do not already know it but wish to learn. To assist that communication, chapters are divided into sections, summaries are provided after each section, and an Afterword is provided at the end of each chapter to make transitions easier to follow from one level to the next. Many of the endnotes provide additional explanations. Discussion questions occur after each chapter. In addition, key words or ideas that are explained in the glossary are shown in boldface print in the text when they first appear. Finally, the index is as thorough as careful attention can make it. Everything possible has been done to facilitate communication. This book is not a test of superior intellectual skill, but a common sense attempt to teach a complicated subject to as many people as possible.

The first edition was published in 1987, well before the momentous changes in 1989 and 1990. This second edition clarifies the conflicts present during early implementations of Marxism and includes the new parts of the story—not just in Europe but in Latin America, Africa, and Asia as well. I have also added a final chapter on the future of communism that seeks to describe rather than predict. Although weakened, communism is not yet history; it is *in esse* rather than *in extremis*.

I am grateful to the Hoover Institution on War, Revolution, and Peace for research support, and to the numerous people who read and commented on the manuscript of the first edition: area experts, professional educators, students, my wife, my children, and individuals with little formal education. Reviewers of the second edition who helped to shape the final product were Daniel L. Burghart of the U.S. Military Academy at West Point, Larry Elowitz of Georgia College, Richard Gripp of San Diego State University, and Joseph Nyomarkay of the University of Southern California. My thanks to all of you.

James R. Ozinga
Oakland University

Communism

Introduction

The term *communism* frightens people. Instead of connoting community sharing and happy cooperation, the word suggests terrorism, gulags, and Soviet
activities designed to embarrass or damage the Western world. For a great
many Americans, communism has come to mean the *other* side, particularly
after the onset of the cold war between the USSR and the United States. When
communist is used to describe someone in the United States, it is usually a
strongly negative commentary on that person's views and implies that the
person is un-American in some way.

A negative response to communism, however, is by no means the only
reaction. The idea of communism has had a long history—much of it before
Karl Marx in the nineteenth century—and sometimes the response to the
idea was positive. For example, prehistoric peoples seemed to live
communistically—social sharing was a dominant characteristic of their
simpler societies. In addition, about four hundred years before Christ, Plato
speculated in *The Republic* that communism among his philosopher kings
and queens would help protect them against the corruptive influences of
money and greed and help them rule for the good of the whole. In the sixteenth century, Sir Thomas More's fictional account of *Utopia* had the island
people happily living in communism, suggesting once again that concern

for the social whole and community sharing was a higher way of life than the materialism and fractious politics of his own day in England and Europe.

The contrast of the idyllic, sharing community with the competitive, acquisitive character of everyday society, has long made communism appear to be a desirable if nearly impossible goal that has appealed to a great many people. The success of utopian novels testified to that popular appeal.[1] Communism to many people became synonomous with idyllic living—a sort of heaven on earth that one can dream about even if it isn't very realistic or practical—but representing, nonetheless, a goal toward which societies could aspire. People who believed that history constantly and gradually progresses from lower to higher forms of social organization found it simple to imagine a communistic future that would naturally emerge from history's evolving.

As a result, when the Bolsheviks took control of Russia in 1917 and for the first time established a state dedicated to the ideals of communism, many *Western* intellectuals felt strongly that the new experiments in the USSR were the progressive wave of the future. Some travelled to the Soviet Union and saw both what they wanted to see and what they were intended to see. These very positive views of the Soviet Union, detailed in Paul Hollander's *Political Pilgrims,*[2] disintegrated just before World War II, only to be replaced in the 1960s and early 1970s by admiration for Mao's China or Castro's Cuba.

A neutral attitude toward communism is possible as well. This view, which neither accepts nor rejects communism, is indifferent to the ideological basis of another society, just as you might ignore a neighbor's different religion. The important thing about a neighbor, in your review, would be how he or she behaves in your relationship regardless of the religious basis underlying this behavior. Similarly, many people view the USSR, China, or other communist states as potential trading partners wherein the important thing is not the ideology, but investment potential, financial stability, and size of the market.

However, the negative view of communism has been more common in history because attempts to establish some form of communism have normally involved attacks on the existing political and economic culture. For examples, think of the German peasant revolts in 1524–1525 and Gerrard Winstanley's small group of Diggers or True Levellers in the middle of England's chaotic seventeenth century, which the establishments of those times saw as serious challenges to their power. A modern anticommunist perspective similarly views socialism or communism as a threat to the preferred, established way of life. Because in modern times the ideology has the power of a state behind it, it is often difficult for people to distinguish between the two—whether, for example, one's hostility is directed against the Soviet Union as a world power, against its alleged communism, or both.

When either pro- or anticommunist beliefs become strongly held, it is difficult to discuss the matter rationally. People wearing ideological blinders see what they wish to see. They value what supports their side of the issue and ridicule opposing arguments. In these circumstances asking questions or simply carrying this book is suspicious.

Communism is a controversial subject wherein objectivity is understandably difficult, a bit rare, and often taken by the already convinced as weakness. A sympathy expressed for *some* aspects of communism is often taken as support for the whole; conversely, a preference for an Adam Smith sort of consumer sovereignty in the market, rather than central economic planning, is imagined to be an apology for the whole of capitalism. Only two sides seem possible. In reality, however, *there aren't just two sides—the pro and the con*. It is quite possible to seek simply to understand without the constant need to condemn or support either "side."

As we approach the twenty-first century it seems increasingly obvious that the "other side" and the "we versus them" attitudes are not only quite outdated and irrelevant but are positions that stand in the way of necessary solutions to global problems. The reduction of the shrillness of ideological combat through a quiet understanding of *both* sides may be labelled naive by ideologues, but it is the necessary prerequisite for a life of greater peace and harmony among different peoples in the world our children and grandchildren will inherit.

NOTES

1.   See for example James Harrington's *Oceana*, Etienne Cabet's *Journey to Icaria*, and Edward Bellamy's *Looking Backward* and *Equality*. Almost any library would have copies. In addition, an excellent source of information on utopia-making throughout history is Frank and Fritzie Manuel, *Utopian Thought in the Western World* (Cambridge, Mass.: Harvard University Press, 1979).

2.   Paul Hollander, *Political Pilgrims: Travels of Western Intellectuals to the Soviet Union, China, and Cuba, 1928–1978* (New York: Oxford University Press, 1981).

1

The Background of Marxism

The story of contemporary communism begins with Karl Marx (1818–1883), whose youth and early adulthood were spent in the Germanic area during the first half of the nineteenth century. Three factors, which Marx would eventually pull together as he developed intellectually, dominated the intellectual climate of the time: the excitement and economic changes caused by the Industrial Revolution: a French socialism, which grew out of the frustrations of egalitarians who saw the French Revolution as incomplete; and the philosophy known as Hegelianism.

Karl Marx grew up in an area exposed to each of these factors. His birthplace, Trier (Treves), was a city of about twelve thousand people located in the Moselle valley. The Industrial Revolution was moving in an eastward direction from Great Britain where it had begun, and Trier's location in the western or Rhineland portion of the still rather medieval Germanic area caused it to feel the impact of economic change well before Berlin and Prussia did. Consequently, impulses toward industrialization and modernization were experienced more strongly there than in the rest of the German area. In addition, Trier's location made it open to French influences in an interesting way. In 1818, when Marx was born, Trier was some twenty miles from the French border, although the city had been a part of France from 1794 to 1814. Thus, Trier was more deeply affected by the French Revolution and later, by French socialism than its German location in 1818 would indicate. Furthermore, the University of Berlin, which Marx began attending in 1836, had been deeply influenced by the historical and philosophical teaching of Professor Georg W. F. Hegel, who had died just five years earlier. Marx's interest in history and philosophy made it impossible for him to avoid the Hegelian philosophy and the interpretations of Hegel by his colleagues and friends.

Because comprehending these three major influences will make it easier to understand the gradual development of Marx's ideas and to grasp the system of thought known as Marxism, let us examine each of them in more detail.

INDUSTRIAL REVOLUTION

The Industrial Revolution began in Britain around 1780. The date is rather arbitrary and the word *revolution* is a bit exaggerated, for it did not happen in a brief, tumultuous fashion, but emerged over time as water power phased into steam power, and decentralized or cottage industries evolved into the factory system.

These changes occurred in Britain because several elements were present there at the same time. Energy from coal was available from deeper seams because of the newly improved steam engines which could pump water out of the coal mines as well as drive machinery in factories. Patent laws deliberately encouraged a climate of inventiveness by ensuring rich financial reward and this resulted in a technological explosion as innovations in the textile industry spread into other areas. Steam power for land transportation led to railroads, which in turn led to the development and use of stronger metals like iron and steel. Capitalized agriculture or farming to provide a sellable surplus was already very visible, most notably in wool production. This helped the textile industry expand and, as subsistence agriculture declined, created a supply of surplus laborers. The worldwide British empire provided both a source of raw materials and a market where finished products could be sold with little competition. The fact that Britain was an island made international transportation easier, while ample rivers permitted an easy internal movement of goods. Sufficient money was available for investments (risk capital). All these essential ingredients had come together around 1780 to bring about the dramatic change in the British economy.

The Industrial Revolution brought about a tremendous alteration in the life-style of most British families. A great many more goods, which would eventually raise the standard of living for all of the population, were being produced by the new industries. However, as the novels of Charles Dickens revealed, in the early 1800s the working **class** did not seem to benefit at all. The workers' cottages were in the lowest, dampest, and worst sections of the city, and each house usually had several families living in one or two rooms. Although disease was rampant, medical care was expensive and often not sought. Workers and their families may not have been worse off than they had been before in the rural areas, but in the countryside their poverty, their wastes, and their diseases were scattered instead of concentrated. In the rural areas they may not have had more income or more food but they did see the light of day, work outdoors, and hedge against hard times by tilling a small garden. In the cities the rhythms were not the seasons and the rising and setting of the sun, but the needs of machines and the factory foreman. The factory shift started and ended in darkness, interior ventilation was extremely poor, and women and children were often preferred by employers because they could be paid even less than the pittance paid to males. The lives of entire families centered around the factory from very early in the morning until evening. Breaks in the day for meals or any other purpose were very grudgingly given. Those who complained were fired. Hunger and malnutrition were common. And this described the good times.

The bad times were the eras of industrial crises when people lost their jobs. This brought about increased pauperization or an often futile return to the countryside where anticipated relief could not be obtained because capitalized agriculture and the Enclosure Acts had reduced available land. Bad times caused banditry, which resulted in prison sentences, begging, prostitution, the work farm, abandoned children, and overpopulated poorhouses.[1] The workers were almost entirely uneducated and illiterate. They didn't have the right to vote, and, if they tried to strike, they were soon forced to join other comrades in the terrible prisons. Life in the poorly lit, crowded, and seldom policed working-class sections of the city was barely endurable.

Usually over half of a worker's income went to purchase food. Life expectancy was very low. In the rural areas, on average the wealthy lived until they were fifty-two years old, while the poor averaged only thirty-eight years. In nineteenth-century Manchester, one of the industrial cities, things were worse: on average the wealthy lived thirty-eight years whereas the workers had a life expectancy of seventeen years![2] Those who survived to age six could begin working in the factory, and life in the factory was the only hope of continuing survival.

The plight of the working class had three decisive consequences, none of which is entirely exclusive of the others. The first was a developing humanitarian concern with the condition of the working class that sought to broaden the existing laws designed to help the poor in order to benefit the new **proletariat** (industrial working class). England had had laws that provided some relief for the poor since the time of Elizabeth I in the 1500s, but they referred more to earlier, rural times. The desire to change this—to help the industrial working poor—gradually found expression in acts passed by Parliament in 1802, 1819, 1825, and 1833. The most important of these was the Factory Act of 1833.

This act provided that children under nine were no longer to be employed in the factories. Children between the ages of nine and thirteen could work no more than forty-eight hours per week and must receive two hours of schooling per day. Those between the ages of thirteen and eighteen were prohibited from working more than sixty-eight hours per week.[3] The act applied only to the large textile industries, and it was poorly implemented and enforced. Although it would take subsequent laws and the passage of decades before real reform was clearly visible, this legislation was an advance at a time when any step, however small, was an incredible improvement.

A second consequence of the workers' conditions was the beginnings of organized union activity. Initially prohibited as a result of fears of worker unrest encouraged by the French Revolution, labor unions became legal in 1825. But the law that gave them life was not intended to give them effective life. When unions moved beyond the strictly local level, they met strong opposition. For example, an attempt was made in 1830 to bring all the small unions together into one large Grand National Consolidated Trades Union. When workers formed subunits of this new union, they were promptly arrested and sentenced to seven years in prison. The Grand National quickly dissolved.[4] In 1838, the labor struggle became political in the form of the Chartist movement, so-called because it presented its demands by means of a charter. Its goals were, among other things, universal suffrage, the secret ballot, and the payment of members of Parliament so that those who weren't wealthy could run for office. These mild demands appeared revolutionary at that time. Over a million signatures were gathered in support of the Charter, and this success helped bring about intense opposition from established interests. Due to this pressure, by 1848 the movement was no longer an active force for change.

A third consequence of the plight of the working class was the development of British socialism. One of the people behind the Grand National movement was Robert Owen, a factory owner concerned about his own workers. As a socialist, Owen improved conditions for his own laborers by improving conditions within his factories, providing decent housing, and by insisting on education for the children of his workers. Owen wanted his ideas to become the model for British industry but he had great difficulty in getting the necessary legislation passed by successive parliaments. His frustrations made him more distinctly socialist; however, Owen's socialism was reformist or nonrevolutionary. He wanted to achieve socialism by the gradual passage and enforcement of new laws—by *using* the government rather than by *overthrowing* it. This reformism would characterize British socialism throughout the nineteenth century, but it *was* socialism—workers through their **cooperatives** would become the joint owners of the production process.

The 1820s and 1830s also saw a more theoretical socialism emerge from a group called the *Ricardian* socialists. Following a concept articulated by both John Locke and Adam Smith that labor created wealth, this group of economists argued that, since the workers created the values of the commodities they produced, the workers should get all the rewards, including the profits. Workers produced the wealth, and that wealth belonged to them rather than to the owners of the factories. This sort of thinking enjoyed a brief heyday and much Owenite thinking blended with that of the Ricardian socialists, but it made little impression on the developing capitalist system.

The Industrial Revolution—centralized factories, urban concentrations, rational and efficient new ways of organizing the productive system, and the push toward continuing, creative investments—spread from England to Belgium and France in the early nineteenth century and soon penetrated the Germanic areas from the west. Most intellectuals saw the new industrial methods as a beneficial and progressive wave of the future, while politicians and monarchs sensed a means of simultaneously increasing both their country's military strength and its general economic health. In the path of that seemingly irresistible movement from west to east lay the Rhineland where Karl Marx was born.

For an area like the Germanic, still quite medieval, the biggest barriers to the new economics were the tariff and tax laws that each little community maintained. Growth in trade and real economies of scale were made nearly impossible by these laws. But already in 1833, when Karl Marx was just fifteen years old, the *Zollverein,* or Customs Union, had been established, which reduced these parochial impediments in large parts of the Germanic area. By 1852, this Customs Union had spread over most of the country. In other words, before the area was politically unified (1871), an economic unity was created by the needs of industrial capitalism to have raw materials, labor, and markets unfettered by local taxes or tariffs that had been in place since the Middle Ages. Marx grew up in the midst of these changes.

*   *   *

The Industrial Revolution was profoundly influential because as new, central factory methods of production were introduced, great changes were brought about in the way people lived their lives. Broadly speaking, the major change was from a rural, agrarian to an urban, industrial way of life. In the process, concentrated poverty among the working classes (proletariat) became a social problem of some magnitude, in part because this pauperization occurred in a context of vastly improved **commodity production**. The obvious dilemma of the working class created at least three attempted solutions: (1) parliamentary concern expressed in the Factory Acts, (2) the slow growth of labor unions to give the proletariat a better edge when dealing with

Map 1 Western Europe 1850

bourgeois employers, and (3) the development of a reformist socialism, which would gradually improve the workers' position by giving them a greater share of the values they had themselves created.

FRENCH SOCIALISM

The French Revolution of 1789 affected the rest of Europe for several decades into the nineteenth century. One reason, of course, was the conquest of Europe by Napoleon Bonaparte, which had the effect of spreading French revolutionary ideas. In addition, the revolution impressed intellectuals of other areas as a progressive political event needed in their own country to clear the way for the desired industrialization. Many people, including Marx, thought that the political aspects of the French Revolution would come to other, less advanced areas. After all, England's political revolution had taken place in the 1600s and industrialization had followed it in the next century. France had had a late-eighteenth-century revolution, and industrialization had followed in its wake. Thus, it seemed that a liberating political revolution would soon come for the Germanic area, along with the early signs of the new industrialization. The more evidence of *German* industrialization there was, the more obviously immediate was the coming political upheaval. A revolutionary excitement existed, therefore, no matter how mistaken that attitude later proved to be.

In addition, this hoped-for progress had a decided socialist-communist[5] tinge that was vague enough to be mixed up with all sorts of other revolutionary hopes—for a greater degree of democracy that did without the monarchy, for removal of medieval barriers to peasant and female mobility in the economic and political system, for improvements in workers' conditions of life, and for the great progress in people's rational thinking that would occur when the masses were universally educated. These liberal hopes were articulated in the context of the vague socialism that emanated from France after the revolution had subsided—a socialism that was born out of the frustrated need to reenergize a revolutionary pendulum that had stopped moving toward full human equality.

The 1789 revolution had been a most exciting time: evolution of a new social system seemed to take only weeks rather than centuries and, for a time, it appeared that real liberty, real equality, and real fraternity were attainable. The king was arrested and executed, a new republic was formed, new constitutions rapidly replaced the old, and hopes generally ran high. But the Jacobin Reign of Terror (1793–1794) was followed by a conservative reaction. Those people who in 1795 had genuinely hoped for greater equality in their political systems felt betrayed by the new conservative governments. To them the revolution had been aborted in midlife, and the conservatives were damming up the revolutionary flow. In 1796, people who wanted to complete the revolution by confiscating all wealth and by generalizing equality attempted a coup d'état. This group called itself the Conspiracy of the Equals and was led by Francois Noel **Babeuf**. The coup attempt failed, Babeuf was arrested, and his Conspiracy of the Equals group had to disband.

Babeuf, rather than Karl Marx, is considered the father of European socialism or communism because he was the first clear advocate of the *abolition* of **private property** rather than a better *distribution* of that property. Babeuf argued in his *Manifesto of the Equals* that the urban and rural poor should seize the power of the state, dispossess the rich, and make property communal rather than private. In other words, this socialism, unlike that developing in Britain, was squarely placed in a revolutionary context. The state had to be overthrown so that consumption could be socialized by placing the fruit of every person's work in a common store from which all could draw according to their needs. As long as the cause of the problem, private property, was still around, this could not be done piecemeal. Private property, Babeuf argued, had created masters and slaves, and it must be destroyed rather than equalized in order to move beyond master-slave relationships to brotherhood and sisterhood. The creation of communal property would teach everyone, he felt, that *no one* could ever become richer or more powerful than one's fellow equals, and would assure to all as much sustenance as they needed, but no more.

Babeuf called for absolute equality with no equivocations. If something could not be divided up equally, it should be prohibited—not even made or grown. His communism tolerated *no* distinctions between people and contemptuously rejected any milder versions of equality. Babeuf was executed in 1797, but his ideas were preserved by one of his group, an Italian named Philippe Buonarrotti, who transmitted his theory to the revolutionary liberals of the early nineteenth century. In the process Buonarrotti, without a thought of any potential difficulties involved, turned Babeuf's *agrarian* socialism into an *industrial* communism that seemed to fit the changing economic scene better.[6] Remember this small fact when questions are later raised about why Marxism's success has been in societies more agrarian than industrial.

Although Babeuf's ideas were the major thrust behind French socialism or communism, Paris of the early nineteenth century became the European melting pot for many other radical ideas—some fairly mild, some rather strange, and some quite extreme. They ranged from the unusual socialism of the disciples of Saint-Simon, to the anarcho-syndicalism of Proudhon and Flora Tristan, and to the unabashed preference for violence in the camp of Louis Auguste **Blanqui**. These different ideas and leaders were united by their demand for radical redistribution of wealth and separated by their own inability to tolerate each other, which allowed apparently minor differences to assume major proportions. Such an inability to tolerate ambiguity is a characteristic of the ideological person; as with the angry father who tells his son or daughter "my way or the highway," it is a belief in the absolute rightness of one's own position that makes all other thinking seem wrong.

Between 1827 and 1871, Paris became a volatile city to govern, erupt-
ing into frequent insurrections and protests. A strong part of the radical
unrest was French socialism. This revolutionary activity and radical thinking crossed the new borders with the Rhineland and became a part of west
German liberalism.

*   *   *

Because the French Revolution did not go beyond liberty (repub-
licanism) and fraternity (nationalism) to the equality that many radicals expected, some, like Babeuf, pushed for absolute equality made possible by
the destruction of private property through revolutionary violence. Among
the milder forms of socialism some, like Saint-Simon's, were more gradualistic
and were cast in terms of a new golden age of technology that would benefit
both employers and workers. Others were more radical, including that of
the anarcho-syndicalists, who called for a society of labor without any political
authority, loosely coordinated by the trade unions which the French called
syndicats, and who believed that, because the French Revolution had not gone
far enough, *another* revolution was needed. A strong component of that
radical enthusiasm was a belief in the need for the abolition of private property. This made an antiproperty revolution appear to be the next progressive
step an evolving history would take. Karl Marx grew up very near to this
intellectual excitement.

HEGELIANISM

The important thing about Hegelianism is simply to understand it in broad
outlines. It may sound silly or utterly confusing, but the fact is that most
intelligent people are baffled the first time they encounter Hegelianism. One
does not have to agree with Hegel's philosophy in order to understand it.
In order to understand Marx's development, it is important to develop a
feeling for Hegel's philosophy and its interpretations by the left at the University of Berlin. Not to discuss this third factor, simply because it is difficult,
would be to provide only an incomplete picture of Marx's evolution.

Georg Wilhelm Friedrich Hegel (1770–1831) adhered to **idealism** in
the philosophic sense of that word; that is, he believed that *idea* was more
real than *matter,* and that material things were pale reflections of ideas. Normally today everyone believes just the opposite, and this difference makes
Hegel hard to comprehend right from the beginning. Imagine a small rock
that you can hold in your hand. You think of it as real because it is material—
it has weight, takes up space, can be measured, and so forth. A philosophical
idealist sees that rock differently. The rock is a collection of ideas like round-
ness, hardness, brownness, and smoothness. It is a rock *because these ideas have
come together* in that rockish way. Similarly, a rose is called a rose because

it reflects a number of ideas in a combination that we have learned to describe as roseness. To an idealist, physical things (matter) are reflections of an idea-reality. The ideas are separated from human brains or human consciousness and treated as though they have a separate life of their own. To show that separation, that abstraction from human thinking, the word is normally capitalized as Idea. Plato, another of the few idealists, even called them Divine Ideas. Hegel referred to this idea world as Reason, Spirit, or Idea.

Imagine for a moment, whether you are male or female, that you have taken the best qualities of all the women you have known or read about and built some sort of model woman out of all those qualities or ideas. Imagine further that you have begun to believe that this mental image or ideal woman actually exists in space somewhere as a standard against which flesh-and-blood women can be compared. Stop right here for a second. What you have done is taken qualities of real people and turned those attributes into a mental concept that you treat as though it were real. You feel that real women ought to measure up to the ideal standard, forgetting that this universal ideal standard has no real existence outside of your imagination.

In a loose way we do this sort of thing frequently—make up something and then treat "it" as though it really exists. But the word *existence* or *exists* is one we usually do not use carefully enough. Strictly and philosophically speaking, *exist* is a word that refers to material, measurable things that can be sensed by the human brain. Now the ideal woman you constructed a moment ago does not exist in that sense, but our minds are capable of making "her" exist in a different way, a nonprovable way, in our heads and projected as a universal concept.

If you treat that ideal woman as real, and treat flesh-and-blood women as *less* real because they are imperfect or not ideal, you are doing in a simple way what philosophical idealists do in a more complicated fashion. You have taken human qualities from real people and fashioned them into a concept that you treat as "more real" than the source of the abstraction. If you go further and give that ideal woman power to influence real events in the world, you have created a superhuman or divine idea and may even think of "her" as a god of some sort. The *gap* now felt between a real human woman and this "Woman" can be called **alienation** or a separation.

Hegel's ideal concept was Reason, and he thought that history was the march of that Reason through time. Hegel took real human reasoning abilities, just as you did with the best qualities of women, and elevated that abstraction, Reason, to the lofty position of a god. History was, Hegel thought, the unfolding of World Reason just as a Christian might think of history as an unfolding of God's plan or providence. At any rate, Hegel's concept made history a single, unfolding story of an evolving Idea called Absolute Reason or Spirit.

In treating history in such a way, Hegel created a gap or separation between real people and his newly created Absolute—a gap he called alienation—just as we did when we created the ideal woman. But Hegel did not realize that *he* had created the alienation by his abstracting; he believed that his abstraction, Reason, was *real,* and that the alienation or separation was a problem to be overcome by this World Reason rather than by the human who had done the abstracting. Alienation should not exist, Hegel felt, between humans and the Absolute Spirit or between people and spirit manifested in nature. So the goal of Reason's or Spirit's historical unfolding was to overcome alienation so that people would realize that *they* and nature and the Absolute *were all one.* This may sound strange but it is not that different from a Christian trying to become mystically in tune with, or even a part of, God. Hegel believed that, as history progressed through time, people would gradually come to see they were a part of (and not separate from) World Reason, and that a society or state permeated by that World Reason was one in which *rational* laws were self-created expressions of human reason. His concept of *freedom* involved people obeying the laws of their own creation—rational laws emerging from, or mystically a part of, World Reason. Becoming free meant becoming one with Spirit, and that, of course, meant overcoming alienation entirely.

As if these concepts were not complicated enough, Hegel believed that progress in history resulted from something he called **dialectics**—the simultaneous confrontation of opposites, which create a conflict that nature has to resolve. This idea is merely an expansion of a fairly simple phenomenon. One example might be the fact that, although we are alive, we are simultaneously "wearing out" or in the process of dying. Not a very pleasant thought, but living and dying, growth and decay, appear to coexist simultaneously. Conflict between the two forces is expressed as sickness and healing until the organism loses the ability to fight off decay. Another example would be the sudden awareness by a new bride that through marriage she has acquired a set of terrible in-laws whom she is supposed to respect even though she finds this impossible. This simultaneous confrontation of opposites often leads to a conflict that resolves the tension between the opposites. Hegel's dialectics, an important part of Marxism as well, taught that the forward motion of history (progress) was the result of conflicts trying to resolve the tensions created by simultaneous opposites.

The dialectical method explained progress or movement over time as forward motion or by ascribing names to the parts of the process that give a sense of dialectical meaning. The forward motion description comes from his *Encyclopedia.* His example is of a flower on a tree. First there is the branch and at the end of that branch a bud, which, when conditions are right, opens to reveal the flower within. At each stage there is a new feature, and the old has been left behind. Yet there is no point at which the bud becomes "not-branch," or the flower becomes "not-bud." This illustrates Hegel's statement, that in the dialectical process each previous element has been negated *but preserved.* The process transcends the past while preserving what is of enduring value in that past. Each successive stage derives its existence and its definition from that which preceded it. So the total dialectical process is a natural process achieved through the resolution of conflict caused by the simultaneous presence of contradictions, a progress that both transcends and preserves that which is left behind.

A second way of describing the dialectic is by giving parts of the process names. *Thesis* is in conflict with *antithesis* and this tension results in *synthesis*. Then the synthesis becomes a new thesis which meets a new antithesis requiring a still different synthesis. The forward movement would look something like this:

Thesis——Antithesis

Syn(thesis)——Antithesis

Syn(thesis)——Antithesis

Syn(thesis)——etc.

This is not good Hegelianism, but it normally helps make Hegelianism easier to understand. The progress in history to which Hegel referred has occurred as a result of the resolution of the dialectical tension—each synthesis was a step forward. This was how the World Reason or World Spirit (that ideal concept) "marched" or "unfolded" through historical time. The unfolding or development of World Spirit particularly occurred in human consciousness and was then reflected in the institutions and customs of the particular age. Hegel believed that all of this took place in three visible stages of world history: the Oriental stage, the Greco-Roman stage, and the Germanic stage (which referred to his own era) when all alienation could be resolved.

Presented graphically such a view of history would look something like this even though such a chart oversimplifies outrageously.

HEGEL'S VIEW OF HISTORY

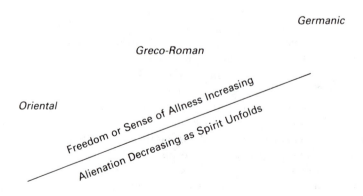

Why was this difficult philosophy important to the radical left in the early decades of the nineteenth century? For two reasons. First, because Hegel had assigned the working out of World Reason in human consciousness to *labor*—already a primary concern of the left in Europe because of the Industrial Revolution. As Hegel used the term, *labor* referred to the purposeful activity of people who were instruments of the World Spirit in furthering its own development. Those who labored were people who did the skilled, creative work. Throughout history labor transformed nature through human activity that progressively *humanized* the world and made it part of the *human* whole. Applying this notion to today's world, we might say that a parking lot or a set of tall buildings, for example, "humanizes" the former woods area and forces connections between nature and humans that were not there before. Today we might well be concerned that such "humanizations" have gone too far in the direction of distorting ecological balances, but this is a late-twentieth-century concern—not one shared by either Hegel or Marx.

To Hegel, in other words, it was labor that was changing the world—labor performed by those whom Hegel called "slaves" or "bondspersons"—even though the "masters" received the credit. For example, we say that the *Pharaohs* built the Pyramids even though we know that thousands of slaves actually did the work. The slaves in Hegel's historical scenario, however, would gradually recognize their ability and their power and, in time, would negate or overthrow their masters. True, this idea about labor—the tremendous importance of its role in history, and how the slaves would eventually transcend their masters—was couched in an obscure and difficult-to-understand philosophy. But nonetheless his idea fit in very well with that aspect of socialism that romanticized the proletariat as the "real people" and the agents of revolution in industrialized societies.

Second, both the philosophy and the view of history were attractive to the left because Hegel built his concept of progress on *change* and *conflict*. History was a long journey in stages, and, as World Reason unfolded, people would overcome their alienation. In this dialectical development progressive change came about through conflicts and even wars that played a major role in facilitating Reason's unfolding in human consciousness. Conflict, in other words, was not to be avoided, but deliberately sought so as to facilitate Reason's progress. All this supposedly culminated in a sense of total freedom linked to obedience to the rational laws of "one's own making."[7] Freedom was a goal of history, but Hegel meant freedom *within* the state—within an ideal rational state—a cultural unit that was a collective outgrowth of the developing World Reason. The state, according to Hegel, was a natural unit wherein common interests bonded people together, a conception Marx would repudiate in favor of "class" as the natural social unit (see Chapter 2). Later communists, such as those in the Soviet Union and elsewhere, would again find the state attractive, but that is to anticipate later chapters.[8] Hegel's philosophy provided a universal and intellectual rationale to radical criticisms and to revolutionary activities that they would not otherwise have had. Radical effort, it could be thought, was not self-serving; it was important to help *society* reach its own important goals.

Because the social goal of the German radicals who became known as *left-Hegelians* was a more rational, less traditional society, one of the first things they began to criticize was the Christian religion. Why? First, because to them Christianity was irrational; they could attack it in the name of reason. Second, because in criticizing Christianity they felt they were also attacking the state religion of Prussia, and in so doing attacking the irrational basis of the Prussian state. The official reception given to that religious criticism, understandably, was anything but kind. David Strauss, one of the left-Hegelians, created a storm of controversy with his book *The Life of Jesus* in 1835–1836. He claimed that Christ's supernatural actions and attributes came from the mythological projections of the eyewitnesses—they didn't *really* happen that way. Strauss felt that he was developing a more rational Gospel, but most readers felt that he was denying a critical and necessary component of the Christian beginning. They did not value the Hegelian rationality that Strauss and others offered.

Despite the criticism, or perhaps even because of it, a strong contingent of left-Hegelian philosophers (students and instructors) developed at the University of Berlin. Karl Marx attended this prestigious school in the capital of Prussia for several years and became a part of this left Hegelian group of radicals. The essence of their position was to criticize society for the good of society—to force the more rapid emergence of the inevitable progressive changes toward which Hegel had pointed and which society needed before true freedom under wholly rational laws could exist.

*   *   *

Hegel was a philosopher who argued that history represented an unfolding of Reason in time—an unfolding that took place in human consciousness. The development or progress of World Reason was dialectical and inevitable, the result of tensions between contradictory and conflicting elements that nature, not being able to stand the tension, forced to resolution. The goal of the whole historical story was to overcome alienation, understood basically as an unnatural separation between people and World Reason, as though if people could understand the rationality of the universe they would not be alienated. Human labor played an important role in the historical story; it transformed the world by humanizing it. The three stages of history culminated in the Germanic period of Hegel's own day in which, this belief assumed, full freedom (no alienation) was possible. The left-Hegelians criticized those elements of society that seemed to impede realization of that unalienated human consciousness, beginning with a critique of the Christian religion. Although this got them into trouble with the authorities, that only seemed to encourage them—as though the conflict they had generated was proof of the correctness of their position. Marx became a part of this movement.

AFTERWORD

This is the general background underlying the development of Marxism. How these three factors specifically affected Karl Marx's development is the story of the next chapter. Chronologically speaking, Marx first felt the influence of Hegelianism and its leftist interpretations at the University of Berlin, then moved to Paris where French socialism had an impact, and finally— influenced by Friedrich Engels and by French historians—determined to study the advanced economics of the country most influenced by the Industrial Revolution: Britain. All three factors intertwined in mature Marxism and became the basis for his own contributions.

NOTES

1. See E. P. Thompson, *The Making of the English Working Class* (New York: Pantheon Books, 1964).

2. Robert J. Goldstein, "Political Repression and Political Development: The 'Human Rights' Issue in Nineteenth Century Europe," *Comparative Social Research*, 4 (1981): 173–174.

3. See Friedrich Engels, *The Condition of the Working Class in England*, trans. W. O. Henderson and W. H. Chaloner, (Stanford, Calif.: Stanford University Press, 1958), p. 194, for details of the Factory Act of 1833.

4. George Lichtheim, *The Origins of Socialism* (New York: Praeger, 1969), p. 116. Also see David Caute, *The Left in Europe Since 1789* (New York: McGraw-Hill, 1966).

5. The words *socialism* and *communism* are used interchangeably in this and subsequent chapters. In the beginning there were few distinctions between the words. In a book, *Socialism and Communism in Contemporary France*, commissioned in the 1820s by the Prussian government to study this new phenomenon, Lorenz von Stein did distinguish between the two in the sense that communism was identified with the aspirations of the volatile French proletariat and was therefore something the government ought to watch carefully. Socialism, on the other hand, was considered to be a vague, leftist liberalism that did not represent a danger. In the *Communist Manifesto,* Marx used the term communism mainly because the group that sponsored the *Manifesto* had just renamed itself the Communist League. In his "Critique of the Gotha Program" written in 1875, Marx separated the terms socialism and communism by referring to socialism as the initial phase of the new society after the revolution wherein people would still be remunerated for work according to the amount of work they had performed. The final phase of the new socialism was called communism—people would be compensated according to need. Other than these distinctions, there really was not much difference between the two terms until Lenin and the Bolsheviks introduced the Third International in 1919. One of the conditions for membership in the Comintern, as it was called, was that parties rename themselves the Communist party of X country. This forced a separation in the ranks of world socialism—people had to choose whether to link up with Lenin's Bolsheviks or not. Those who did were thereafter called communists. Those who did not became known as socialists. Because the Comintern em-

phasized the need for revolutionary overthrow of capitalist governments and socialists tended to focus more on evolutionary change within government systems, the two words became quite separate in meaning from 1920 to the present. An example of the distinction is the difference between French socialists and French communists: the socialist government of President Francois Mitterand in the 1980s was distinctly separate from the French Communist party. The common, contemporary understanding of socialism as fairly mild and communism as revolutionary and more dangerous is, therefore, an interesting confirmation of Lorenz von Stein's 1820s analysis.

However, those countries ruled by communist parties are called communist countries even though the Soviet Union, for example, never attained the final phase of communism in Marx's terms (see Chapter 4). Until very recently, the Soviet position was that they were moving from socialism to a future communism. Since Gorbachev, however, the Soviet goal has not been communism but a redefined, market-oriented socialism. Confusion is almost inevitable. One has to develop a sense for the difference, and attribute different meanings to the words depending on who is doing the speaking or the writing. In this book, the term socialism can almost always be linked to communism. Exceptions to this understanding will be clearly indicated.

6.   See Lichtheim, *Origins of Socialism,* for a thorough description of the leading characters in this French drama on the left. The details reveal the complexity, the chaos, and the jealousies that pervaded the period.

7.   See Carl J. Friedrich, *The Philosophy of Hegel* (New York: Random House, 1954), particularly the selections from Hegel's *Phenomenology of the Spirit,* pp. 399–519. Also see Charles Taylor, *Hegel* (Cambridge, England: Cambridge University Press, 1977), particularly the overview in Chapter 1; and H. B. Acton, "Hegel, Georg Wilhelm Friedrich," in *Encyclopedia of Philosophy,* ed. Paul Edwards (New York: The Free Press, 1967), Vol. 3: 436, 443. Also see W. T. Stace, *The Philosophy of Hegel* (London: Dover Publications, 1955), for a less political interpretation of Hegel.

8.   Such communists in the 1990s are considered conservative or right-wing because they would prefer a strong, centralized state and economy. This "right" and "left" distinction comes up in a variety of places in this text, particularly in Chapter 5 and the discussion of the Second International. The terms "right" and "left," often used very loosely, refer back to the physical seating arrangements in the French National Assembly. The conservatives sat on the right of the presiding officer while the revolutionaries sat on the left. In subsequent history, these positions came to stand for political philosophies. The term *right wing* was used to describe those who favored conservative or reactionary political and economic programs, restrictions on the power of the masses, and oligarchical rule. Support of laissez-faire economics and strong executive powers also came to characterize the right, with extreme rightist positions supporting fascism. The term *left wing* was used to describe those who favored radical, sometimes revolutionary programs that gave more power to the masses, expanded democracy, and encouraged welfare-statism. Obviously each of these opposing positions can *themselves* have right and left wings if they are large enough, and the extreme right and extreme left seem to have few differences. Lenin was left wing in the Second International because he advocated revolution, but he became right wing after 1917 because he understandably became conservative about change and very protective with reference to the state. See Jack Plano, Milton Greenberg, Roy Olton, and Robert Riggs, *Political Science Dictionary* (Hinsdale, Ill.: The Dryden Press, 1973), pp. 220, 331.

DISCUSSION QUESTIONS

1.   What does it mean to say that idea is real while matter is less real? How does philosophic idealism differ from common language in calling someone idealistic?

2.   Hegel believed that history represented positive progress in a variety of ways. What developed or evolved? Explain.

3.   What factors came together in Great Britain around 1780 to cause the Industrial Revolution?

4. What general changes did the Industrial Revolution bring to countries that experienced it?
5. Describe the condition of the English working class in th early nineteenth century.
6. What responses were stimulated by the conditions of the working class in England?
7. What did Babeuf's Conspiracy of the Equals seek to accomplish in 1796?
8. How did Babeuf's ideas become so influential in French radical thought in the early nineteenth century?
9. What frustrations did radicals feel about the French Revolution's developments in the mid-1790s?
10. What did *dialectics* mean to Hegel and Marx?
11. What factors made Hegelianism attractive to the left?
12. Why did left-Hegelians criticize Christianity?

2

Karl Marx and the Development of Marxism

THE EARLY YEARS

Born into a relatively affluent Jewish family, Karl Marx enjoyed a pleasant youth, much of which was spent in the company of other children, and with the friendly von Westphalens next door. His teachers in the Trier *Gymnasium* demanded rigorous performance, and inspired in him **humanism**, the values of the Enlightenment, and ideals of service to society. At seventeen, Marx's life goals were sweeping in scope and hinted of his wish to save the world. Some six years later he would write that idealism is not an illusion but is the true reality.[1]

In the fall of 1835, when he was seventeen, Marx left home for the University of Bonn, located in the small city several miles to the northeast on the Rhine River. He was not a serious student, however, and his father insisted that Karl transfer to the more demanding atmosphere of the University of Berlin. While at Bonn he spent too much time writing poetry to Jenny von Westphalen back in Trier. At Berlin, a year later, he continued this poetry writing for a time. He wanted to become a great poet, but when he realized he simply did not have the talent to do so, he became intensely involved with legal studies and tried to make his mark in this field by writing a new history of law. He was an ambitious young man with a strong ego, who was out to influence the world right from the beginning of his university career. He tried in law as well as in poetry, but all he succeeded in doing was to make himself overtired and ill. He wrote his father that he was also struggling with philosophy instead of merely criticizing it in his romantic poetry as he had before.[2]

Actually he lacked a philosophy to hold together his history of law—a theory that would bind the various parts together in a coherent whole. Such a philosophy existed, however, in the form of Hegelianism, then in vogue at the University of Berlin. Although Karl Marx did not like it at first, he reluctantly came to accept it even though this meant that he was accepting someone else's theoretical framework. He wrote of his "conversion" to Hegelianism as being borne ". . . into the clutches of the enemy."[3] After having made the first step of acceptance, his second step was to master Hegelianism by studying it so thoroughly that he quickly became an expert.

However, his Hegelianism was deeply influenced by the left Hegelian interpretations followed by the group of university instructors and students at the University of Berlin. The group, called *Die Freien* (The Free Ones), and led by the brothers Bruno and Edgar Bauer, was the Berlin center of the young or left Hegelian movement. This group became Marx's "world" and his "university," and in a short time this ambitious young world-changer became one of the group's stars because he knew Hegel in such depth. Marx had a great capacity for absorbing new information, and such a capacity for believing that *his* version of things was right and others wrong that he soon achieved a reputation among the group as a ferocious critic.

Most of Marx's study was outside of class. He remained in Berlin for several years as a student, happily pursuing knowledge, secure in his place within The Free Ones, and confident that he and his friends would make a dramatic impact on the world of scholarship. But the world he was living in was an idea world that had very little practical application. Just as a modern college student might do very well spinning theories from a barstool and even become known as the local philosopher in the student center, such success—being a big frog in the small pond of local ideas—does not normally translate very well into the practical world in which most people live. In addition, such a parochial success gives an individual a stronger sense of confidence than might be wise. The idea world in which Karl Marx lived from 1836 to 1841 gave him that sense of intellectual leadership, but several events threw the cold water of reality on his philosophical theorizing.

First, one of his favorite professors at the university, Eduard Gans, had become a follower of French socialism and wrote approvingly of the socialist Saint-Simonians who described the continuing existence of slavery in the factories of the new economic era. Gans asked why these hundreds of emaciated and miserable men and women were sacrificing their health for the service and profit of the shop owner. Factory workers, he said, were exploited like animals and their only freedom was to die of hunger. Couldn't these miserable proletarians be awakened in order to accomplish progressive change?[4] Could Marx fit this proletarian cause into his philosophy of Reason's march through history and dialectical change? Why would he want to? It didn't seem appropriate at first.

A second intruding element was more personal: his father died in March of 1838. Heinrich Marx had been a major influence on his son, and after his death Karl began to have much weaker relations with his family in Trier. Karl seems to have felt that his family would financially support him indefinitely, but this was not to be the case. Within a few years after his father's death, his relations with his mother were strained—in large part because of Karl's continuing need for money from a family increasingly unwilling to subsidize him. They asked why Karl didn't go to work and support himself. An understandable question, but doing what? This problem came to a head in 1841 when he was twenty-three years old.

Just at that time reality intruded again. Marx found that he would be unable to get a university teaching position because The Free Ones' continuing critiques of religion were making Prussian authorities very hostile to them, and Marx was an active part of that movement. The group brought the conflict on themselves deliberately. In fairness to their common sense, they may have felt that, because the current Prussian Minister of Culture, who could influence academic appointments, was sympathetic to them, they didn't need to worry about future jobs. They didn't regard the hostility of other officials as a problem that would later hurt their chances. Moreover, they valued the conflict with political authorities as an expression of the dialectical tension that prefigured positive change. Their problems with the established powerholders encouraged them in the belief that they were *implementing* Hegelianism—helping to bring the philosophy of Hegel to real life in society. They convinced themselves that what they were doing was engaging in the critical activity they called *praxis:* informed, ruthless criticism of existing institutions so as to bring practical philosophy into concrete reality. By using their understanding of Hegelianism as the basis for their criticisms, they hoped to clarify and resolve contradictions in the *empirical* world that blocked the emergence of a philosophized society.[5]

In 1845, this atmosphere of criticism led Johann Kaspar Schmidt (Max Stirner) to write *The Ego and His Own,* a most individualistic denial of the state's right to exist at all. Marx's close friend, Bruno Bauer, who had just taken a teaching position in the *theology* department at the University of Bonn, was encouraged by that "praxis" atmosphere to attack Christianity, arguing that historically Christ had not existed at all. Bauer wanted to teach a "rational" sort of theology. This type of criticism, and Bauer's plans with Marx to establish a new journal of atheism that would bowl over the professors of theology at Bonn, had a decidedly negative impact on both men's chances for university employment. In 1840, the Prussian minister of Culture, who had been sympathetic to the ideas of Bruno Bauer, died. The new Minister,

Johann Eichhorn, wanted no part of the sort of praxis Bauer and Marx were talking about. Bauer lost his position as instructor at the University of Bonn where he had been hoping Marx would join him, and Marx lost any chance for an academic career under this new dispensation in Prussia or in Prussian-controlled areas such as the Rhineland.

The following year, in 1841, Marx received his doctoral degree in philosophy from the University of Jena, an older school just south of Prussia. Because the climate in Prussia under Minister of Culture Eichhorn (as well as under a new, more religious rector at the University of Berlin) had caused Marx to fear trouble over his degree at Berlin, he had sent his dissertation to Jena and was awarded the degree in absentia—a fairly common practice at the time.

*   *   *

Karl Marx came from a relatively well-to-do family of Jewish background and an educational system that stressed idealism and service to society. His first year of college at Bonn was a disaster according to his father. The University of Berlin, however, was a fateful choice because the move to Berlin exposed this young romanticist to left Hegelianism. Being the kind of person he was, Marx had to excel within the group. He achieved a reputation and developed ideas that would last a lifetime. The penchant for religious criticism of the left-Hegelians, which severely irritated most of the establishment, caused Marx to run afoul of the official who determined academic appointments and destroyed his chances for academic employment. He even felt it necessary to get his Ph.D. from the University of Jena, a school outside of Prussia. However, despite his controversial associations, Marx was not yet a revolutionary.

THE YOUNG DEVELOPING RADICAL

His student days were over but Marx did not yet know what he would do for a living. He wanted to marry Jenny von Westphalen, his Trier neighbor, but his mother had made clear that he couldn't rely on his family in Trier for support. So when an older member of his left Hegelian group, Arnold Ruge, asked Marx to write articles for his journal, the *Deutsche Jahrbuecher,* he quickly accepted. Ruge commissioned an article criticizing the new Prussian censorship laws. This helped Marx financially and showed him how he might use his education and skills outside a classroom. Marx wrote several articles on different subjects for *Deutsche Jahrbuecher,* but that particular journal never appeared. Ruge was forced to publish a new journal, *Anekdota,* out of Switzerland in which only one of Marx's articles appeared and that was the only issue of the new journal that was ever published. So, despite the prospect of supporting himself by writing left Hegelian social and political criticism, this work did not provide much income or employment.

Marx next worked as an editor of a newspaper in Cologne, but, after a few months, the Prussian government shut it down. While writing for the newspaper, Marx became aware of the socialism and communism that others had begun to advocate, but he did not yet accept such ideas as his own. To very careful readers of his editorials and articles, Marx might have seemed close to socialism, but Marx himself didn't appear aware of it. For example, he wrote that property and wealth caused an *externalization* of self in the things that were owned—as though something owned was a physical part of the owner, an extension of self. The issue was whether peasants who needed fuel could pick up dead, fallen wood in the forests owned by the wealthy. The owners objected strenuously, and they acted, Marx felt, as though the peasants were asking for the owners' arms and legs rather than the useless, ungathered fallen branches of thousands of trees. Beginning to pull away from Hegel's cherishing of the state, Marx wrote that such externalization of self into the objects owned was visible in the whole political system and resulted in Prussian legislators representing *property* rather than *people*.[6]

At this point, Marx was more liberal than socialist. He was trying, in a modest way so as not to offend government censors attached to the newspaper, to stress the need to overcome such externalizations that divided society. To Marx, the externalizations were artificial divisions or separations and were empirical examples of the alienation Hegel had sought to overcome. Although Marx was still more a philosopher than anything else, his job on the newspaper was forcing him to relate that philosophy to practical events. Actually, he felt negatively about the socialism he encountered at the time. After he had left Berlin, The Free Ones had become more radical—Bruno Bauer and the group were advocating socialism as the final answer to social problems. Marx wanted no part of this change. It irritated him when members of his former group sent him socialist-communist material to use in the newspaper. In November 1842, he wrote to Arnold Ruge that he considered the efforts of The Free Ones in Berlin to disguise socialist or communist dogmas in the theater criticisms they sent to the newspaper as inappropriate and unethical. Communism, he felt, required a different and thorough discussion if it were to be discussed at all.[7]

Marx *was* aware, however, that his increasingly negative view of the state, influenced perhaps by Max Stirner's ideas, as well as by his own difficulties in getting and keeping a decent job, was moving him away from Hegelianism that valued the *state* as the social collective in which human alienation would disappear. After he had lost the battle with the bureaucracy and the newspaper was shut down in early 1843, Marx came to grips with the philosophical issue by examining and criticizing Hegel's views on the state, although he still did not accept socialism as a description of his "new" views. Marx could not accept socialism-communism as the next stage in history simply because such a step would be desirable. History moves dialectically, Marx felt, through the resolution of conflicting opposites as the World Reason unfolds. The fact that communism seemed desirable was not enough, because it was not a *necessary* or an *inevitable* step in the steady march of Reason through history.

Marx's reluctance, however, was not shared by men like Friedrich Engels or Mikhail Bakunin. Although both of these men had also been left Hegelians, they became socialists before Marx and were very important in Marx's later life. Bakunin would go on to become a well-known proponent of socialist **anarchism** whose main difference from Marx would be his detestation of *any* authority in the future society. Many years later, this division between the two men would destroy the First International Workingmen's Association. Friedrich Engels also became a communist and after 1844 became Marx's closest friend, confidant, financial supporter, coauthor, and almost Marx's alter ego. Engels' father was a partner in Ermin and Engels, a textile firm, and Friedrich took over the running of the firm's offices in Britain in order to support himself as well as the Marx family. In addition, Engels' observations and conclusions about the working class in England were to be critically important in Marx's switch to revolutionary communism in 1843–1844.

In 1843, however, Marx, although increasingly antistate, still thought in Hegelian terms as he moved toward a more revolutionary position. His hostility to the state's representation of property interests rather than people was pushing his revolutionary development. He had become convinced that the only solution that made sense with respect to Prussia was a democratic or republican kind of revolution like the French Revolution in 1789. The Prussian monarchy, he wrote, operated on the principle of a despicable, dehumanized citizenry.[8]

What did he mean by "dehumanized" people? He meant people whose human essence had been torn from them, people who were forced to externalize themselves by projecting their human essence onto things external to them to which they gave their human powers. Critical in helping Marx make this distinction, which became a very important part of his philosophy, were the ideas of Ludwig Feuerbach, another member of the left Hegelian group.

In his 1841 critique of religion, *Essence of Christianity,* Feuerbach argued that people had created God rather than the other way around. We created God, Feuerbach felt, by projecting and externalizing finite *human* experience and then worshipping what we had fashioned out of ourselves. We made God out of our own best qualities and then treated our creation as though it were "other" or separate from us. In this way we externalized our own human essence and then acted as though this creation had power over us. In order to understand the essence of the Christian religion, Feuerbach argued, you have to reverse the order of the subject and predicate: instead of God creating humans, humans had created God. The deity was a predicate of humanity, and the rise of religion was a particular historical fact. The God-concept of that religion, however, was a projection of the human essence that people had abstracted from themselves. The essence of religion, said Feuerbach, was real people who *forgot that the source of the God was themselves* and foolishly worshipped their own creation as "other," as something external to them that had them in its power. Religion, in short, was a prime example of self-alienation or externalization. Religion was a *problem* rather than the *solution* that so many people made of it. This God-concept must be destroyed in order that people could regain their own lost human essence.

In an 1843 article, which appeared with Marx's article in Ruge's *Anekdota,* Feuerbach applied the same critique to the philosophy of Hegel. This German philosophy, he argued, represented the same abstraction of a limited, local feature of human experience, reason, into an absolute universal principle, called Reason, that Hegel imagined to be both real and powerful. Since this is nonsense, Feuerbach argued, it cannot be what Hegel meant. Hegel should be read differently by substituting the empirical word *human* for the idea abstraction *Spirit* in order to preserve the real truth in the Hegelian system. Feuerbach thought that Hegel had mistakenly mystified material reality with his theories, and had given an ideal quality to the empirical order that led to an uncritical acceptance of empirical evils.[9]

The same notion can be put another way. If you believe, for example, that poor people have their deserved rewards in heaven *after* this life is over, you don't worry too much about the poverty all about you. Your theory or your religion is mystifying or giving an ideal significance to empirical reality, which has the effect of discounting the need for any action to correct the problem. This was what Feuerbach was driving at; Hegel, by arguing that ideas were more real than material things, made ideas more important than material, empirical things, which allowed empirical evils (assuming poverty to be an evil for the moment) to go unchallenged. If you consider an ongoing, real conflict such as the religious struggle in Northern Ireland to be a pale reflection of Reason's struggle to overcome its alienation through human consciousness, you tend to take a relatively indifferent approach to which side is right. According to Hegelian theory, the right side will be the winning side. The theory encourages passivity. The important thing, Feuerbach argued, was to read Hegel "transformationally" to overcome this problem and make the idealist philosophy into a materialistic one so that *real* living, breathing people and *real* life conditions become more important than ideas about them.

During the summer of 1843, all these conceptions came together for Karl Marx. Although he was unemployed, he had received a settlement from his father's estate and had married Jenny von Westphalen, and now he had time to think and write. His experiences on the newspaper, his critical attitudes concerning religion and the state, and now the penetrating analyses of Feuerbach pushed him to a critical investigation of one of Hegel's major political works. Marx's *Critique of Hegel's Philosophy of Right,* written in 1843, revealed his continuing distaste for Prussia and traditional German institutions, although he still recommended a democratic revolution.

Sounding very much like Feuerbach rather than how Max Stirner would sound in 1845, Marx wrote that people have species needs (needs as humans in general) as well as individual needs. The human essence that Feuerbach had described is social, Marx said, and the *social forms* of society embedded in the culture and institutions are the expression of that social human species. Culture and institutions reflect human essence in that they derive from people's needs and in turn fulfill those needs. This built-in reciprocity can be described as the communal being *(Gemeinwesen),* which species-humans need as much as they require air to breathe. The actual forms of the communal being, such as family, society, and state, reflect and fulfill real, empirical human needs. This tight togetherness between people and social institutions, this reciprocity, is a sine qua non of human existence; to describe one side is to describe the other.

Moreover, people are conscious of the bond with others, and this self-awareness and consciousness of species, Marx felt, helps elevate humans above the animal world. Therein lies a problem, however, for this awareness of species-existence, this bond with others, demands that there be *no* separation between the individual and society as there is between the believer and God. Yet that separation or alienation exists—there is a gap between the state and society. The state seems external to people, as an "other" or another's power to them, and represents the interests of private property far better than those of common people. That separation must be overcome by pulling the artificially externalized state back into the social humans it supposedly reflects, just as in religion the solution is to pull God out of the heavens and back into the people from which the concept had originally been drawn. Marx wrote that Hegel had solved this problem *but only in the world of ideas*—in abstracted human consciousness. Hegel had transcended the problem without solving it, which had the effect of justifying the alienative status quo. Instead of making private property a civil quality, something that everyone shared, Hegel made political citizenship, existence, and sentiment a quality of private property.[10] In other words, the cart was before the horse—private property was considered far more important than the real human needs it was supposed to reflect.

Marx's vehicle for overcoming this alienation in human political life was universal suffrage—a radical idea at the time, but still some distance from socialism. Marx believed that when everyone was permitted to vote in elections, universal suffrage would erase the separation between society and the political state.[11] Communism still seemed to Marx to be a dogmatic, ready-made answer that was grossly inferior to his own idea of a representative political system created by a revolution through the ballot box.[12] The fact that universal voting seemed to Marx to be an almost mystical expression of human species unity indicated that, even though he was trying to turn Hegel upside down, or make Hegelianism an *empirical* philosophy, the idealism of Hegel still colored Marx's empirical arguments. When everyone voted, Marx felt, a new state would emerge that would express the political sentiments of the entire civil society and be indistinguishable from its human components. Alienation would be overcome. *Gemeinwesen,* an institutional expression of reciprocity, was still thought of as the "state" rather than the commune distinct from the state it would later become.

Although this was still a philosopher writing, Marx's words carried revolutionary connotations. One could expect the existing state to resist a reform that would result in its own abolition. In the face of hostility from official quarters, insisting on universal suffrage could be considered revolutionary. Marx didn't really come to grips with that issue because his pragmatic sense wasn't as well developed as his philosophical one. He acted as though, somehow, universal suffrage would simply vote the old state out and bring the new one in, as though having the right idea absolved him from considering the problems of implementation. Remember this point. This attitude would be visible later, even when Marx was writing about the proletarian revolution. His attitude and his suffrage position would be visible again in the revolutionary period of 1848–1849. After Marx's death, this preoccupation with the ballot box in the 1890s would appear again as reformist socialism began to take over the supposedly revolutionary Second International. Lenin and others would later correct this Marxist "flaw," but in dramatically different circumstances in backward societies.

In 1843, however, Marx was still developing. He had come to see that it was not simply in religion or with reference to the state that alienation was visible, but that significant separations were everywhere. Money worship was also a symbol of human alienation in that it made money a **fetish** with apparent human powers. Even the relationship between a man and a woman revealed alienation or externalization. Such human relationships were actually commercial transactions in which the woman was bought and sold in the sense that her beauty and character were far less important than financial considerations such as dowry or potential inheritance.[13] But even though the effects of alienation could be seen everywhere, religion still exhibited it best. In religion a person's own nature is objectified, and human power is given to an alien entity called God. Therefore, as long as people were captivated by religion, other forms of alienation evolved out of it. Marx believed that humans were conditioned by religion to anticipate being confronted with alien, powerful "others" in a variety of forms.[14] *A strong indictment of religion, therefore, was a necessary prerequisite to human emancipation from all alienation.*

*   *   *

The period from 1841 to 1843 was a most critical time in Marx's development. Two major factors in his evolution were his need to find remunerative work and the writings of Ludwig Feuerbach. The work experience brought him in touch with practical problems—such as the issue of the peasant's right to deadwood in the forest. Marx instinctively and immediately placed himself on the side of the underdog—the peasants—but he explained his position in a philosophical manner. What peasants were combatting was the tendency for property owners to externalize themselves into their property, and this, Marx felt, tarnished the whole state that Hegel had apparently valued.

Feuerbach paved the way for Marx to see that the externalization of self in the things one owns reflected what humans had done in religion as well as what Hegel had done in philosophy. From this point on, Marx would argue that the criticism of religion—as by Feuerbach—was the beginning of all criticism in the sense that all of society was pervaded by alienating externalizations of self that were given humanlike powers. The state, for example, was seen by people as a powerful "other." Marx believed universal suffrage would overcome that tendency to externalize.

THE MATURE SOCIALIST

A real change in Marx's thinking surfaced after he moved to Paris in October of 1843 and began mixing with radicals. His ideological shift was almost immediate. Marx had agreed to be the editor of a new Paris-based journal that would be free of Prussian censors and would bring together German and French radical criticism. Within a short time he found his resistance to communism had crumbled and his vehicle for revolutionary change had switched from the universal suffrage of just a few months before to the *proletarian revolution*. His ideas, philosophical concepts pushed into solutions for real empirical evils, had now found a new home in socialist or communist theories that seemed to give his previous concepts a more vigorous life.

Perhaps, Marx felt, Feuerbach had unintentionally given communism a philosophical foundation with his critiques of Christianity and Hegelianism. Alienated people, with their tendency to externalize their own powers into forces that confronted them as "other," desperately needed a frame of reference that encouraged human wholeness and an awareness of connection with nature and other people. Socialism-communism no longer seemed to be *merely desirable* but philosophically *necessary,* naturally growing out of his "de-idealized" Hegelianism. Once communism became philosophically acceptable to Marx, his two years of resistance evaporated. Friedrich Engels helped the change along because he also came at socialism from a Hegelian perspective. In making this transition, all Marx really had to alter in his democratic philosophy was the vehicle of radical change: to accept the no-

Karl Marx   1818–1883

tion of the revolutionary working class, rather than universal suffrage, as the primary agent of the transition to a better future. But in order to do that, Marx had to romanticize the proletariat much as Engels had done. In a letter to Feuerbach, Marx described French workers as having a "... virginal freshness and nobility," and British workers as having made giant steps; he proclaimed that "history is preparing among these 'barbarians' of our civiliz-ed society the practical element for the emancipation of humanity."[15]

Note that Marx did not see workers so much as people with their own needs, but more as the *means of revolutionary change*. This is a very important point that people often miss because it seems somewhat unkind to Marx to say it or because it seems so obvious as to not require mentioning. But this attitude is just like that of a missionary who sees heathens (nonbelievers) as souls to convert rather than as real people with real needs that may or may not be solved by the missionary's activities. Marx "knew" what the proletariat needed without asking a single worker. He thought he knew what the proletariat would do, what the proletariat would have to do—driven by the inevitable dialectical forces in society. As with Feuerbach, Marx had changed Hegel's focus from idealism to materialism, but he hadn't discarded Hegelianism. He had brought the Hegelian framework into his acceptance of French socialism by combining French and German ideas. The proletariat did not become a force that would act to improve *its own condition only;* it now became the revolutionary agent for overcoming alienation *for all humanity.*

Moreover, the new association with Friedrich Engels did more than help Marx alter his means of revolutionary change. Engels persuaded Marx to believe that the transformation of society by the proletariat was expected imminently, creating a sense of revolutionary crisis that ultimately proved frustrating to both men. Engels had no doubt that the inevitable war of the poor against the rich must come by 1846 or at the latest by 1852.[16]

Once Marx had altered his vehicle of radical change, moreover, many other ideas rearranged themselves. Believing there was still time to lay the philosophic foundation of the movement, he began with his criticism of religion, which was the basis of every other criticism.[17] The whole world was pervaded with the principle of separation and alienation seen so clearly in religion. The point was to change that by unmasking religion's "other forms" or analogs in empirical society.

Marx saw the proletariat through his philosophical spectacles. Unmasking religion's other forms meant a materialistic reading of Hegel's idealistic philosophy, as Feuerbach had suggested. Where Hegel wrote the word *Spirit* or *Reason,* one had to substitute the word *human* in order to help Hegel actually say what Feuerbach and Marx thought he *should* have said. The Absolute was not Idea externalizing itself into the material world and bridging the gulf between humans, nature, and Absolute; rather, humans had externalized themselves and in the process alienated themselves unnecessarily.

For example, human mastery over nature—the taming of nature—had not made the world of nature a part of human essence. People still treated it as "other." They did not see that external world as a part of themselves, even though nearly the whole of that natural world revealed a human impact. It was a humanized world and, therefore, a part of the human whole, an extension of human nature and a bond between individual people in the society.[18]

Moreover, that alienating externalization was present in the heart of social production. Who were the real *producers* in society? The "bondspersons" or "slaves," Hegel's actual "doers," were in fact the proletariat: humans par excellence. Just as religion represented alienation in the heavenly sphere, so the working class revealed it in the empirical world of social production. This meant that alienation existed in the very heart of human essence: in labor. The productive activity that distinguished species-humans from animals, the creativeness that united all humans and nature into a *human* wholeness, was deeply divided. And not only nature confronted people as alien and "other," but so did all products of human labor. Things that people had made confronted them as "other," as not belonging to the makers but to someone else. The alienated character of labor resulted in the universal dislike of work—a dislike of one's own productive human essence. One's needs were not satisfied by work as an end; instead, labor was the *means* to satisfy lesser needs.[19]

In other words, the whole world of productive activity that ought to have been the fulfillment of *human* nature had become the means for the maintenance of people's *animal* nature. A person worked in order to live, rather than lived in order to work. Members of the working class symbolized in the secular, material world what religion symbolized in the heavenly world: alienation or unnatural and unnecessary externalization of their human essence. Their labor resulted in products that confronted them as commodities, as capital, as alien others, and this externalization of self in one's labor must be overcome or negated before freedom could be realized and they could be at home with themselves. Hegel had seen human alienation as lessening over time, but Marx saw it steadily increasing in severity and extent. In this sense, Marx clearly felt that he had stood Hegel on his feet, or stood him right side up.

Actual observations of working-class conditions fleshed out the concept and gave it empirical weight, but Marx's concept of the proletariat derived essentially from an inversion of Hegel and the analysis of religion, not from an analysis of working-class problems. The proletariat would become the redeemer of humanity, freeing everyone by freeing itself.

At the same time, the workers represented an *economic class* in society. Marx's developing appreciation for communism from a philosophical perspective opened up to embrace economics as an important part of his new thinking. When he moved to Paris, Marx began an intensive study of French history to give himself a better understanding of the French Revolution. He concluded that French history, indeed all human history, was a story of the conflict between classes in society. And since one's class was a description of where one stood with respect to owning or not owning the **means of production**, the economic factors that made up the **mode of production** in any given era were important to understand. Those economic factors were empirical indicators of deeper, philosophic truths.

In order for history to exist at all, Marx wrote, the production of goods necessary to sustain life must occur. Production, thus, is the basis of human history. But it was alienated production right from the beginning, and this fact caused the production *classes* to emerge: those who owned the means of production and those who did not. The separation into two basic classes was the division of labor in society. Conflict was implicit in the division of labor, and the dialectical resolution of that conflict moved history forward in historical materialism (see Chapter 3).

In Paris, Marx was in the center of revolutionary socialism, and his use of the proletariat as the agent class of the forthcoming revolution pushed him in the direction of economics—and, with Engels' assistance, the advanced economics of Britain. Marx now saw that a solid economic analysis would demonstrate the accuracy of his blend of philosophical and empirical perspectives. The study of economics became the prime necessity of his life. He and his family had been hounded out of France because Prussian officials had put pressure on the Paris government to expel him, and then they had been forced out of Brussels because of his authorship of the *Communist Manifesto*. Partly to study economics, partly because Engels was in England, and partly because he was running out of countries that would permit him residence, Marx moved to London where he remained for the rest of his life.

However, his planned critique of political economy was never really completed. He was diverted from his economic studies by the philosophical struggles still going on in Germany, by the need to refute the activities of other revolutionaries, by joining the League of the Just (1836–1847) as it became the Communist League in 1847 and, a year later, writing the *Communist Manifesto* for the group, by his brief involvement in restarting the Cologne newspaper during the revolutionary years of 1848–1849 in Europe, and by his leading role in the International Workingmen's Association that began in 1864.

Marx's long hours in the reading room of the British Museum resulted in much writing that was not published until the 1920s and 1930s, such as the *Economic and Philosophical Manuscripts of 1844* and the *Grundrisse (Main Principles)*.[20] In 1859, he published a part of his conclusions, the *Contribution to a Critique of Political Economy*, and in 1867 the first volume of *Capital*, the work for which he is best known. The second and third volumes were published after his death by Engels, and a fourth by Karl Kautsky, the leader of the German Social Democratic party.

Living in London had not caused Marx to forget Germany. It was always on his mind in the sense that what he described in England, he believed would soon take place in Germany. Industrial capitalism was the wave of the future, sweeping from Britain into Europe, from west to east. By describing it, he felt he was helping Germans understand what was coming in the near future.

Throughout Marx's life, the monetary returns on his literary activity amounted to almost nothing. His inheritance and Jenny's were soon spent and the family thereafter lived in severe poverty. For all his productive life, Marx and his family were supported by Friedrich Engels, who continued to work in his father's textile business largely because of Marx's financial needs. That support from Engels was sporadic and at fairly low levels during the early years in England because Engels did not command a good salary until later. And yet Marx did not find a job. He applied once for a position as a railway clerk, but was rejected because of his terrible handwriting. He felt he had more important things to do than to find and keep a job. His poverty was real, but so was his dedication.

In March 1883, Marx died in his sleep. Engels lived until 1895, and during the next twelve years he continued their work, but the revolution they both had sought failed to come. Nonetheless, Marx's legacy included a full description of how and why history was inevitably leading to the revolution that would usher in the truly human age.

*   *   *

Marx's move to Paris in late 1843 was as fateful as had been his move from Bonn to the University of Berlin. In Paris he was thrust into the middle of radical socialist politics. Almost immediately Marx substituted the revolutionary working class for universal suffrage as his vehicle of change, and the class struggle as the main conflict in history. This pulled Marx in the direction of economic studies. The philosopher-turned-socialist phased into the radical economist. In this transition, Marx's earlier philosophy never left him. It deeply affected his approach both to French socialism and English economics. The proletariat was an earthly example of alienation carried to its fullest, just as religion was the main example in the heavenly sphere. Because the working class represented alienation at its worst, it could, by redeeming itself through revolution, redeem all people everywhere.

AFTERWORD

For all of Marxism's supposed empiricism, it was more theory *applied* to practical reality rather than theory *derived* from practice. Instead of practice determining theory, as Mao Zedong would later expect in China, theory kept expecting practice to go in the directions that theory indicated. As the next chapter should make clear, this approach kept running into trouble. Events, the bourgeois employers, and the proletariat itself would all fail to do what theory expected them to do.

NOTES

1. David McLellan, *Marx Before Marxism* (New York: Harper & Row, 1970), p. 40. The sentence is part of Marx's Ph.D. dissertation dedication to Ludwig von Westphalen and represented a part of what Ludwig had taught him during their frequent long walks when Marx was a young man in Trier.

2. Karl Marx, "Letter to His Father: On a Turning Point in Life (1837)," in *Writings of the Young Marx on Philosophy and Society,* eds. Loyd D. Easton and Kurt H. Guddat (New York: Doubleday Anchor, 1967), p. 47.

3. Ibid., p. 48.

4. Eduard Gans, *Rückblicke auf Personen und Zustande* (Berlin: 1836), cited in McLellan, *Marx Before Marxism,* p. 51.

5. Ibid., p. 65.

6. Karl Marx, "Leading Article in No. 179 of the *Kölnische Zeitung,*" in Easton and Guddat, *Writings,* pp. 118, 120.

7. Karl Marx, "Arnold Ruge (Dresden), Cologne 30 November, 1842," in *The Letters of Karl Marx,* ed. and trans. Saul K. Padover (Englewood Cliffs, N.J.: Prentice-Hall, 1979), pp. 20–21.

8. Ibid., p. 26.

9. J. O'Malley, ed., *Karl Marx—Critique of Hegel's Philosophy of Right* (Cambridge, England: Cambridge University Press, 1970), p. xxxvii.

10. Ibid., p. 111.

11. Ibid., p. 121.

12. Karl Marx, "To Arnold Ruge (in Dresden), Kreuznach, September, 1843, in Padover, *Letters,* pp. 30–32.

13. Karl Marx, "On the Jewish Question," in Easton and Guddat, *Writings,* pp. 245–246.

14. Ibid., p. 248.

15. Karl Marx, "To Ludwig Feuerbach (in Bruckberg), Paris, 38 Rue Vaneau, August 11, 1844," in Padover, *Letters,* p. 35.

16. Friedrich Engels, *Conditions of the Working Class in England,* cited in Gertrude Himmelfarb, *The Idea of Poverty* (New York: Alfred A. Knopf, 1984), p. 270. This citation is a different translation from that given by W. O. Henderson and W. H. Chaloner in Friedrich Engels, *The Conditions of the Working Class in England* (Stanford, Calif.: Stanford University Press, 1958), pp. 334–335. The virtue of the Himmelfarb citation is that it is a translation by Florence Wischnewetzky approved by Engels himself for the American edition in 1887. The disadvantage is that where Engels writes that in the original 1844 book that the revolution *must* come, the approved English version fails to italicize the word *must,* most likely because forty-three years later that emphatic prediction of an imminent revolution was somewhat embarrassing.

17. O'Malley, *Critique of Hegel's Philosophy,* pp. 131–132.

18. Karl Marx, "Economic and Philosophic Manuscripts (1844)," in Easton and Guddat, *Writings,* pp. 305–306.

19. Ibid., p. 292.

20. Both Marx's *Economic and Philosophical Manuscripts of 1844* and the *Grundrisse* have been published, even though long after his death, in 1932, and 1925, respectively. Easton and Guddat, *Writings,* is a good source for the former and the latter has been published in English by David McLellan as *Grundrisse* (New York: Harper & Row, 1971). The 1844 material and the *Grundrisse* written in 1857–1858 provide a needed synthesis between Marx's philosophic past and his later economic studies by pointing back to the Hegelian and Feuerbachian period as well as forward to the critique of capitalism and the coming of communism. The notebooks make it clear that Marx the economic critic was still the philosopher-social critic, for human alienation was manifested in economic history as well as in the capitalist mode of production. Even though he did not mention alienation in his later works on economics like *Capital,* the economic factors he described were the predominant influence in an organic, social unity wherein the externalization of the human essence had reached its peak.

DISCUSSION QUESTIONS

1. Explain Marx's belief that the criticism of religion showed the way to criticize nonreligious things in society that were permeated with the religious principle of externalization. Give examples.
2. In what way would Marx consider that the following list of words all expressed alienation? Wage-labor, state, proletariat, money, bourgeoisie, private property, division of labor, nature, produced commodities.
3. Explain: Humans work in order to live rather than live in order to work.
4. Was Marx an atheist or a humanist who sounded like one?
5. How did Feuerbach influence Marx's development?
6. In what ways did Marx turn Hegel upside down?
7. Show how influential Marx's moves to Berlin and Paris were.
8. What was the left-wing Hegelian movement? Name a few leaders.
9. What prevented Marx from becoming a professor at the University of Bonn with Bruno Bauer?
10. Describe Marx's association with Friedrich Engels.
11. What was the League of the Just, what did it become, and what was Marx's involvement?

3

Historical
Materialism

OVERVIEW

Historical **materialism** was the name given to Marx's explanation of how past events marched together inevitably to the proletarian or worker revolution. Marx adapted Hegel's idealist saga of the unfolding of the World Spirit into a materialist story of the developing, empirical human caught up in relations of production. Engel's conception of **dialectical materialism** is different and should be distinguished from historical materialism.

Philosophers have often used history to show how their own particular interpretations of contemporary life have *necessarily* developed out of events in the past. These philosophers wanted to *ground* their individual perspectives in history. If their interpretations of the past were accepted, they felt that their arguments about the present day would be believed. In seventeenth-century England, for example, Thomas Hobbes had demonstrated the need for a strong sovereign, at a time when this issue was being hotly debated between king and Parliament. To make his idea more acceptable, Hobbes imagined that human history had begun with a danger-filled state of nature that demanded a strong authority to create the social order needed for civilization to exist. About forty years later, John Locke wanted a parliamentary form of English government rather than a monarchical one, so he imagined a milder state of nature at the beginning of history that needed less in terms of powerful, focused authority to maintain civil order. Like Hobbes, Locke created a view of history that supported his beliefs about political life in his day.

In addition, scholars in the nineteenth century frequently described history as progressing in *stages* of development from lower to higher forms of social organization, just like the growth of a biological organism. As we shall see, Marx's historical materialism reveals both of these nineteenth-century tendencies: the use of history to support present-day arguments, and the notion that the past inevitably grows into the present and future through stages of evolution.

The *primary* elements of Marx's history were social, producing humans. It was impossible to imagine a person living entirely alone; people lived in societies—they were social. Moreover, that social life could not exist for long unless humans produced the goods that made life possible. Thus history itself was dependent on the social production of the wherewithal of life. The description of that past story, therefore, ought not to be the saga of kings and empires, but the story of social production: how the material forces of production combined in different historical periods.

The telling of that story led directly to an analysis of the capitalist mode of production as well as to a prediction about the socialist-communist future. Historical materialism was a single progressive story that highlighted progress in the way people made their living—the way that people, raw materials, machines, and tools were arranged in a mode of production within a given era. Progress—the movement from one stage to the next—was the result of the dialectical conflict between classes that represented the two sides of the social division of labor: the owners and the nonowners of the means of production.

People were born into a definite era and their mode of production or relations of production were *determined* or *shaped* by the stage of development of the material productive forces of that era.[1] These relations of production that Marx also called relations of property made up the economic structure of the society, which was the real basis of the whole society. A **superstructure** of legal, political, and cultural institutions developed on that economic foundation and reflected that economic base. Even the social and intellectual *consciousness* of the age—how people thought and expressed themselves—reflected the dominant economic base of that period.[2]

Although people were born into a society characterized by a particular mode of production and existing superstructure, they developed these productive relations further by inventions and new discoveries. Workers weren't just the end product of the existing relations of production, they also helped to determine what those relations were or what they would become. Society was the result of human reciprocal action.[3]

Gradually, succeeding generations of creative, inventive producers challenged the existing relations of production. The mode of production characterizing a given historical period could not grow and expand indefinitely; like a rubber band, it would break if pushed or pulled too far. Marx felt that new inventions and discoveries, new ways of doing old things, created such an accumulated pressure on the existing mode of production that the system could not expand any further. As additional development was hampered or restricted by the lack of elasticity in the mode of production, a class struggle would occur, and the subsequent revolution would establish a new mode of production—a new stage of history.[4]

The emerging stage would have a new ruling class that would confront a different nonowning class of workers. The new owners of the means of production, however, would not spring up overnight. They had been evolving in the womb of the old society, to use Marx's expression, quietly gathering maturity and strength until they were ready to emerge. The "birth" of the new class was dependent on two appropriate economic conditions: the exhaustion of the old relations of production so that they could no longer absorb new challenges, and the maturing of the new class in the womb of the old. When both factors were present, a revolution occurred that opened the way for a new set of production relations to go through a similar cycle of flexibility, growth, and eventual inelasticity until it was replaced by another.

Thus, to Marx, human history seemed to be a series of stages of economic development. But Marx was really describing European history—economic structures that evolved through stages of primitive communism to the ancient or slave society, then to the feudal period, and finally to the capitalism of Marx's own day. This would in turn be followed by the communism of the future described in Chapter 4. However, Marx was aware of another possible sequence, namely, Asiatic society or oriental despotism. Despotic societies emerged from primitive communism in areas where the state held a monopoly over the irrigation systems on which the agricultural societies depended. Oriental despotisms such as those in Egypt, China, India, and elsewhere had a history different from that of European development because these Asiatic societies did not go through the same stages and they proved astonishingly durable over time.

Aside from this exception, which Marx noted but ignored, historical materialism was a story of progressive stages of economic development, moved by the dialectical confrontation implicit in the division of labor, and resulting in class warfare. The record of the conflict of classes is the story of the human past and present represented in the stages of production in the following chart.

MARX'S STAGES OF HISTORICAL MATERIALISM

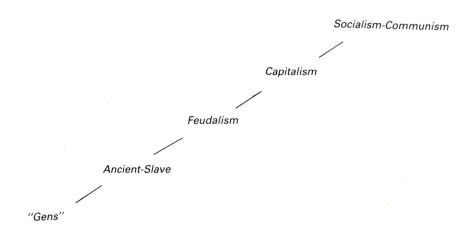

TECHNOLOGICAL ABILITY *AND* ALIENATION INCREASING

The first stage of historical materialism was a primitive period at the beginning of civilization that has been called the *gens* or beginning stage.[5] Society then consisted of hunters and gatherers organized into sharing, communal systems of tribes and clans. The primitive communism that existed then centered on the extended family. Although variations certainly existed, the society was often matriarchal. A small account of manufacture existed that produced some goods for trade, although most commodities produced were for consumption within the community. People in the system produced for *use,* in other words, rather than for *exchange,* even though trade existed.

When agriculture developed as a significant means of food production, private property became visible in the economic base. Lines of descent and inheritance switched from the mother's line to the father's, polygamy gave way to monogamy, and *individual* or *private* possessions began to supplant *social* or *common* possessions. At this point, Marx taught, slave labor was introduced to increase production of agricultural goods. The surplus products that resulted made trade more important, and production for exchange became common. This made slavery an even more necessary institution. When the old communal relations in the *gens* stage became a barrier to further progress, a social revolution occurred and a new relation of production emerged: the ancient-slave society. Private property was then enshrined in the relations of production in the form of the two major classes—the owners and the nonowners (in this case the slaves). Thus began the *division of labor,* which might also be described as a division *within* labor.

By associating labor with slavery, people increasingly became alienated from the productive and creative *essence* that defines a human. Working became a despised activity, easily externalized, and no longer seen as an intrinsic part of oneself. Expansion of slavery to increase surplus production pushed the volume of trade higher and higher and resulted in the emergence of merchants and money to facilitate trading. Economic expansion was worldwide in the Greco-Roman period, based on slave labor, and supported by military conquests. But when the Roman armies no longer had rich new territories to conquer and began to fight each other, economic expansion began to reverse. Soldiers released from the armies found neither land nor employment and met with increasing corruption at the top of the social system.

The new class of impoverished free people physically manifested the tensions within the dying economic order. Revolution again changed the relations of production. The large landed estates previously worked by slaves were broken up, and smaller-scale subsistence agriculture reappeared as thousands of people began fending for themselves. However, the new class was relatively powerless, and, as the old empire disintegrated, feudalism and a new class division was born.

In feudal systems, the division of labor was between the serfs and the lords of the manors (local opportunists). In general, workers might own the tools used in production, but otherwise they were serfs who owed labor to the lord, paid high rents to the manor, and were seldom able to leave the lord's service. Towns dotted the landscape, but they were rural in nature. Cities were simply large towns made more prominent by a seaport or by royal residences. The small amount of manufacturing that went on in the towns was performed by hand, protected from competition by strong guild restrictions.

Merchants came back as stability returned. Initially, however, trade was very local, but several developments changed this: the introduction of the compass in Europe permitted more distant travel, particularly on uncharted oceans; the Crusades expanded trade horizons; and geographical discoveries dramatically increased the amount of available gold and silver. All these changes contributed to a tremendous increase in trade and a desire for the production of commodities for exchange or trade rather than simply for one's own use. Increasingly, the old relations of production became dependent on the merchant, and the nobility and the serf became outdated. The rise of those who controlled the money that greased the wheels of state could not be suppressed. The old feudal relations became a fetter on continued development, and they had to be transcended. Again, a revolution occurred and a new set of production relationships emerged that resulted in a new division of labor: between the *proletariat* (nonowners of the means of production, workers) and the *bourgeoisie* (owners of the means of production, capitalists).

*   *   *

Marx, as did many others, used history to show how events appeared to develop inevitably in such a way as to lead to his specific analysis of his own age. He saw history as progress, pushed by dialectical tension between opposing economic classes, and developing through specific stages from lower to higher, with the stages understood as different relations of production. The *gens* period was followed by the ancient-slave society, which in turn was supplanted by feudalism, which gave way to capitalism. At this point, historical materialism turned from a description of the past to an analysis of Marx's present—with the goal, of course, of showing exactly how and why the final revolution would occur that would usher in the future society of socialism and communism.

MARX'S CRITIQUE OF CAPITALISM

Marx believed that capitalism (the relations of production of his own day) was the final period of alienated "prehistory," which led to a vastly improved future that would emerge from the proletarian revolution. Historical materialism now changed from a description of the past to an analysis of capitalist relations of production, which had evolved out of the past as a process of natural history,[6] according to a rational dialectic (his own) rather than the mystical dialectic of Hegel. There were two related reasons for Marx's analysis of capitalism beyond the need to justify his own advocacy of socialism: to show the temporary nature of capitalism and to reveal capitalism's self-destructive nature. To demonstrate that capitalism was a stage in humanity's development like other stages, Marx had to combat the general tendency to see in one's own institutions eternal and sacred givens that could not be touched.[7]

Why was capitalism temporary? Because it demonstrated the depths of human alienation and the widening separations that had grown along with great progress in technological ability. Capitalism represented both a high point of technical progress and a nadir of alienation—a simultaneous best and worst that could not long coexist. But it was also temporary because it was self-destructive, containing within itself the seeds of its own destruction. Marx believed that the working class had to become aware of both the negative aspects and the temporary character of capitalism. Spreading this knowledge of capitalism's nature would create **class consciousness**, hope, and revolution.

Marx began his analysis of capitalism with the question of value. What was the value of a commodity in the marketplace? Assume that value equals price and then ask, Why that price? For example, say that a pair of scissors is priced at five dollars. Why that price? Why not four dollars or six dollars? On what basis does one determine value (price)?

To understand Marx here, one must leave behind traditional explanations such that the scissors cost five dollars because someone calculated costs and profits and came up with five dollars; or that the price is five dollars because the market indicates that is the level of balance between supply and demand. Remember that Marx was a philosopher who was delving into economics, not an economist delving into philosophy. Forget those traditional explanations for the moment.

Marx argued that the basis of value (price) is *labor*. He deliberately used a concept called the *labor theory of value* that John Locke had developed and that economic theorists such as David Ricardo had popularized. This theory stated that the value of any commodity is a reflection of the *labor* that has gone into its production. Human labor time is the sole determiner of value in this theory. To account for slow or lazy workers as well as fast or ambitious ones, Marx rephrased the statement so that it read as follows: the value (price) of any commodity is the result of the *socially necessary* or average labor time used in its manufacture. Thus, a commodity that takes eight hours to make is twice as valuable as one that takes only four hours.

At the root of this theory is the notion that all value is created by labor. In an agricultural milieu, the theory justifies fencing in land and calling it private property because the farmer has mixed his labor with the soil and made it more valuable than it was before. That increased value belongs to the particular farmer, and the only way to protect the new value is to call the land private property so that the fruit of that labor will belong to that farmer. In the industrial milieu, the labor theory of value points to the factory workers as the sole creators of commodity values and implies that those workers deserve to receive the full measure of the value they have created.

However, in a factory there are also raw materials and machinery. What about them? They are commodities also, Marx insisted. Machines have to be made by laborers, and raw materials must be extracted from the ground or grown by workers. So in those cases, too, the value of the machine or specific raw material is the amount of socially necessary human labor time expended in its manufacture or development into usable form. Machines and raw materials represent "stored" or "frozen" human labor. The commodity concept refers to all levels of the producing process. The general public are consumers of finished products like automobiles, but the capitalists are consumers of machines and raw materials for those finished products. On each level, the value of the commodity can be determined by the amount of socially necessary, *living* labor.

Labor is also a commodity. According to Marx, in the bourgeois (capitalist) relations of production, workers were paid wages that reflected the laborers' value or the cost of sustaining the individual worker as worker. Wages below this level caused starvation, and wages above this level assumed a philanthropy among capitalists that Marx did not believe was there. Wages, therefore, tended to hover around the subsistence level, even though they were influenced by supply and demand—numbers of available laborers and jobs.

In the production process, living labor is combined with frozen or stored labor (machines and raw materials) to create new commodities. To the capitalists, costs are expenditures for the three commodity categories: raw materials, machines, and human labor time. These costs to the capitalist are passed along to the consumer. However, the market price (value) of the finished product does not reflect this cost base alone. An article that cost five dollars to produce is priced at seven dollars. Where did this extra value of two dollars come from? Marx insisted it came from **surplus value**, a value created by laborers *that is not part of the costs of production because workers were not paid for a part of their labor time.*

Imagine a worker hired for ten dollars per day. During the workday, living labor is combined with stored human labor to produce items of value. Further imagine that during the *morning* hours, the worker produces ten dollars worth of goods. If the laborer goes home at noon, the capitalist would receive an equivalent return for the wages paid. However, the worker cannot go home; his or her contract with the employer will not permit it. During the labor time of the rest of the day, therefore, the worker would create products but receive no remuneration. None at all. This unremunerated labor created the surplus value that is the basis of profit.

Creation of surplus value is thus an essential part of capitalism. If capitalists had to pay the full equivalent to the workers, if they couldn't have surplus value, they would cease to be capitalists. Profit is based on exploitation and theft, according to Marx, but without it the system would not operate as a capitalist system.[8]

Was Marx intending to deny the bourgeoisie a return on their investment? By no means, even though the capitalists did not creatively produce anything the way *labor* did. Marx was writing a scientific analysis, not a moralistic tract, when he wrote *Capital.* He was not trying to *improve* capitalism through this or that reform effort, nor was he really interested in improving the proletariat's lot within capitalism. Instead, he sought to explain the true nature of the economic system so that his readers would know exactly how and why they were being exploited and impoverished. By seeing *themselves* in capitalism, laborers could develop what Hegel called a mind of their own. "Thus precisely in labor where there seemed to be merely some outsider's mind and ideas involved, the servant becomes aware, through this rediscovery of himself by himself, of having and being a 'mind of his own.' "[9]

The other side of the exploitative character of capitalism, a fact sometimes ignored by revolutionaries, is that labor only becomes productive, according to Marx, when taken into capital (or under capitalism) and utilized under capitalist discipline (the industrial factory). Of course alienation increases and the workers confront stored or frozen labor as an alien "other." However, in order for capitalism to exist, labor must be turned into wealth. Wealth has been created by a productive process stimulated by the greed of the capitalist that, however deplorable, has dramatically increased both productivity and the amount of goods available for consumption.[10] The chains of minimal subsistence that characterized all previous economic history would be broken forever because of the wealth produced by capitalism.

Marx saw capitalism as an ongoing and valuable stage of historical materialism. But it was destined to perish as have other earlier stages. Within bourgeois society, a force was growing that would destroy the system: the proletariat, maturing within the womb of the capitalist relations of production. And around that developing proletariat, the future mode of production was growing: socialism.

Although capitalism is based on private property, Marx believed that the proletariat experienced collective work in the factories and communal living conditions outside the factory. Large numbers of factory workers were brought together under one factory roof where, through the discipline of capitalism, they were taught to work *together* in commodity production. The goods produced were not the result of a single worker's activity, but resulted from the labor of them all. The commodities were a joint product, a social product. To whom did it belong? To the capitalist, the owner of the means of production. If the bourgeoisie were ignored for the moment, then the real owner of the product was the producing collectivity and not a single individual. Moreover, the workers were concentrated in living quarters around the factories. They not only worked together but they also lived together and were bound together by their propertyless condition. Within the framework of capitalism, socialism began to emerge.

Within this capitalist system, the dialectic was also visible. Contradictions abounded. For example, where did the capitalist get money to invest? From either personal labor, theft, piracy, confiscation, or similar efforts by ancestors. Invested money came back with a return in the following year. But where did the extra money—that return—come from? It came from capitalized surplus value owing its existence to unpaid labor. The proletariat, by its own surplus labor, created the capital destined to employ additional labor in the following year. Bourgeois or capitalist relations of property ensured the legal right to appropriate the products of unpaid labor. This kept the whole system moving and expanding, but not forever.

For another example, the primitive assembly lines utilized in nineteenth-century factories resulted in greater productivity, but by means of an extensive overspecialization of labor,[11] which converted the worker into a crippled monstrosity. The assembly line forced dexterity in a very limited area while ignoring the rest of the worker's creative potential. The individual was turned into a machinelike creature, performing over and over again the same skills that could not be sold anywhere else. Capitalism's production of wealth, however valuable as a prerequisite for the later sharing under socialism and communism, crippled the worker in the process.

In addition, the proletariat was usually not paid enough to be able to consume the products that it made. As capital expanded, production expanded, and this ought to have meant increases in wages due to shortages of labor. However, just the opposite happened. Ruthless competition among capitalists reduced the number of bourgeoisie by forcing the unsuccessful competitors into the ranks of the working class, while the successful remaining capitalists became monopolists. This concentrated industry permitted better economies of scale; utilization of even more machinery and greater efficiencies of production that produced cheaper goods but caused overall profits to fall at the same time.

Why would this concentration of capital cause profits to fall? Because of lower surplus value. Concentrating one's industry in a larger factory where more machinery could be used *reduced* the size of the active work force. This was why the expansion of production did not cause a rise in wages—another contradiction in capitalism. The shortage of laborers imagined by some economists to be the result of capitalism's expansion became instead, according to Marx, the shortage of jobs as workers were replaced by machines. But the capitalist did not realize that *profits were based on surplus value*, which was in turn based on *living* labor. Living labor represented a variable cost to the capitalist, unlike the fixed costs of raw materials and machines. Living labor was therefore the only cost factor the capitalist could manipulate so as to increase profits. The smaller size of the *active* work force in the new larger factories meant that less surplus value could be extracted. The product was cheapened because less socially necessary human labor time had gone into its manufacture. It would sell for less and the volume of sales might rise, but this would quickly increase competition and further aggravate the situation. One's share of the market would decline and one's profits would shrink because profits could only be realized from the unpaid work of laborers in one's own factory. Reductions in the active work force had to be matched by intensifying the pressure to produce on the remaining workers or by expanding the workday still further (or both) to keep profits at the same level. But these were merely temporary measures; inevitably, profits would fall.

This meant several things. First, along with the capital necessary for production expansion, the laboring class produced the means by which it was itself made superfluous in the economic system. The ranks of the unemployed, the industrial reserve army, grew larger. This put pressure on those who still had jobs to put up with more intense exploitation if they wanted to stay employed. Classical economists had argued that, as capital expanded, wages would increase until a greater supply of laborers caused by better food and conditions brought the wages down again. Marx insisted that this would never happen. Long before workers could benefit, the increasing concentration of industry into monopolies would introduce so many new machines that the proletariat would be worse off rather than temporarily in a better position. He called this the *absolute general law of capitalist accumulation*—the greater the social wealth, the greater the absolute mass of the proletariat whose ranks were swelled by unsuccessful bourgeoisie, and the greater the size of the industrial reserve army. The greater the ranks of the unemployed in the absence of any unemployment compensation, the greater the scope of pauperism and poverty. On the one hand was social wealth, the production of which was capitalism's historic vocation; on the other hand was constantly expanding misery.

Second, this worsening of conditions was made even more dreadful by the periodic crises that both Marx and Engels believed to be endemic to capitalism. Why would these crises occur? Basically because of the organic concentration of capital. Marx argued that weakening profits would accelerate the monopolistic concentration of capital, which in turn would stimulate overproduction to recover diminished profits. But this tendency to overproduce would cause profits to fall even faster. A vicious spiral would emerge. Markets would become glutted with products, warehouses would fill up, more workers would be laid off, and the entire economic picture of capitalism would exhibit an immobilization of productiveness until sufficient time had passed and production could again resume—but with fewer bourgeoisie, more proletariat, more members of the industrial reserve army, and less living labor involved in production. These economic crises would occur on a steadily increasing timetable. It was inevitable.

Thus, capitalism was inevitably eroding from within, helplessly creating the seeds of its own destruction. Capitalists could not stop the degeneration. The misery of the proletariat would deepen, new monopolies would contain fewer and fewer capitalists, and the industrial reserve army of unemployed workers would dramatically enlarge. The increasingly pauperized proletariat would finally discover that they *themselves* were the overwhelming majority of the population, opposed by a handful of capitalists. At this point, the giant contradiction implicit in this relation of property from the beginning would become clear. The thoroughly socialized proletariat would face relations of production that permitted a very small group to benefit from the poverty of the vast majority of the people. Those capitalist relations that had created so much wealth would now exhaust their historic function; they would become fetters on continued progress. Marx believed that the proletariat would see this, and see themselves for what they really were: the real basis of the whole social system. Their consciousness of unnecessary servitude, coupled with a sense of their own power, would bring about the proletarian revolution.

Just as revolution had altered previous modes of production, so it would the present system. The mode of production would radically change and, in the process, would abolish the old superstructure based on capitalist relations of production. Although the existing state, as part of that superstructure, would be smashed, that was the consequence of the social revolution, not its primary purpose. The end sought by the ongoing dialectic was the resolution of the class conflict within the economic base of the society.[12]

Although it would probably begin in one country, the revolution would quickly become worldwide. Workers had no country in this type of struggle, Marx thought. Nationalism, he argued, was part of the bourgeois mystique and would be a restraint on proletarian development. Workers all over the world would quickly ascertain that they had nothing to lose but their chains and everything to gain—a world based on the fruits of their own collective labor, organized into a society that would, for the first time, inaugurate a really *human* history.

*   *   *

In Marx's judgment, capitalism was a valuable historical stage. Without it future socialism would not have any wealth to share. But even so, capitalism, once understood, was an economic system riddled with contradictions. What made the system flourish was profit, which Marx showed to be surplus value extracted from an exploited work force. Even capitalism's growth contained seeds of self-destruction. Growth was based on money derived from unpaid labor. Production techniques in the new factories turned workers into stunted fragments of their former selves. The majority of the population did not have the wherewithal to purchase the products they themselves made. Inevitable concentrations of capital caused profits to fall, and this in turn stimulated overproduction, which resulted in worsening crises.

Inevitably, capitalism would become so riddled with contradictions that the class struggle between the proletariat and the bourgeoisie would arise. When the workers realized the cause of their acute misery, the depths of their alienation, and how few people stood in the way of their taking over, the proletarian revolution would occur.

THE REVOLUTION—CONFUSED EXPECTATIONS

According to Marx's descriptive analysis of capitalism, capitalism was destroying itself, and the expected revolution was the result of those self-destructive features that helped develop the proletariat and contribute to the inelasticity of capitalist relations of production. Revolution was not an afterthought to Marx, but it was as much the consequence as the cause of change. When Marxism was later applied by others, particularly Lenin in the context of imperialism, revolution was given a more starring role.

Part of the reason for this variation in emphasis is the different circumstances in the areas where Marxism will be implemented. But another part of the reason for varying interpretations of the role and place of revolution was Marx's own ambiguity about revolution, an ambiguity that arose both from his philosophic background and from the frustrations of a prophet whose predicted developments did not materialize. There was something apocalyptical that could be drawn from Marx's description of the proletarian revolution—the coming revolution more intense, more far-reaching, and more enduring than those that occurred in the past. When Marxists talked of the proletarian revolution still to come, they invested it with great significance, as though it would be a climactic end of things as previously known, and the beginnings of something very new.

When this view of revolution was coupled with Marx's reluctance to discuss the future postrevolutionary society, his entire theory began to take on the appearance of a "never-never land" or utopia. Eduard Bernstein, a friend of Engels and a German Social Democrat, described this problem as one that Marxists could not ignore: that neither the revolution nor the society that should follow it was correctly portrayed in Marxist theory (see Chapter 5).

Part of the confusion can be attributed to the fact that Marxism has been applied in areas and times that Marx did not foresee—such as Russia in 1917 (Chapter 6) and Ethiopia in 1978 (Chapter 9). Some of the confusion about revolution and the future, however, can be attributed to Marx and Engels themselves. Neither of them liked discussing details of the post-revolutionary society because they felt that too much talk about the future made them sound like theorists of **utopian socialism**. But oddly enough, the two men were not all that clear about the proletarian revolution either. They seemed to be confused about what would cause the expected revolution, when it would occur, whether a radical party was necessary to lead it or whether the proletarian masses would be able to do it themselves, and whether the forthcoming struggle would be violent and sudden or peaceful and gradual. The revolutionary legacy that the two men left was, in other words, confusing enough that practically any later interpretation could be called Marxist.

Let's examine the elements individually. First, regarding the cause of the revolution, why would it happen? The theory of historical materialism insisted that the revolution was an outgrowth of the obvious and extreme contradiction between capital and labor—just a few capitalists controlling all the wealth in a confrontation with a large and impoverished working class. When events did not unfold that way in the last half of the nineteenth century, Engels himself argued that their revolutionary predictions were a romanticized version of the French Revolution of 1789, Engels wrote that ". . . our conceptions of the nature and course of the 'social' revolution proclaimed in Paris in February 1848, of the revolution of the proletariat, [were] strongly coloured by the memories of the prototypes of 1789 and 1830."[13] In their minds, the proletarian revolution became too much of a struggle of good against evil, or progressive forces against the exhausted minions of the old order in which the deprived would triumph over the depraved.

They continued to think this way even though the European revolutions in 1848–1849, in which they themselves were involved, failed to gain anything significant for the workers. Their thinking did not include enough real analysis and included too much "ought to be." As the hindsight of a century later makes clear, they did not realize that revolutions occur when the crisis of modernization in a specific country confronts the old politico-economic system that is unable to meet the new demands. They failed to appreciate the flexibility of capitalists in responding to new crises or demands; instead, they attributed to the bourgeoisie all of the rigid attributes of the old monarchical orders that had emerged from the Middle Ages.

In 1895, Engels stated that he and Marx had failed to correctly analyze what was taking place in 1848–1849.[14] Marx, however, never became that reflective. He simply became frustrated when the revolution did not come. He was convinced that a new economic crisis would bring it about.[15] When that didn't happen, he began hoping that significant new events, such as the discovery of gold in California or the development of steam locomotives, would bring about the crisis that would usher in the revolution.

In 1895, Engels believed that he and Marx had been wrong because economic conditions had not sufficiently ripened.[16] But really their analysis was off. They just did not pay enough attention to how the revolutionary fervor of workers was being sapped by late-nineteenth-century developments such as the extension of political suffrage and the growth of effective unions in countries such as Britain.[17] Actually the revolution they envisioned made more sense in the 1840s, during capitalism's more primitive period, than it would later in the century.

Second, the timing of the revolution also seemed more confused than necessary. Marx wrote to Engels in 1856 that the proletarian revolution in Germany depended on the possibility of backing from an occurrence similar to the Peasant War of the sixteenth century.[18] If the proletariat needed help from serfs when the critical time came, the stages of historical materialism were not as clear as Marx had thought. Could it also be that the proletariat might attain power "ahead of time"? This was a real possibility to Engels—a seizure of power *before* economic conditions were ripe! The proletariat would then be undertaking *untimely communist experiments.*[19] What had seemed so clear in 1844 or 1850 about the timing of the revolution was evidently not clear at all.

Third, was a radical party necessary or would the proletarian masses suffice? Who or what would lead the way when class consciousness fully developed? Did the existence of an "advanced party" cancel out the need for a proletarian majority of the population? In 1848 Marx had described the Communist League, formed in 1847 out of the old League of the Just, as a group that *alone* knew the line of march, the correct path to follow.[20] In 1867 he described the International as a powerful engine in "our hands."[21] Near the effective demise of the First International in 1872, Marx and Engels wrote a resolution for the Hague Congress that said, "In its struggle against the collective power of the possessing classes the proletariat can act as a class only by constituting itself a distinct political party. . . . This . . . is indispensible to ensure the triumph of the social revolution."[22] In 1875, Engels identified the Eisenacher wing of the German Social Democrats as "our" party.[23] The masses were important, no question, but the correct party was important as well.

Fourth, would the revolution be violent or would peaceful reforms gradually add up to "revolution"? Should one work against the system, or for reform within it? Theoretically the answer was simple: against the system in a violent revolution. Material force against material force was necessary to overthrow the bourgeoisie, Marx had argued. Perhaps because of the existence of the German Social Democrats, a Marxist party that formed at Eisenach in 1869; perhaps because he simply changed his mind; or perhaps because Marx had never intended to sound so much in favor of violence, he said in an 1872 speech delivered in the Netherlands:

> We know of the allowances we must make for the institutions, customs and traditions of the various countries; and we do not deny that there are countries such as America, England, and I would add Holland if I knew your institutions better, where the working people may achieve their goal by peaceful means. If that is true, we must also recognize that in most of the continental countries it is force that will have to be the lever of our revolutions; it is force that we shall some day have to resort to in order to establish a reign of labour.[24]

Although qualified, this statement allowed for the possibility of a peaceful transition to socialism in the democratic countries where suffrage was already meaningful by 1872. In 1895, Engels went so far as to suggest that perhaps the ballot box might replace the barricades in Germany as well.[25] He qualified this by alluding to the possible need for violence, but certainly both Engels and Marx confused the issue of whether the method of change was violence or voting. If violence, then revolution could be expected. If peaceful voting were the means of achieving reforms, then gradually enough reforms might accumulate so that one could speak of a revolutionary change in the society, but it would come through a much longer process.

Thus, the legacy left by historical materialism was not very clear. But even though history quietly refused to step into the pattern that Marx had constructed, he believed until his death that revolution was imminent. Regardless of whether or not others agreed with him, Marx felt that he had solved the riddle of history and found the means to end the enslavement and alienation of human beings everywhere. That solution, he believed, was communism.

*   *   *

From 1848 onwards, both Marx and Engels would have liked historical events to fit their predictions. But when this did not happen they did not change their theories; instead, they continued to reinterpret empirical reality to maintain the correctness of their theories. As a result, they confused their revolutionary legacy, especially in regard to the cause of revolutions, their timing, whether a radical party was necessary, and whether the revolution would be peaceful and gradual or violent and imminent.

AFTERWORD

Whether Marx was right or wrong is not important. The discussion of historical materialism would not be taking place if Marxist communism had not become the operative ideology of *over one-third of the world's population.* But, because it has been applied in so many revolutionary situations in the twentieth century, there is a tendency to grant Marxism a greater significance than it deserves.

For instance, why did Lenin, the leader of the Russian Bolsheviks, apply Marxism to the relatively underdeveloped Russia in 1917 when Marx expected the revolution to occur in advanced industrial societies? Why do we imagine that Lenin misapplied Marxism instead of seeing that Marx himself was wrong?[26] And second, why *did* the widespread application of Marxism occur in underdeveloped societies? *Could it be because Marx's vision of the future rather than his description of the past fit the crisis of modernization in those countries?* The next chapter moves closer to an answer to those questions.

NOTES

1. A summary of Marx's views on historical materialism can be found in Karl Marx, "Preface to *A Contribution to the Critique of Political Economy,"* in *Marx-Engels Selected Works* (Moscow: Progress Publishers, 1970), vol. 1:503–504.

2. Engels felt that those who believed that Marx and himself were rigid economic determinists were wrong, even though Engels felt that he and Marx were partly to blame because they did not always take the time to put in the necessary qualifiers. Engels argued that the superstructure also had an impact on the economic foundation of society. See Friedrich Engels, "Letter to J. Bloch in Konigsberg" (September 1890), in *Selected Works,* vol. 3:487–488.

3. The foregoing paragraph is paraphrased from Karl Marx, "Letter to P. V. Annekov in Paris," in *Selected Works,* vol. 1, especially pp. 518, 522.

4. Marx, "Preface to *A Contribution to the Critique of Political Economy,"* p. 504.

5. For extensive detail, see Friedrich Engels, "The Origin of the Family, Private Property and the State," in *Selected Works,* vol. 3:191–334. This work was partially based on Lewis Morgan's *Ancient Society* (1877) and Marx's notes on that book to which Engels added his own research.

6. Karl Marx, "Preface to the First German Edition of the First Volume of *Capital,"* in *Selected Works,* vol. 2:89.

7. Karl Marx, "Afterword to the Second German Edition of the First Volume of *Capital*," in *Selected Works*, vol. 2:98.

8. Karl Marx, "Productive Power in Capitalist and Communist Society," in *Grundrisse*, trans., ed. David McLellan, (New York: Harper & Row, 1971), p. 151.

9. G. W. F. Hegel, *The Phenomenology of the Spirit*, in *The Philosophy of Hegel*, ed. Carl Friedrich (New York: Random House, 1954), p. 409.

10. For a fuller discussion of this point by Marx, see "The Contributions of Labour and Capital to the Production Process," in McLellan, *Grundrisse*, pp. 87–93.

11. The term *overspecialization of labor* is used here to avoid confusing it with the more common *division of labor*, which had a more general, alienative meaning in most of Marx's writings.

12. See an excellent discussion of these points in Robert Tucker, "The Marxian Revolutionary Idea," in *Why Revolution?* eds. Clifford Paynton and Robert Blackey (Cambridge, Mass.: Schenkman, 1971), pp. 214–229.

13. Friedrich Engels, "Preface to Marx's Class Struggles in France, 1848–1850," in *Selected Works*, vol. 1:189.

14. Ibid., p. 187.

15. Karl Marx, "The Class Struggles in France, 1848–1850," in *Selected Works*, vol. 1:289.

16. Engels, "Preface," pp. 191–192.

17. Marx, "Class Struggles," p. 223.

18. Karl Marx, "Letter to Engels in Manchester, April 16, 1856," in *Selected Works*, vol. 1:529.

19. Friedrich Engels, "Letter to J. Wedemeyer, April 12, 1853," in *Marx-Engels Selected Correspondence* (Moscow: Foreign Languages Publishing House, n.d.), p. 94.

20. Karl Marx and Friedrich Engels, "The Manifesto of the Communist Party," in *Selected Works*, vol. 1:120.

21. Karl Marx, "Letter to Engels, September 11, 1867," in *Marx-Engels Selected Works in Two Volumes* (London: Martin Lawrence, Ltd., 1942) vol. 2:614.

22. Karl Marx and Friedrich Engels, "From the Resolutions of the General Congress Held in the Hague," in *Selected Works*, vol. 2:291.

23. Friedrich Engels, "Letter to August Bebel, March 18–28, 1875," in *Selected Works*, vol. 3:31.

24. Karl Marx, "The Hague Congress," in *Selected Works*, vol. 2:293.

25. Engels, "Preface," p. 201.

26. Note, for example, the words of Alfred G. Meyer: "It should be obvious that the thoughts of Marx and Engels about the nature of the revolution or about political strategy could not serve as an adequate guide to their Russian disciples." Alfred G. Meyer, *Communism* (New York: Random House, 1984), p. 30. Also note George Lichtheim's words: ". . . if anyone introduced a profound 'revision' of Marxist doctrine, it was none other than Lenin himself." George Lichtheim, *Marxism: An Historical and Critical Study,* (New York: Praeger Publishers, 1965), p. 330.

DISCUSSION QUESTIONS

1. Was Marx as much of a materialist as he himself thought he was? Explain.
2. Describe Marx's stages of historical materialism in outline form.
3. Exactly how does one stage dialectically develop into another?
4. What is economic determinism? Does this describe Marx's position?
5. Why does Marx's revolutionary theory appear ambiguous?
6. What is surplus value?
7. What is the absolute general law of capital accumulation?

8. What is the industrial reserve army?
9. Why did Marx ignore the Asiatic societies?
10. What is the division of labor in historical materialism?
11. Why was the proletarian revolution expected to be the culmination of human prehistory?

4

The Communist Goal
of the Future

In the early months of 1844, shortly after he arrived in Paris, Marx became convinced that the future would be a communist one. His correspondence and the memoirs of Arnold Ruge mark the change in Marx's thinking.[1] Marx came to believe that when awareness of alienation—its cause and its cure— had spread among workers to the point where they saw life itself as a living contradiction, they would become revolutionary in order to transform the conditions of their existence. Arising from the absolute low point of human alienation, degradation, and destitution, the revolution would be total: a universal emancipation by the class that represented everyone. In freeing itself, the working class would liberate all humans from the crushing bondage of alienated existence.

Communism represented the key that could unlock previously frustrated human forces, a solution to the riddle of history, a positive rather than a negative direction for future human development. Marx described the goal in philosophical language, but this is what he meant.

> *Communism* as *positive* overcoming of *private property* as *human self-alienation,* and thus as the actual *appropriation of the human* essence through and for man; therefore as the complete and conscious restoration of man to himself within the total wealth of previous development, [is] the restoration of man as a *social,*

that is human being. This communism as completed naturalism is humanism, as completed humanism it is naturalism. It is the *genuine* resolution of the antagonism between man and nature and between man and man; it is the true resolution of the conflict between existence and essence, objectification and self-affirmation, freedom and necessity, individual and species. It is the riddle of history solved and knows itself as this solution.[2]

To Marx, the proletarian revolution was *much* more than a revolution in the normal sense of that word. The working class would initiate a climax of human history, establishing a philosophical watershed where the difference between the prerevolutionary past and the postrevolutionary future would be very clear. But Marx and Engels were not very specific about that communist future. They did not describe postrevolutionary society because they did not want to be classed with popular utopian socialists who provided too many imaginative and minute details about the future. Although Marx and Engels occasionally referred to the communist future, their references are scattered over a long period of time and in many different contexts. In this chapter, these views of the communist future are gathered and presented with a greater consistency and organization than Marx and Engels themselves provided. Although they would probably agree with a coherent view built from their writings, there is a risk in presenting it. Remember, too, that Marx and Engels described the future from their vantage point in the nineteenth century. They projected what they believed would come to pass, but they were *not* in any sense describing actual communist systems as they later developed in the twentieth century.

COMMUNISM AS A MEANS TO AN END

For Marx, communism was both means and goal. Recall that his struggle against religion had become a battle against the society that required religion. Although overcoming human alienation would be the great task of the revolution, in the process atheism would become unnecessary. Previously, the denial of God had been an affirmation of the human spirit, but after the revolution the human would be affirmed in every aspect of life. Thus, not atheism but the return of the human to full essential being was the goal of the future.

In a similar fashion, communism comprised the essentially negative means, which Marx characterized as the **negation of the negation** for arriving at a positive communist future. The abolition of private property and the expropriation of the expropriators or the smashing of the state, the militant arm of the ruling class—were not, after all, things that one did for long; they would be done *in order that* practical communism, Marx's concept of humanism, might come into being. In one of the last of his 1844 Paris manuscripts, Marx wrote:

The position of communism is the negation of the negation and hence for the next stage of historical development, the necessary *actual* phase of man's emancipation and rehabilitation. *Communism* is the necessary form and dynamic principle of the immediate future but not as such the goal of human development—the form of human society.[3]

The abolition of private property, therefore, would be the *first step* taken by the proletarian revolutionaries. This would be accomplished not by burning down people's houses, or by redistributing the wealth of society, but by basically altering the mode of production. A socialism that depended on redistribution of wealth was, according to Marx, vulgar socialism. Marx was not intending to prune the property "tree," but to uproot it. The means of production would be socialized and the division of labor in the relations of production would be forever ended. No longer would there be owners and nonowners of the means of production; all would own collectively. Private property would be *abolished,* not merely equalized.

To do this, however, the proletariat would need power and the willingness to use it. Their power would come from the state they had conquered.

> ... the proletarian class will first have to possess itself of the organized political force of the State and with this aid stamp out the resistance of the Capitalist class and reorganize society ... [carrying out] that economic revolution of society without which the whole victory must end in a defeat and in a massacre of the working class like that after the Paris Commune.[4]
>
> Between capitalist and communist society lies the period of the revolutionary transformation of the one into the other. Corresponding to this is also a political transition period in which the state can be nothing but *the revolutionary dictatorship of the proletariat.*[5]

Anarchists such as Mikhail Bakunin (1814–1876) or Pierre Joseph Proudhon (1809–1865) wanted to destroy the state, which would cause capitalism to collapse. Marx and Engels reversed this. They would destroy capitalism and the withering of the state would follow. But before the state collapsed, they would use its power to socialize the means of production and to crush opposition from former capitalists. Engels wrote that the temporary use of the state by the proletariat would not be in the interests of freedom, but in order to hold down workers' adversaries by force.[6] Actually, he continued, the notions of *freedom* and the *state* were unlikely as simultaneous concepts. In that sense, Marx and Engels agreed with the anarchists. As soon as it became possible to speak of freedom after the revolution, the state would cease to exist and be replaced everywhere, Engels said, by *Gemeinwesen,* a good old German word that conveys the meaning of the French word *commune.*[7].

In the meantime, Engels felt, the state would be useful to the working class. Workers would not forget that the state was actually a machine used for the oppression of one class by another. An evil thing *at best,* the state would be amputated of as many of its worst parts as possible before it was used in the dictatorship of the proletariat.[8]

Such use of the power of the state would only be temporary. When the means of production were socialized, the division of labor would be abolished and classes reflecting a division of labor would be unable to arise. The need for an oppressive arm of the ruling class in a context of classlessness made no sense. Therefore the state would function only for the transition. How long would that be? Engels answered, rather ambiguously, ". . . until such time as a generation reared in new, free social conditions is able to throw the entire lumber of the state on the scrap heap."[9]

> When at last [the state] becomes the real representative of the whole of society, it renders itself unnecessary. As soon as there is no longer any social class to be held in subjection; as soon as class rule, and the individual struggle for exist- ence based upon our present anarchy in production, with the collisions and excesses arising from these, are removed, nothing more remains to be repressed, and a special repressive force, a state, is no longer necessary. The first act by virtue of which the state really constitutes itself the representative of the whole of society—the taking possession of the means of production in the name of society—this is, at the same time, its last independent act as a state. State inter- ference in social relations becomes, in one domain after another, superfluous, and then dies out of itself. . . .[10]

These ideas were based on the belief that the socialized relations of production would dramatically influence the new environment and the peo- ple in it. Failure to comprehend this key element in scientific socialism will make Marx's comprehension of the future read like a fairy tale, out of touch with what is called reality. Marx believed that what one might call "human nature" was, to a large extent, a reflection of the dominant mode of produc- tion—not entirely caused by it but deeply conditioned nonetheless. People were products of heredity, of course, but to a much greater extent they reflected the environment that they had created—the institutional superstruc- ture that surrounded them from birth. Although humans had always been social (a part of their essence), previous relations of production, reflecting the perniciousness of private property, had obscured that natural character by forcing all kinds of "separations" into it. What passed for human character in the bourgeois period was actually a travesty of real human nature. Social- ization of the means of production meant overcoming alienation in real life, and that meant a return to true human nature. The bourgeois individual with a passion for private acquisition at the expense of society would fade away. The new person would be a *social* person.

This new essence was superior to the one humans began with in primi- tive communism. In that earlier period people had been alienated from nature, from a world considered outside themselves, because they could not understand it. All of subsequent history, however, had demonstrated an increasing human ability to conquer that "outside nature" and to impose human will on it. By the time of communism, therefore, the nature that surrounded people would be understood as a part of *human* nature and a bond with other people. The new human nature would thus be the most complete human essence—and real *human* history could only then begin. Like the prodigal son, in their long history people had squandered their essence and, as a result, had eaten of the bitter husks of alienation. Now, rejecting that past, they would return to themselves wiser and richer.

*　　*　　*

In the view of Marx and Engels, communism as means to an end would comprise the abolition of private property, socialization of the means of production, establishment of the dictatorship of the proletariat that would seek and destroy enemies of the revolution, and the beginning of a changed human nature that would reflect the altered status of the economic foundation of society. Ownership of anything important would become social rather than private. Although state power was to be only temporary, it would be used on behalf of worker interests. In addition, people would find that their alienated existence, taken for granted for so long, was gradually being left behind.

COMMUNISM IN PRACTICE

The revolutionary dictatorship of the proletariat, according to Marx and Engels, would be communism as means, socializing the means of production, destroying capitalist opposition, and abolishing institutions that reflected the alienated past. But in employing those means, the proletariat would be proceeding dialectically, that is, building a qualitatively new phenomenon on the basis of what was of enduring value in the old. Property that was the basis of production and that separated people into classes of have and have-nots was to be abolished. Articles of consumption would belong to all people as a human right, but they would be consumed individually. In communism, one could say that this dress or that shirt was a personal possession, but property as a privilege for the few would be abolished and replaced by the private possession of social property for the purposes of consumption.

This was a general description of what was expected to develop from the socialization of the means of production. Details of how this would work in specific situations were not provided. Think of private cars, for example. Would they all be the same model, color, and year? If not, would they not be property that separated one person from another? Would the production of such cars accord with Babeuf's idea that anything produced must be available to all or else it should not be made? All sorts of questions can be asked but Marx and Engels are poor sources for answers. They refused to provide details. Their answer to all such questions probably would be, Let the future society make the decision.

Other institutions would follow a path similar to that of property. Liberal democracy, for instance, for all of its freedoms and pretensions of freedom, was nonetheless a bourgeois state. Vulgar democracy, Marx wrote, saw the millennium in the democratic republic. Proponents of liberal democracy did not suspect that such democracy was actually the last form of the state in bourgeois society—the one in which the class struggle had to be fought to a conclusion.[11] Much later, Engels described the democratic republic as the last form of bourgeois rule and the one in which that rule crumbled.[12] *Bourgeois* democracy was to be transcended by a new, more truly democratic form that exchanged past illusion for reality. With the withering of the state, the new society would see the administration of *things* rather than *people.*

Communism in practice would flow out of communism as means. The new social form would be called *association* or *community.*

> The working class in the course of its development will substitute for the old civil society an association which will exclude classes and their antagonism, and there will be no more political power properly so-called, since political power is precisely the official expression of antagonism in civil society.[13]

Abolition of the division of labor could not endure without a communal organization of society. Instead of the pretense of a democracy made impossible by the division of labor, the genuine community was an organization in which individuals gained their freedom in and through their association. If people were really to assert themselves as individuals and to rule themselves, they had to do so through community with others.[14]

The new association, therefore, would not be political in the sense of factional politics, but it would be democratic in a real sense of the word. The people would really rule. People would become their own masters; they would shape their institutions instead of being shaped by them. Exactly how this association would work in practice was not described; this was one of many details left to work itself out. Engels provided a clue to the possible mechanics of the association, however, when he generalized about the worth of two methods used by the **Paris Commune of 1871.** He spoke highly of filling all posts by universal suffrage, with easy recall provisions, and paying those elected officials no more than what other workers were paid.[15]

The association, therefore, was not anarchic; there would be authority in the new system. Not political authority, of course, but an authority similar to self-discipline, arising from *social* consciousness and *voluntary* cooperation, and guided by leaders or coordinators. For example, an orchestra is a disciplined group of people who are coordinated by a conductor, who in turn is guided by the music or plan. If everyone in the orchestra played the notes that pleased him or her individually, music would only rarely emerge. Self-disciplined performers would do better, but guidance and coordination must be added to self-discipline in order for real music to emerge.

Remember that this was to be a different sort of democracy. People would be masters of their own society, but humans were not simply individuals—they were simultaneously social. Marx and Engels were writing about all people, not just a few. The human collective would have to be disciplined and coordinated, and the people would have to provide this discipline and coordination for the society as a whole, not just for themselves. Some people would be given the task of coordinating the whole. The bread had to get to the grocery stores, the wheat to the mills, and the milk to the children. This would require that people perform their tasks, under guidance, in concert with each other.[16]

As a matter of common sense, Marx wrote:

> . . . all labours, in which many individuals cooperate, necessarily require for the connection and unity of the process one commanding will, and this performs a function which does not refer to fragmentary operations, but to the combined labour of the workshop, in the same way as does that of a director of an orchestra. This is a kind of productive labour which must be performed in every mode of production requiring a combination of labours.[17]

The whole point of the plan was to be production for consumption; production for use, not for exchange. The products that people wanted would be produced. Production required discipline and coordination, a plan of operation that developed from below, but that represented social authority nonetheless.[18] The social authority, the plan, would function as the head controls the body, making progressive development possible. The result would be an unbroken, progressive development of industry and a practically limitless growth in production, an abundance made possible by unfettering the very productive capitalist system. By removing private extraction of profit and proceeding according to a rational plan, wealth would be created that would change human life much as a river flowing over former desert sands would bring new green life. Engels wrote that the new society would do away with extravagance and waste, end the devastation of productive forces and products, and free the producing system to provide a fully sufficient existence for everyone.[19]

Communism in practice would mean association, planned production, and abundant wealth. People would have to work, but work would be different. Formerly, work had been merely a means to satisfy the needs of a person's animal existence, but now work would be the expression of *human* life. Productive labor was an opportunity for the individual to develop and utilize all of his or her faculties, both physical and mental. Productive labor would become more like a hobby, something a person would want to do because he or she could do it well, and because it would be fun; it would be especially pleasant, because no one could place his or her labors on another group's shoulders; there would be no privileged class. To add to this pleasure, people would be able to work at different tasks rather than be bored with only one. Associational labor would bring an individual worker's varied interests into daily life. One might, for example, be a teacher in the morning, a bricklayer in the afternoon, and a movie critic in the evening. Talents of people, heretofore only latent, would be allowed to flower. People would labor still, but with a profound difference.

Private housework would be transformed into a public industry. This implied childcare centers, public dining facilities, and perhaps a corps of "maids" performing vital cleaning functions as part of their social labor. The domination of women by men, a necessity so long as the division of labor made the male the breadwinner, was already being undermined in capitalism. Under communism the woman would be an equal partner with the man, married for love and only as long as love endured. The entire relationship between men and women, and between women and society, would dramatically alter.[20]

Agriculture would also be transformed by associational, rationally planned labor. Land would be withdrawn from private ownership, transformed into social property, and worked by cooperative associations of agricultural workers as part of their social labor. Communal activity on the combined farms would allow for greater production, which would be coordinated in the single rational plan for the entire worldwide association. The differences between town and country would diminish. Large cities would be broken up and rural areas would lose their sense of stuporous isolation. Scattered industry would receive purer water and cleaner air, and the rural areas would benefit from the nearby industries. City sewage would be used as agricultural fertilizer. Mixing town and country together would even out the population distribution and combine the best of both urban and rural worlds.[21]

Extensive coordination would require that some people be entrusted with the administration of the social plan, but such positions were not understood as potential platforms of power. The elected administrators would have talents for that job, but like everyone else, they would do other tasks as well. Perhaps an administrator would fish in the morning, administer in the afternoon, and be a school teacher in the evening. The administrator's position was not, therefore, one of privilege. Easy recall was to be built into the system in case of need, but most of the details would be worked out by the people in the association.

Communism in practice would also mean an economics of time; the amount of time required for human labor would be reduced both by the rational plan and by the production for use rather than for exchange. The time saved would allow more production of different things or more time for intellectual development. The massive introduction of machinery that had reduced surplus value in capitalism would have a different impact in communism; it would lower work requirements without lowering consumption levels. Greater amounts of leisure time could be used to gain more education in the arts and sciences, and education would now be available to all.[22] Even under capitalism, semi-automated industry was placing production on the level of an automatic process requiring supervision and regulation and little else. Under communism, savings in labor time that allowed for more education would result in improvements in production and qualitative differences in the workers themselves. Humans living and working in the association would be renewing both themselves and the world of wealth that they had created.[23] What was really worth preserving in historically inherited culture, science, art, and human relations would be preserved and converted into the common property of the whole society where it would be developed further.[24]

Communism in pratice would have a final social benefit: peace. In its revolution, the proletariat would already have demonstrated that it had left behind the narrow confines of bourgeois nationalism. The association would be worldwide, and the conflict between classes would have disappeared. Since needs would be satisfied and talents directed into social channels, hostility between groups of people or between individuals would wither away, just as the state would. Engles wrote glowingly about the American Iroquois tribe practicing primitive communism:

> Everything runs smoothly without soldiers, gendarmes or police; without nobles, kings, governors, prefects or judges; without prisons; without trials. All quarrels and disputes are settled by the whole body of those concerned.[25]

Although the primitive society, however wonderful, which had been reflected by the Iroquois, had been doomed to perish, all of the subsequent history of human progress in mastering nature and improving production did not diminish the beauty of that primitive communist beginning. The communism of the future would be far richer because it would be totally unalienated, fully human, and worldwide. The socialized means of production proceeding according to the rational plan for the benefit of everyone would put an end to crime and an end to war. A new society would spring up, Marx wrote, whose international rule would be peace, because its national ruler would everywhere be the same: labor.[26]

*   *   *

According to Marx and Engels, communism in practice would mean not only social property, but democracy in a new and different context: association or community. This association or commune organization would see the expression of people's will without class antagonism and without political power. Exactly how this would work was left to the future to determine for itself; in broad outlines, the commune would work on the principle of a town meeting in which everyone was equal and each person found it possible to voice an attitude or opinion. All social posts would be filled by universal suffrage and it would be easy to recall elected officials if necessary. The pay of the administrators would be the same as that of an average worker.

The commune concept would be worldwide and, in general, it would function as the master coordinator of all important activities much like the conductor of an orchestra pulls individual performances together into a harmonious whole. All production would proceed according to this notion of a rational plan. How such a concept could be implemented on a global scale was left unspecified and the possible tensions between participatory democracy and central planning were left unexplored.

Commune organization would result in an increase in leisure time that individuals would use to further their education. A second result would be worldwide peace. Class antagonisms would have ended, and the commune network would have covered the world. A third result would be shared social wealth that was greater than any seen before. Waste, extravagance, and private profit would be eliminated, and people working for themselves would labor with far more zeal. The wealth to be shared was expected to be real affluence.

COMMUNISM AS DISTRIBUTION OF SOCIAL WEALTH

The new society, as Marx and Engels envisioned it, would also have a new mechanism for the distribution of social wealth to individuals. In general terms, that mechanism varied according to which phase of the future one was in. Two such phases were expected: socialism, followed by communism. This was one of the few times that Marx distinguished between the two words. *Socialism* referred to the initial phase just after the revolution, and *communism* to the final phase.

The proper distribution of social wealth could be realized only when the means of production had already been socialized. *Property was to be abolished, not equalized or shared in some better way.* To Marx, anything less was vulgar socialism. His goal was to help society implement a fundamental alteration that would kill off the disease itself, not simply attack the symptoms with partial solutions. Distribution was important, but *it was to flow out of the socialism* rather than constitute the means of achieving it.

Before one could speak of distribution to people as individuals, Marx wrote, the association would need to make sure of the basis of their lives—the engine of production. First, society should replace the used-up portions of the means of production such as raw materials and worn or outdated machinery. Second, society should budget for production expansion. Third, a reserve fund for contingencies should be established. Fourth, an allocation for nonproducing but associated costs of production, such as administration, schools, public health, and unemployment compensation should be made. This would come off the top. The remainder would be divided as social dividends among the individual producers in the society.[27]

The manner of distribution to individuals would depend on the character of the society. In the initial period following the revolution, the society would still be economically, morally, and intellectually scarred with the birthmarks of the old capitalist system. In this first phase, workers would not exchange their products as social wealth belonging to all of them, even though there would be a direct relation between labor and product. The *value* of the product would still be expressed in external "monetary" terminology, resulting in the laborers being individually rewarded. A person's labor time would entitle the worker to a certificate stating that, after deductions, he or she should receive from the common store goods equivalent to that labor time. The workers would each receive back from the society the exact amount, less deductions, that their labor had contributed.

Distribution in the initial stage of socialism would differ from that of the past because money would not exist as a medium of exchange: a given amount of labor would simply be exchanged for an equivalent amount of products. At this stage, however, such distribution would be an equality, Marx insisted, that papered over inequality. As part of their natural endowment, some workers were stronger, both physically and mentally, and could produce more and work longer hours than others. While the labor of everyone was valued, an individual's labor would still be measured and rewarded on the basis of how hard or how long he or she worked. In addition, some workers required more of a reward than others just to stay equal. Some would be married with families, others would be single. In other words, this initial equality, raised to a social right, ignored the unequal natural endowments and/or unequal needs of the people. The result would not be new classes, but some would clearly be better off than others. "From each according to ability, to each according to work" was not yet communism.

To overcome this problem, social right, instead of being equal, would have to be unequal. Equal social right in socialism led to inequality. When society had sufficiently distanced itself from the capitalist past, social right could be made unequal so that equality of needs satisfaction would result. At this point the transition to communism, the second phase, would have occurred.

> In a higher phase of communist society, after the enslaving subordination of the individual to the division of labour, and therewith also the antithesis between mental and physical labour, has vanished; after labour has become not only a means of life but life's prime want; after the productive forces have also increased with the all-round development of the individual, and all the springs of cooperative wealth flow more abundantly—only then can the narrow horizon of bourgeois right be crossed in its entirety and society inscribe on its banners: From each according to his ability, to each according to his needs.[28]

Distribution of social wealth would be unequal. Needs that people formerly spent their entire lives trying to satisfy would be easily fulfilled. With everyone working and producing according to need rather than according to potential sales, consumption and production would both be parts of the rational, coordinating plan. As in More's *Utopia*, as needs of consumption rose, production would also rise. As needs fell, leisure time would rise.

Distribution stores would be accessible and would contain everything important to people. A person could simply go to the distribution store and select whatever was needed for the day or more. No money would change hands. The goods available to that individual would not be tied in any way to that individual's *personal* work performance. The commodities had been produced by people who, as Babeuf had conceived it, had deposited the fruit of their labor in the common store. The rational plan, implemented by social administrators without the market mechanism, would assure that sufficient goods found their way to specific stores or outlets. The commodities in that particular store would represent social wealth to which the individual was entitled on the basis of need alone.

Under these circumstances, one might ask, what would prevent people from taking more than they needed? The answer is that these would be different people—socially, not individually, oriented. They would not want to take more than what they needed because they would no longer possess the drive to acquire individually at the expense of others. The entire concept of taking more than one needs would have been left behind.

*   *   *

Marx made it very clear that distribution *followed* the socialization of the means of production; the question of how the social wealth should be shared was an aspect of socialism, *not* the essence of socialism. Before distribution could be considered, various allocations were to be made off the top: replacement of used-up or worn-out elements of the production process, expansion of production, a reserve for contingencies, and allocations for nonproducing, socially necessary categories such as public health and teaching. In the initial socialist phase, distribution would be equal and based on one's work time, but as soon as possible, the basis for distribution would shift to need. The person with greater needs would then receive more than one with lesser needs, even though both had contributed equally to the society.

AFTERWORD

Marx and Engels saw the communist future described above as the goal of human striving, what all of history had been in the process of becoming.

The internal dynamic of history would culminate, they thought, in the start of a *human* history that was in some ways a return to the past—to the beginnings of prehistory—but that also incorporated the wealth of centuries of technological progress. The dialectic, moving through classes in history, would finally come to rest in the dramatically altered, classless relations of production. Instead of Hegel's rational state, where people obeyed self-created laws, Marx's collective was the association following a rational plan of the people's own devising. The proletariat, representing universal interests, would create a plateau of plenty by socializing the means of production. Communism as means would result in communism in practice and a new form of distribution of social wealth that was able to satisfy individual needs.

In 1837, Marx had written to his father that he was seeking the Idea in the real itself so that he could establish that human mental nature was just as determined, concrete, and firmly established in its broad outlines as was physical nature.[29] By blending his understanding of a transformed Hegel with French revolutionary politics and British economic factors, Marx believed he had unlocked the secrets of history and was pointing the way to human emancipation for all time.

Was he correct? Even partly correct? Before rushing to answer that question we should see what happened to Marx's ideas as people tried to incorporate them into their thinking and to implement them in their own parts of the world. Marx wanted to change the world. He died without doing so, but his ideas accomplished what he himself could not do during his lifetime. The world has been changed, and is still changing, because of the ideas of Marx and Engels. But in what direction? An unbiased answer will not be easy to find, and it will require careful consideration of how these ideas were implemented by others.

NOTES

1.   David McLellan, *Marx before Marxism* (New York: Harper & Row, 1970), p. 184.

2.   Loyd D. Easton and Kurt H. Guddat, eds., "Economic and Philosophic Manuscripts 1844, *Writings of the Young Marx on Philosophy and Society* (Garden City, N.Y.: Doubleday, 1967), p. 304.

3.   Ibid., p. 314.

4.   Friedrich Engels, "Letter to Phillip Van Patten, April 18, 1883," in *Marx-Engels Selected Correspondence* (Moscow: Foreign Languages Publishing House, n.d.), p. 437. See Paris Commune of 1871 in the Glossary.

5.   Karl Marx, "Critique of the Gotha Problem," in *Marx-Engels Selected Works* (Moscow: Progress Publishers, 1970), vol. 3:26.

6.   Friedrich Engels, "Letter to A. Bebel, March 18–28, 1875," in *Selected Works*, vol. 3:35.

7.   Ibid.

8.   Friedrich Engels, "Introduction to 'The Civil War in France,' " in *Selected Works*, vol. 2:189.

9.   Ibid.

10.   Friedrich Engels, "Socialism: Utopian and Scientific," In *Selected Works,* vol. 3:147.

11.   Marx, "Critique of the Gotha Program," p. 27.

12.   Friedrich Engels, "Letter to Eduard Bernstein, March 24, 1884," in *Selected Correspondence,* p. 445.

13.   Karl Marx, *The Poverty of Philosophy* (Moscow: Foreign Languages Publishing House, n.d.), p. 167.

14.   Karl Marx and Friedrich Engels, "Feuerbach, Opposition of the Materialistic and Idealistic Outlook" (chap. 1 of *The German Ideology*), vol. 1:65–66.

15.   Engels, "Introduction to 'The Civil War in France,' " in *Selected Works,* vol. 2:188.

16.   See Friedrich Engels, "Letter to T. Cuno in Milan, January 24, 1872," in *Selected Works,* vol. 3:425–426.

17.   Karl Marx as quoted in Irving Fetscher, "Marx, Engels, and the Future Society," in *The Future of the Communist Society,* ed. W. Laqueur and T. Labedz (New York: Praeger, 1962), p. 101. In fairness to Marx, this preference for a planned economy over the alleged anarchy of the market was made about a century before experience revealed the severe limitations of planned economies. However, in these and similar works, Marx revealed a tendency to ascribe reality to collective abstractions reminiscent of Rousseau's error with respect to the General Will. Even though Adam Smith expected political coordination and guidance for the economy, his "invisible hand" was most definitely not the Plan. Marx may be accused of setting up the later problem with planned economies, but it needs remembering that Marxism was applied in areas where command economies initially made a great deal of sense and, except for agriculture, performed well for decades.

18.   Friedrich Engels, "On Authority," in *Selected Works,* vol. 2:378.

19.   Friedrich Engels, "Socialism: Utopian and Scientific," in *Selected Works,* vol. 3:148–149.

20.   Friedrich Engels, "Origin in the Family, Private Property and the State," In *Selected Works,* vol. 3:248–255.

21.   See Friedrich Engels, *Herr Eugene Dühring's Revolution in Science (Anti-Dühring)* (New York: International Publishers, 1939), pp. 323–324; and his *The Housing Questions* (New York: International Publishers, n.d.), pp. 36, 95–96.

22.   Karl Marx, "The Position of Labour in Capitalist and Communist Society," in *The Grundrisse,* trans. David McLellan (New York: Harper & Row, 1971), p. 142. Also see "General and Specific Labour," ibid., pp. 74–76.

23.   Karl Marx, "Leisure and Free Time in Communist Society," in McLellan, *Grundrisse,* pp. 148–149.

24.   Engels, *Housing Question,* p. 29–30.

25.   Engels, "Origin of the Family," p. 266.

26.   Karl Marx, "First Address of the General Council of the International Working Men's Association on the Franco-Prussian War," in *Selected Works,* vol. 2:193–194.

27.   Karl Marx, "Critique of the Gotha Program," in *Selected Works,* vol. 3:16–17.

28.   Ibid., p. 19.

29.   Karl Marx, "Letter to His Father: On a Turning Point in Life (1837)," in Easton and Guddat, *Writings,* p. 46.

DISCUSSION QUESTIONS

1.   Why did Marx believe that people's consciousness and behavior would become less selfish and more socially oriented after the proletarian revolution?

2.   Did Marx believe that the redistribution of wealth caused socialism to exist or that socialism caused a redistribution?

3. What do each of the following slogans mean? "From each according to his ability, to each according to his work." "From each according to his ability, to each according to his needs." To what phase of the future does each refer?

4. What did the term *dictatorship of the proletariat* mean to Marx? Was it a dictatorship by one person over the proletariat? Why would it be temporary?

5. What does it mean to socialize the means of production when traditional government has been destroyed?

6. How would society arrive at the general plan of production and distribution that would be followed in the new age?

7. Distinguish between communism as means and communism as a practical guide to social activity.

8. How long would socialism last prior to the emergence of full communism?

9. What does it mean to say that the establishment of socialism-communism negates the negation?

10. Would the dialectic stop operating in the new society?

11. Is Marx's vision of the future an implementable possibility or just a persisting human dream?

5

The Initial Implementation, 1870–1917

When ideas are put into practice something is always lost in the transition. Not only are people imperfect implementers of ideas, but ideas themselves can never be articulated in a vacuum; they compete with other ideas and lose some of their sharpness in the process. Marx's ideas, never that clear to begin with, were understood very differently during his lifetime and applied in almost contradictory ways after his death. *Where* his ideas were applied dictated *what* part of his legacy was stressed.

THE IMPLEMENTATION PROBLEM

Most people who have some knowledge of Marxism would imagine that any problem of implementation would arise from the impossibility of attaining Marx's communism. They would point to the utopian character of Marx's vision of the future, to the Kingdom of God on earth aspects of such a total solution to human problems, and smile knowingly about any suggestion of difficulty in implementation.

The problem that arose, however, was not that Marx's ideas could not be applied, but that they were applied so differently. The difficulties were visible even before Marx's death. The people who made up the First International Workingmen's Association, for example, were by no means unified; they represented deep political, economic, and ideological differences. Yet they all imagined they were involved in a single struggle. Marx was actively involved with this organization from its inception in 1864,[1] and yet it was a disappointment in terms of implementing Marx's ideas. It created a little excitement and the illusion of international solidarity, but it accomplished nothing except to be there for fearful governments to blame for the radical nature of the Paris Commune of 1871. Both the International and the Paris Commune of 1871 were thus given greater significance than they merited. For a time, as a result, involvement in international organizations representing worker interests was banned, which had the effect of postponing the problem. When that governmental fear faded and the Second International was founded in Paris in 1889, it was still full of untested revolutionary rhetoric and international zeal, but little substance. From the beginning in 1889 to its demise in 1914,[2] the Second International was an orchestra whose members played vastly different music.[3]

The chief cause of differences among Marxist revolutionaries who sang the same songs and rallied to the same slogans in the International was the presence in some of the countries they represented of an evolving democracy accompanying an increasing industrialization. If political activity were permitted, as it increasingly was in Germany, France, and Britain, working-class representatives ran for elective office, and worked *within the system* to achieve benefits for workers. Even if the democracy in question was weak and tenuous, as it was in Germany, the longer that putative revolutionaries participated in their own political system, the stronger their tendency became to value compromise and incremental reforms over conflict and revolution. Those revolutionaries, however, who came from areas that permitted no democratic activity, such as tsarist Russia, could not work in the open to achieve incremental reforms. The only goal that made sense continued to be violent revolution. They *had* to overthrow the entire system in order to accomplish anything.

This difference, which began to divide east and west, was not absolute because advocates of violent revolution were still present in the more democratic areas, and reformers could be found in the areas still under autocratic despotism. But the dominant percentage changed from west to east: to the west of Berlin the prevailing weight in Marxist groups evolved into peaceful and gradual evolution to socialist goals, while east of Berlin the dominant strain continued to be revolution.

This general difference had further ramifications that altered the concrete meaning and significance of words common to both sides. Internationalism was one example. The Second International sought to further *international* socialist/communist goals. But, in areas where the revolutionary aspect of Marxism was watered down by parties working within their own system, it increasingly became clear that their goals could best be achieved

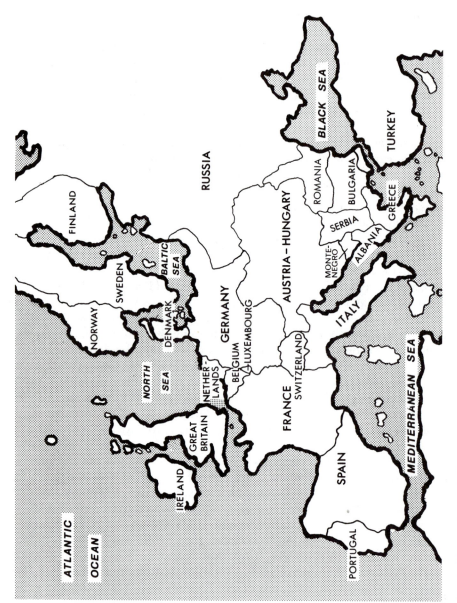

Map 2 Western Europe 1900

74

within their own nation. On the other hand, members of the International who represented the less developed and nondemocratic areas led weak, clandestine revolutionary organizations for whom the internationalism of the movement was a source of necessary strength. The internationalism of the Second International, therefore, became a pious abstraction for some members who were enjoying success within their own nation, but it became an absolute and practical necessity for others who continued to depend on that internationalism as their only hope for ultimate revolution.

Labor unions were another example. This difference was related to *when* either party or labor unions emerged in a country. In the more democratic and industrialized west, labor unions often emerged ahead of parties or at about the same time. This timing made it difficult for the more ideological parties to dominate the unions—indeed, the pragmatism of the unions helped make the Western parties less revolutionary, and the parties often became representatives of the union interests in the legislature. But in areas where neither party nor union was legal, the ideological fervor of the party, the all-or-nothing revolutionary approach, remained unchallenged by any day-to-day union activity within the system. When unions finally developed there, they became appendages of the party.

How the national party structured itself internally also seemed to flow from these differences. The degree of internal democracy in the socialist parties and/or unions tended to reflect the amount of democracy in the society as a whole. As one might expect, a significant amount of democracy was present in socialist parties and unions within and to the west of Berlin. Socialist leaders such as France's Jules Guesde (1845–1922) and Germany's Karl Kautsky (1854–1938) worked in this context. These leaders were in fact democrats, as well as socialists, who felt that the "revolution" they talked about needed the assent of the majority of the people. These liberal attitudes dominated Western Europe where the permissible, legal method of struggle was in fact altering the Marxist goal. In the clandestine parties to the east, however, internal party authoritarianism pushed out any real party democracy.

Consideration of these differences in the supposedly unified Second International clarifies two things. First, Lenin's adaptation of Marxism to fit Russia was by no means the only significant adaptation of Marxism. Other leaders representing very different countries were doing the same thing. Second, when adaptations reached the point of significantly reshaping Marxism, new theories were needed to explain and justify the new interpretations. On one side the new theory was provided by Eduard Bernstein's Revisionism, while on the other side the new theory was provided by Lenin's Imperialism.

Germany and Russia in the 1870–1917 time period were examples that help clarify all this. Germany represented those parties in the Second International that evolved into reformism, whereas Russia illustrated the opposite direction—a greater emphasis on violent revolution.

*   *   *

The implementation problem was only partly due to vagueness in Marxism itself. It was also due to the differences that arose between countries that were already becoming democratic and more open and nations in which a feudal autocracy still prevailed. Four significant differences developed: reformism among the western parties overcame the revolutionary ideology, whereas the opposite was true in the east; internationalism weakened in western parties but remained very strong in eastern parties; parties in western countries came to be either dominated by or cautious of the union movement, while in the east the party dominated the unions when they finally emerged; and parties in western areas operated with more internal democracy whereas those in the east (except for Rosa Luxemburg's) became authoritarian.

THE WEAKENING OF THE REVOLUTIONARY MESSAGE

In the Second International the German Social-Democrats (SPD) seemed the closest to Marx. It was well organized and had youth programs as well as a women's wing. In addition, it functioned as the model party for others in the Second International. Nonetheless, the SPD exhibited the weakening of the revolutionary ideology very clearly.

The Germanic area, not an independent country until 1871, was dominated during the nineteenth century by Prussia, a southeast Baltic area that became known for its harsh discipline and militarism. Prussia led the rest of Germany into active and significant involvement in European affairs. Economically the area was industrializing while politically the importance of parliaments, elections, and political parties was increasing even though Prince Otto von Bismarck (1815–1898) personally maneuvered things as he saw fit. In this context, working-class parties had some difficulties, for officials viewed them as too radical. Marx and Engels had visualized independent proletarian parties that cooperated with revolutionary elements among small capitalists or peasants and that urged on the bourgeoisie in their liberal struggles against the Prussian government. The goal of such parties would be to stay as independent as possible so as to preserve the revolutionary socialist ideology, but to cooperate with nonsocialist groups whenever that joint effort seemed to move history forward to socialism. Such, at least, was the intention, but it did not work out that way.

The SPD began with the General German Workers' Association organized in 1863 by Ferdinand Lassalle (1825–1864). Although Marx and Lassalle knew each other rather well, Lassalle was more a Hegelian than a Marxist.[4] Socialism, Lassalle thought, complemented the developing *spirit* of the German people, which sought expression through a universal suffrage that would transform the state and benefit the entire population. A year earlier, in 1862, Marx had sent Wilhelm Liebknecht (1826–1900) to Germany to begin a Marxist organization. Liebknecht, however, was expelled from the country and when the General German Workers' Association was founded it was without Marx's direct influence or cooperation.

Also in 1863 a more Marxist group formed to represent workers: the League of German Workers' Educational Society. As part of the struggle to gain worker support, Liebknecht and August Bebel (1840–1913) used the League to counter Lassalle's influence and to introduce Marx's ideas into the workers' movement.

As a result of this in-fighting, the German Social Democratic party emerged at Eisenach in 1869. Marx referred to this group as the "Eisenachers," and considered them his own German party. In 1875, after a meeting in Gotha, the Lassallians and Marxists unified under the leadership of the more Marxist Eisenacher group and became the SPD. Marx, not consulted in advance, criticized the Gotha Program for containing too much Lassalle and not enough Marx. Liebknecht, however, suppressed Marx's critique.[5]

But even in "his own" party, Marx's strategy of limited cooperation with other revolutionary or progressive elements brought unexpected consequences. By siding with the more progressive elements of the bourgeoisie against the common enemy—the German autocracy—the workers would create a chance for their own victory; defeating the autocracy was seen as a necessary preliminary to working for a proletarian or socialist victory.[6] The trouble with this idea was that *to the bourgeoisie* victory over the autocracy meant a democratic republic—not socialism. In working with middle-class representatives toward the initial goal, the working-class party's method and goal indicated a willingness *to postpone working for the proletarian revolution*. And the longer the SPD worked for republican or liberal goals, the longer exposure they had to parliamentary politics as the vehicle of progressive change—hardly a revolutionary position in the Marxist sense.

Initially the weakening of the revolutionary ideology was not clear, but as more working-class parties elected socialist representatives to various German parliaments the problem began to surface. In 1867, Bismarck had granted general manhood suffrage to the North German Confederation, and both the leader of the Lassallian group and Liebknecht, among others, had won seats in the Reichstag, the German parliament. To *talk about* cooperating with the progressive bourgeoisie while maintaining independence was easy, but difficult in practice. Both aspects of this strategy were troublesome: cooperate too much and the socialists became reformists rather than revolutionaries, whereas to insist on independence ruined later opportunities for socialists to participate in ruling parliamentary coalitions. The problems of later years grew from such early seeds, but the growth was largely unnoticed.

Hostility from German officials increased after an attempt to assassinate Emperor William I in 1878. Bismarck pushed antisocialism laws through the legislature which remained in force for the next twelve years. The new laws prohibited the existence of any organization that sought to subvert the state or social order by advocating any form of socialism, social democracy, or communism. As if the climate were not sufficiently hostile, in 1878 a negative view of socialism was also voiced by the Vatican. The papal encyclical *Quod Apostilici Muneris* informed Catholics that socialism, communism, and nihilism (anarchic revolutionary violence) were deadly plagues. The effect of both legal and religious condemnation created a decidedly hostile atmosphere for socialism in the newly unified Germany.

SPD leaders were forced underground or into exile in Switzerland, and socialist candidates for elections in Germany had to play down their socialist connections. As a result, the SPD leadership was divorced from involvement in the day-to-day life of the party, which resulted in a preservation of the revolutionary ideology among the leaders while the actual activity of the party still in Germany was quite unideological. The gap between theory and practice widened. The leaders were still speaking and writing in the old revolutionary language while party members, running for public office within Germany, increasingly became reformists as their socialism/communism was diluted in order to make it legal.

When a lessening of the fears of socialism/communism permitted a repeal of the antisocialist laws in 1890, the SPD leaders returned from their exile. An open and full meeting at Erfurt in 1891 was jubilant, but the resulting Erfurt Program described a revolutionary Marxism that reflected past theory, not present practice. Phrases such as the "increasing misery of the proletariat" were articulated in the face of vast improvements in working-class life. The capitalism that Marxism described as dying because of internal contradictions was still growing and healthy. Thus, in the SPD, the dominant party of the Second International established only two years earlier, theory and practice were wide apart.

Karl Kautsky, until 1917 the editor of the SPD journal *Die Neue Zeit,* balanced an orthodox Marxism with reformist methods. He advocated a Marxism that included a large number of by now familiar themes: surplus value as the exploitative basis of capitalism; the contradictions in capitalism; the increasing misery of the proletariat; and the fall of the small bourgeoisie into the ranks of the working class as industrial crises widened the class divisions of society. Kautsky was convinced that the future would bring the destructive monopolization of big business and the progressive socialization of the working class as economic forces prepared the workers to take the leading role from the bourgeoisie. Kautsky's notion of revolution, however, was based on an *evolutionary* model. He had a strong faith in the socialist future that would develop once a majority of the people became socialists. He disagreed sharply with Lenin in 1917 when Lenin established the dictatorship of the proletariat in Russia before a majority of people were on the side of the Bolsheviks. (Lenin responded by calling Kautsky a renegade.) The majority issue was important to Kautsky because *his* workers' state would come about by peaceful methods; he intensely disliked violence. Although he believed that a disciplined and unified proletariat was necessary to achieve victory, the victory would come about through democratic means. *Revolution became synonymous with the coming of socialism rather than the means of attaining it.*

This careful balance could not last long, and a new theory had to be created to justify the transition to reformism. The new theory was called *Revisionism,* a fundamental reassessment of Marxism.[7] Its creator was Eduard Bernstein (1850–1932), a member of the SPD who had lived in England for several years. While there he became a close friend of Friedrich Engels and was deeply influenced by the ethical and reformist socialism of the Fabian Society. Beginning with articles in *Die Neue Zeit* in 1896, Bernstein radically criticized Marxism, stirring up controversy and condemnation within both party ranks and the International. He summarized his ideas in 1899 in a book titled *Evolutionary Socialism (Die Voraussetzungen des Sozialismus und die Aufgaben der Sozialdemokratie).*

Bernstein had no intention of destroying Marxism; he just wanted to purge it of incorrect elements—things he felt that Marx had been wrong about. The difficulty was that his critique went to the heart of Marxism.

First, he attacked Marx's general reticence to discuss the socialist future as fostering the idea that after capitalism a sudden leap into socialism would solve all problems. This eschatological view of revolution was utopian, he felt, and it was Marxism's failure to probe the future that actually created the utopian attitudes.

Second, Bernstein challenged the idea that capitalism was in its death throes. It still had considerable vitality, and this greater longevity for capitalism meant, Bernstein argued, that there would be no sudden leap from capitalism to socialism, no single great act by socialists after they had attained power, but rather an accumulation of piecemeal changes brought about by social action within the limits imposed by economic development. In other words, the transition from capitalism to socialism would be so gradual that it would be difficult to isolate the point at which socialism emerged.[8] Socialists would build support among the electorate, eventually take control of the lower legislative house, then create sufficient pressure on the upper house to persuade it to accept a socialist program for the country.[9]

In making this sort of argument, Bernstein was denying the starkness of the class struggle and repudiating much of economic determinism. He argued, for example, that Marx's predictions about the pauperization of the working class, the shrinking number of capitalists, or the dying out of the middle class were simply not coming true. Because economic determinism was not working according to predictions, and attempts at political reform were achieving successes, Bernstein had no trouble scuttling the former and reinforcing the latter.

Third, Bernstein argued that workers would not be able to take over the many industries in the country immediately; workers wouldn't know how. This was another instance, he felt, of the romanticizing of the working class— the assumption that they would, without training, know how to run factories, administer the distribution of necessities, curb or exterminate capitalists, and set up an entirely new system of life—all at the same time. Bernstein maintained that a longer transition period between capitalism and socialism was needed because the industries would have to remain in the hands of capitalists for a time. During that transition period there would be consumer cooperatives but not producer co-ops, leaving industry temporarily in private hands. Additionally, a dictatorship of the proletariat was inapplicable to this different transition—it was insufficiently democratic and needed to be removed from socialist theory!

Fourth, even the idea of internationalism was attacked by Bernstein. Workers, after all, were also citizens of countries. They should go about the business of safeguarding the interests of their own nations even if that meant colonial expansion. A higher civilization, he believed, had the right to dominate a lower culture.

Naturally, Revisionism had to be officially condemned by the Marxist SPD, but the condemnation was lukewarm and Bernstein was never expelled from the party as many left-wingers wanted. The older leaders were phasing out: Liebknecht had died, Bebel was very old, and even Kautsky's influence was beginning to wane. The mild SPD response gave mute testimony to the strength of agreement with Bernstein's ideas even though they were too radical for official acceptance. New leaders were beginning to take over, and, although they insisted that the old orthodoxy was still important, they increasingly interpreted that orthodoxy to fit their reformism.

For example, the SPD only talked about support for Russian revolutionaries involved in the 1905 revolution in St. Petersburg. But even talking about the *possibility* of a supportive general strike so alarmed the trade unions that they exacted a promise from the SPD that such a strike would not be called without prior consultation with the unions. Internationalism no longer seemed important because conditions for workers *in Germany* were improving and the unions saw little point in upsetting this progress. Although their position denied international worker solidarity, it made pragmatic sense in Germany.

The lack of any real internationalism explained the positions taken by parties in the International when war broke out in Europe in 1914. In the German parliament, the majority of the SPD members voted to go to war, breaking the previous internationalist agreements at Stuttgart (1907) and Basel (1912) designed to prevent imperialist wars. An SPD minority that opposed the war went along with the majority for the sake of party unity until 1917. Most other parties in the International also supported the war, and Lenin began to call them "social imperialists."[10]

Although the SPD was a strong party and the leader of the Second International, its inner conflict, present from the beginning, turned the SPD into a group whose socialism was more a remembered orthodoxy than a program for implementation. A similar scenario was visible in both France and Great Britain. In France even the radical nature of anarchosyndicalism (anarchy guided by unions) and the appeal of the general strike faded. In Britain, the revolutionary rhetoric of socialism became difficult to remember.

The implementation of Marxism in countries with new or developing democratic traditions created a reformist socialism that denied the need for a violent, single-act revolution that would quickly begin an international movement to socialism. As these socialists increasingly became involved with their governments in the early twentieth century, their ideology seemed remote from original Marxism, however ambiguous that Marxist legacy had been.

*   *   *

The German party, the SPD, revealed the tension between revolutionary ideology and reformist practice that gradually resolved into reformism. Because the people involved were ideologues, this transition required a new theory to justify it. Revisionism, the new theory, was supplied by Eduard Bernstein, who, influenced by English reformism, exploded the delicate balance the SPD had maintained between reformism and revolution. His attack on traditional Marxism had four parts: one, the failure to discuss the future led to utopian expectations arising from the revolution; two, capitalism was not collapsing and therefore socialism would come in a piecemeal, gradual fashion; three, most implications of economic determinism were incorrect; and four, he argued that the transition from capitalism to socialism needed capitalists for a long time to run the factories. Additionally, he argued that the dictatorship of the proletariat was insufficiently democratic, and he played down Marx's internationalism. Reaction to Bernstein's ideas was very mild. He was not expelled, nor were his ideas really repudiated.

As the choice was increasingly made to solve workers' short-term problems politically, the proletarian solution to the long-term problem, revolution, was shelved. The result was to postpone indefinitely Marx's communism.

THE STRENGTHENING OF THE
REVOLUTIONARY MESSAGE

Russia, on the other hand, was a backward, enormous empire that entered the modern era centuries behind the West both economically and politically. Its government was an old-fashioned dictatorship unameliorated by constitution; the tsar's will was law. Russia's underdeveloped feudal economy made it militarily weak in contrast to its more industrialized neighbors. The nineteenth-century industrialization that did develop, financed by exporting food from a subsistence agricultural base, was under strict government control, based on state rather than private investment, and skewed to military needs. The result was an uneven state capitalism that permitted neither time nor opportunity for a middle (capitalist) class to develop. The relatively immobile labor force remained essentially peasant in character. The goal was to change enough to become militarily strong, but not enough to alter the power structure and privileges of the autocracy. By the twentieth century, Russia was a curious combination of isolation and backwardness in rural areas and state capitalist development in the urban centers of western Russia.

Because there was no possibility of reform, revolution was the only hope for significant change. Those revolutionaries who became Marxists, therefore, emphasized the violent, single-step revolution. And because the Russian proletariat was new and small in comparison to the peasantry, the tendency became overwhelming (except for Rosa Luxemburg) to think in terms of a revolution led by a *minority* in the name of the majority. Not only did this reflect the autocracy of Russia but it also reflected a fear, reinforced by what was visible in Germany, France, and Britain, that if the majority of workers were left to themselves, the absolutely necessary revolution would never occur.

Rosa Luxemburg (1870–1919), the leader of the Marxist Polish party, was an exception to this general attitude, perhaps due to her long association with the SPD. She believed in a conspiratorial party that would gain the support of the *mass* of Polish workers by struggling for economic gains and democratic liberties. She believed that her party would lead the workers into strikes and from this mass activity would come a revolutionary consciousness and the numbers the party needed for revolution. Her group was organized democratically and as much influence came from the lower levels as possible. She could not conceive of a revolution that did not have a massive following, nor of a party that was too distinct from the masses. Even so, the lack of open opportunity for Rosa Luxemburg's Polish workers caused her to stress revolutionary involvement and pushed her further away from the more moderate SPD and to identify more with Russian Marxists than with the SPD. Her Spartacus League tried to maintain ties to the SPD, but she carried her fervor for mass revolution to her untimely death in 1919.[11]

Feliks Dzerzhinskii (1877–1926), a Polish revolutionary who joined the Bolsheviks, and Lenin represented the radical-revolutionary end of this European continuum by seeking tight control *over* the workers by the party leadership. The two men believed that only an authoritarian approach would bring about a unified, successful revolution. Their impatience with democratic niceties revealed a dedication to revolution that sacrificed anything that might delay the desired goal.

These party leaders were also dependent on the internationalism espoused by the Second International. They mistakenly believed that the strength of revolutionary Marxism lay in advanced industrial nations such as Germany, France, and Britain. Initially at least, they could only make sense of the socialist revolution in such an international framework. Socialism would first come from the advanced capitalist countries and not from backward areas like Russia. Any hope for a socialist future, therefore, lay with those countries to the west. The increasing nationalism of those western parties, therefore, seemed a betrayal of Marxism.

But how did Marxism, a revolutionary ideology apparently designed for advanced capitalist systems, ever find adherents in backward Russia? Quite innocently in the beginning. Peasant-oriented radicals began to wonder if Marx's concept of socialism could work in a country that skipped the capitalist stage entirely. These Russian populists hoped that it would because they fervently disliked what they knew about western capitalism, feeling that it would not help the impoverished and backward Russian peasants they tried to represent. They wanted to overthrow the tsarist government and replace it with a peasant socialism based on the village commune. They romanticized the communes, a nineteenth-century innovation in rural life, failing to see that the chief purpose of the communes was not collective life for the peasantry, but efficiency for government in tax collecting and, after 1861, receiving the serfs' redemption payments required as part of their emancipation.

A letter was sent to Marx to ask his opinion, and, oddly enough, Marx himself agreed with the populists' idea.[12] Marx wrote that socialism based on the village commune might be a real possibility, if Russian capitalism had not yet become firmly entrenched. This was a flexible adaptation of the stages of historical materialism by Marx himself who, in other places, had written of the historical *importance* of capitalism. Marx probably agreed with the idea because he felt that by the time the Russians attempted to implement this rural socialism, a proper proletarian revolution would already have occurred in Western Europe. The "proper" European socialism would then absorb an agricultural Russia into a new global society.

Although this idea never developed much further, it did provide grounds to discuss the possibilities of Marxism for backward Russia. Georgi Plekhanov (1857–1918), a former populist who worked among the urban proletariat in Russian cities, discarded peasant socialism in favor of orthodox Marxist socialism based on the Russian proletariat. This was understandable because conditions of working-class people in Britain during the 1840s, which had helped Engels convince Marx of the imminence of the proletarian revolution, were being replicated for the Russian workers before Plekhanov's eyes. According to investigations in 1882–1883, conditions in Russian factories were deplorable: some factories forced their workers to labor eighteen hours a day; and wages were paid once or twice a year, encouraging workers' continual indebtedness to the factory store for food and clothing. When workers went out on strike, they were punitively fined or drafted into the army. Even so, strikes continued. Although some of the strikes resulted from revolutionary agitation by secret labor organizations trying to follow socialist ideas, most of the strike activity in Russia was based on economic rather than political conditions. Strikers' concerns were local working conditions and wages rather than an interest in overthrowing the tsarist government. The big strike at Orekhove-Zuevo in 1885, for example, was economic in nature even though influenced by revolutionary socialist ideas.[13] The *intellectuals* had revolutionary ideas, but the *workers* did not often share them. Lenin discovered this in the 1890s.

Plekhanov was exiled from Russia because of his radical activity and represented the Russian Marxist movement in the Second International from Switzerland, where, of course, he was isolated from even the small amount of reformism in Russia. In 1883 he established the Emancipation of Labor Group and insisted that Marxism was the *only* answer for Russia's problems.[14] Plekhanov's new group hoped to coordinate and influence events in Russia through the clandestine democratic societies (circles) that had developed at Russian universities. These radical groups in Russia were a mixture of Marxists, anarchists, and terrorists dedicated to revolution and some sort of socialism. Even though they were so ideologically mixed, the university circles provided a focal point for revolutionary agitation.

Map 3   The Soviet Union

Plekhanov's traditional, revolutionary Marxism assumed what the populists in Russia were still denying: capitalism had in fact arrived in Russia and could not be turned back. Plekhanov's position also implied that the new Russian capitalism would have to run its full course before socialism could develop. In terms of the stages of historical materialism, therefore, he seemed orthodox: one stage following another, that is, not skipping capitalism. But within that orthodoxy, Plekhanov adapted historical materialism, much as Marx had done, to fit the different conditions of a Russia still caught in feudalism and seeking a revolution against the tsar.[15]

In historical materialism the revolution against autocracy was led by the bourgeoisie. Plekhanov argued that the Russian bourgeoisie was almost nonexistent—too weak to perform this historic role. The Russian proletariat, however, was *already strong enough to help* the bourgeoisie. Plekhanov therefore urged active working-class support of the *bourgeois* revolutionary attempts so as to create the capitalist preconditions for a later socialism. He urged that the proletariat support a separate bourgeois revolution *only as a necessary first step,* introducing into Russian Marxism the idea of the minimum program (bourgeois revolution) and the maximum program (proletarian revolution) that both **Trotsky** and Lenin would develop further.

Plekhanov's Marxism attracted one revolutionary who would easily eclipse the founder within a few years. That person was Lenin (1870–1924), whose real name was Vladimir Ilyich Ulyanov. He was born in Simbirsk (now called Ulyanovsk), the son of a successful teacher who became an inspector and then a director of schools in the Simbirsk area. His father's work was so well received that he was made a part of the nobility by the tsar, a title his oldest son (Alexander) would inherit. Vladimir's mother was an educated daughter of a retired physician. She spoke German as well as Russian and taught herself English and French. Under her guidance the children put together a weekly newspaper edited by Alexander.

This placid, successful family life was rudely shattered in January 1886 when the father died unexpectedly. Shortly thereafter, at the age of fifteen, Vladimir became an atheist, and Alexander (Sasha) became a revolutionary. By this time Sasha was attending the University of St. Petersburg, where he became a leader of the university's Social Democratic circle. Alexander and a few others decided in 1886 that an appropriate way to commemorate the fifth anniversary of the 1881 assassination of Tsar Alexander II was to kill Alexander III. The plot failed, however, and Alexander Ilyich was arrested. At his trial he tried to assume all the blame himself, refused a defense attorney, and placed the real guilt on the shoulders of the tsarist regime. He was executed on May 8, 1887. The fist Lenin shook at the deity after his father's death became the fist he shook at the tsarist system. Still, there was a third shock to come, which would turn Lenin's cold fury into disciplined dedication to revolution.

In the fall of 1887 Vladimir became a freshman at the University of Kazan, where a rigid inspector strictly enforced the new 1884 University Statutes. In December the students demonstrated, and Vladimir participated. When the police arrived they discovered that another "Ulyanov" was involved in antigovernment activities, and Vladimir was promptly arrested and expelled from school. He was also banished to the family estate at Kokushkino for at least a year, and his family went along with him. His brief exile was critical for his later development because here he read voraciously, studying his school textbooks as well as the works of former Russian revolutionary heroes such as Chernyshevski and Dobrolyubov. From his reading he developed a strong sense of the necessary *dedication* a revolutionary must have to be successful. That dedication to revolution presupposed that *any* means were justified to rid Russia of tsarism, and that there was no substitute for direct, personal involvement in revolutionary activity. He began to read Marx with great satisfaction.

Vladimir (Lenin) never did get back to formal school, but he did pass examinations in 1891 that entitled him to practice law even though a legal career was meaningless for a revolutionary. And by this time he was indeed a revolutionary, already showing signs of the dedication he later exhibited. An early example occurred during the 1891–1892 famine in the Russian countryside—the result of exporting food from a shaky agricultural base. To deal with the famine emergency the government had permitted the formation of citizen groups to aid the peasants—something the tsarist government normally did not allow. Some of the groups were genuinely interested in helping the starving peasants; others were covers for radicals who saw the famine as a desirable phenomenon hastening the downfall of tsarism. Lenin was definitely in the second category. He argued that the famine performed a progressive function that forced peasants to move to the cities and become part of the proletariat, which, in turn, would hasten industrialization. Attempts to ease the conditions of the starving peasants, he felt, were expressions of a saccharine sweet sentimentality that he wanted no part of.[16]

Lenin was expressing a profound dedication to *revolution* rather than *reform,* a focus that took on the characteristics of a holy cause motivated by a morality that few people could comprehend: whatever contributed to that revolution was useful—even famine. He refused to condemn use of terroristic tactics, supposedly avoided by Plekhanov's group. For Lenin the revolution became vitally important, almost more of an end in itself than a means to an end. While Bernstein was in England developing reformist ideas, Lenin's notions were solidifying into a total absorption with revolution.

In August 1893, Lenin began his life as a professional revolutionary by joining the Elders' Circle in St. Petersburg, a group involved in propagating Marxism among factory workers. The Elders' Circle was one of many groups that had evolved from previous attempts by populists to spread education among the peasantry and the working class. Although the circles had become increasingly Marxist under the influence of both the secret Social Democrats and the Marxism already inherent in populism, the methods used by the radical intellectuals emphasized basic education for workers so that they could later be taught Marxism and develop a revolutionary conscious-ness. Often, more time was spent on general education than on Marxism; necessary but nonactivist. Some radicals began to complain that the circle activity was useless because so many of the workers they educated did not become revolutionaries. Some of their pupils emigrated to America; others went on to higher education; some went into business!

This method changed in the 1890s. The spontaneous strike and demon-stration activity of Jewish and Polish workers altered the revolutionaries' view of how these circles should be run. The pressure for change came from workers, not the intellectuals. Polish workers in 1890, following Second International suggestions, celebrated May Day as a day of demonstrations. Each year May Day became a bigger event. In 1891 worker response was much greater than the year before, and by 1892 their activity forced Russian authorities to send troops to the Polish city of Lodz. Confrontation! Far more exciting for Marxists than teaching general subjects to semiliterate workers. By 1893 strikes and demonstrations had spread to Vilna, a Lithuanian border city and a center of Jewish socialism that Yuli Martov and Alexander Kremer had channeled into Marxist directions. In 1894, Martov and Kremer wrote a pamphlet, "On Agitation," summarizing the Vilna group's decision to for-sake the old education methods and begin agitating workers and leading strikes.

This pamphlet had a dramatic impact on revolutionary intellectuals because it advocated a much more satisfying direction for younger Marxists impatient for revolution. The new approach suggested that leaders acquaint themselves with worker issues in specific factories, print up a list of demands agreeable to *those* workers, and then lead them out on strike. The radicals hoped that the employer would call the police, and that workers would find themselves struggling with the local police and, perhaps, even the tsar's army behind the police. What would begin as a strike over a few local issues could thus turn into revolution against the tsarist government.

These hopes were not realized for two related reasons that helped shape Lenin's evolving views. First, revolutionary intellectuals were arrested and exiled for leading the strikes; they were temporarily out of the action. Workers began organizing on their own, and when the central circle *organiza-tion* tried to reassume control by sending in another "revolutionary" to lead that particular group of workers, the new leader was frequently resented by the local workers, who began asking: "Are these revolutionary intellectuals *really* necessary?" Second, striking workers went back to work *too soon*, long before the police were called. The employer would usually concede the need for improvements or compromise, and the workers would return. That was what the strike had been about to the workers—but emphatically not to the revolutionaries who wanted workers to be involved in steps leading to a revolution. The workers seldom got to step two.

Lenin concluded from these experiences that revolutionary intellectuals were vital in leading the workers because the proletariat on its own would never develop *revolutionary consciousness*. He believed the highest level of consciousness workers could ever attain on their own was something he called a trade-union level. Revolutionary consciousness was beyond them.

Lenin's disagreement with Rosa Luxemburg arose from these conclusions; too much democracy in the movement was fatal to the revolutionary cause. *Workers had to be led.* He now argued that only an organization of professional revolutionaries could lead *the class struggle* of the proletariat. The workers could not do it themselves; they would always stop short at the trade-union level. The organization was vital to bring to the workers' movement the necessary class or revolutionary consciousness lacked by the proletariat. The revolution, to Lenin, began to depend more on the organization than on the workers in whose name the revolution was sought.

This organization should coordinate revolutionary activity in different Russian areas and it could accomplish this through a newspaper. While Lenin was in exile in Siberia, the Russian Social Democratic Labor Party (RSDLP) had organized in Minsk in 1898, but its newspaper had been suppressed by the police. Lenin wanted to start a new paper, publish it outside of Russia and smuggle it in. This would allow him to fight what he called "economism," or trade-unionist reformism in Russia, bring unity to the movement, and keep various local events connected with the political struggle for democracy (minimum program) so that the further goal of socialism (maximum program) could be achieved.[17]

The result was a newspaper titled *Iskra* (trans. *Spark*), critically important, Lenin believed, for coordinating RSDLP activities and for combatting the Bernsteinian Revisionism he saw coming from the German SPD. Only a party of professional revolutionaries, he argued, could act as the political *vanguard* of the proletarian struggle, the repository for revolutionary consciousness. Without the party organization the proletariat was incapable of bringing about revolutionary change; without the party the workers were nothing![18] What did not lead to revolution was "nothing," and what did was thereby good. Thus, the party should follow whatever tactic or whatever alliance with other groups that promoted revolution.

The operating principle of the party was **democratic centralism**; the party would be controlled from the center, but debates on issues could be permitted before a party decision. Once the decision was made, all obeyed without exception. In addition, the party was to be small enough to be controllable, secret, and composed of professional revolutionaries. The elite vanguard of the proletariat carried the consciousness that the workers themselves were incapable of sustaining.

Lenin's ideas stimulated strong opposition within the RSDLP from other radicals who didn't want to go this far toward a party so distinct from the proletarian masses. At the 1903 Second Congress, therefore, the famous split occurred that resulted in two factions: the majority, led by Lenin, called the *Bolsheviks* ("people in the majority"), and a minority, led by Martov, called the *Mensheviks* ("people in the minority"). For the next few years these two ideological factions struggled as much with each other as they did against the tsarist regime, and the old organization, the RSDLP, began to fade away.

This split in the RSDLP was quite noticeable by 1905 when trouble erupted in St. Petersburg. On a Sunday in January (the 22nd), the leader of the Union of Russian Workers, a priest named Father Gapon, led a massive demonstration of men, women, and children in St. Petersburg. Their purpose was to petition the tsar for certain changes, but they never reached Tsar Nicholas II. His troops fired on the demonstrators and kept on firing until at least seventy people were lying dead on the pavement, and many hundreds of others were wounded.[19] Revulsion swept over much of Russia. Within a short time the tsar's uncle, the governor general of Moscow, was assassinated by a member of the terrorist wing of the Socialist Revolutionary Party. Protest strikes were called, developing into walkouts and then into a general strike, loosely coordinated by a new workers' group called a *soviet* or council. Within a short time the new St. Petersburg soviet was being led by a young non-Bolshevik RSDLP member named Lev Davidovich Bronstein (1879–1940). His alias was Trotsky.

The Bolsheviks came into the affair late but with great excitement, calling for immediate armed risings and a revolutionary dictatorship of peasants and workers, but few people seemed to be listening. In addition, the tsarist government successfully exploited Lenin's inability to cooperate with less revolutionary groups and kept the workers' organizations split. When the Duma (legislature) was created as a concession to the populace, the more obviously revolutionary activity by the Bolsheviks provided excuses for Nicholas II to reassert his control over the situation; partly because of this the Duma steadily lost its potential for influence. The armed risings called for by Lenin's group were failures, and the Bolsheviks lost still more supporters. Lenin wanted to establish a coalition of rebellious forces that he called the revolutionary dictatorship of the peasants and workers. Such a group, he felt, would quickly be able to establish the *bourgeois revolution* (the minimum program), on the basis of which the struggle for socialism could proceed. Although this did not work out, the revolutionary atmosphere in 1905–06 did cause one of Trotsky's ideas to surface.

Trotsky maintained that in the struggle for the minimum program (the bourgeois revolution), the Social Democrats would be foolish to forget the peculiar conditions of Russia: a relatively strong proletariat and a weak bourgeoisie. Worker activity, he said, initially on behalf of the middle-class capitalists ought to be continued after the success of the bourgeoisie. A permanent revolutionary spirit should carry over, beyond the bourgeois revolution, into the transition period between the minimum and maximum programs. The permanent revolutionary spirit would shorten the duration of the transition period and would spark the international proletariat to initiate revolutions in their own countries. Worldwide socialism, Trotsky believed, would result. The concept of permanent revolution became an influential idea, and after Lenin's death in 1924, Trotsky's continued effort on behalf of an international "permanent revolution" contributed to his difficulties with Stalin.

But the 1905 revolution gave little scope to this theorizing. The tsar made modest concessions, such as the Dumas, and open participation by political parties and unions, but Tsar Nicholas II remained in control until 1917. The revolutionary momentum faded and died by 1907. During the next decade (1907–1917) the Bolsheviks tried to spread their influence against competing radicals and to organize strikes and demonstrations in Russia, but results were disappointing. Lenin's writings from Zurich during this inactive decade ardently maintained that the party represented the *spirit* of the revolutionary advanced workers and would lead the less conscious workers when the time came. Thus, he argued, perfecting the party organization meant a continual improvement of proletarian hopes and should not be despised by those impatient for more dramatic activities.

Although the party's goal was still the bourgeois revolution, Trotsky's notion of permanent revolution and the theory of the spark igniting the international proletariat were beginning to penetrate. However, the success of these ideas had an unexpected consequence. Greater participation by the workers during the transition period between the minimum and maximum programs caused the blurring of the edges of the two programs, and the proletariat lost its distinctiveness as the specific class agent of the *proletarian* revolution. It was fast becoming the agent class of *any* revolution. Plekhanov had at first sharpened the stages of historical materialism, but the permanent revolution idea caused the edges of the stages to fade. Lenin was unperturbed by this. He wrote: "Whoever expects a 'pure' social revolution will *never* live to see it. The socialist revolution in Europe *cannot be* anything other than an outburst of mass struggle on the part of all sundry oppressed and discontented elements."[20] His theory was expanding even though the opportunities to implement the theory were not.

But a proletarian revolution in backward Russia? How could this be? During the long period of nonrevolutionary activity Lenin had time to develop a theory that justified a Marxist, proletarian revolution in Russia. Still a part of the Second International, Lenin probably had to field many uncomfortable questions about why Russians who represented a feudal society were involved in a Marxist organization, or why they were so revolutionary when it was obvious that capitalism was not dying. Lenin's response was his 1916 theory of Imperialism. Building on work done by other economists, Lenin answered the questions and in the process created a new role for backward societies such as Russia.

His theory contended that the highest stage of capitalism had now been

V. I. Lenin   1870–1924

reached in what he called **finance capitalism** or **monopoly capitalism**. In order to last this long capitalism had been forced to expand its markets and investments into foreign areas that were backward or less developed. In other words, monopoly capitalists, assisted by centralized banking interests, had exported capitalism to the underdeveloped world.

Now the whole world exhibited the division of labor *between countries* as had earlier been visible *between classes* within a country. The advanced industrial *nations* were the new capitalists and the poor *countries* were the new proletariat. In other words, Russia stood to Great Britain as proletariat did to capitalist.

The export of capital to underdeveloped areas caused severe strains in the poorer areas where the exploitation of raw materials and the labor force was severe. Conversely, imperialism contributed to *fewer* strains in the advanced country because the superprofits these international capitalists were now able to gather in were used to bribe workers in the advanced industrial countries. The workers in Britain, for example, could be paid more and treated better because of the superprofits being extracted from the underdeveloped areas of the world. This was why the workers in the wealthy countries were no longer revolutionary.

But, by the same token, there existed a very strong force for *revolution* in the exploited areas, Lenin argued, for two reasons beyond the obvious one of raw exploitation. First, the export of capital created *uneven development* in that poor country. Although a poor country might still be predominantly backward, in the midst of that backwardness existed *advanced* capitalism. So to argue that a country like Russia could not even think of Marxism or a proletarian revolution because it hadn't had the bourgeois revolution and its capitalism was not sufficiently advanced was nonsense. Uneven development also created an advanced proletariat. Its members might be small in number, but they were an advanced working class just like in Britain or France.

Second, in underdeveloped countries such uneven development created workers with a *higher potential for revolution* than in the developed capitalist countries! Why? Because, Lenin argued, of *combined development* caused by the doubled need for revolution: the struggle against the autocracy *combined* with the struggle against capitalists. Capitalism, in its last stage of global imperialism, could not avoid creating this new, powerful, international seed of its own destruction.

The theory of imperialism had an air of plausibility about it because advanced capitalist nations such as Britain, France, Germany, and the United States *had acted imperialistically* with respect to the less developed parts of the world. Think only of colonies in Africa or the systematic dividing up of China. Whether this plausibility extended to the conclusions that Lenin drew, however, is another thing entirely. But for someone who believed in the whole theory, revolutions in poor countries that sought a socialist future in the name of Marx certainly became justifiable. The theory of imperialism not only explained why capitalism had not yet collapsed, but provided grounds for implementing Marxism in backward areas where the desire and need for revolution were the strongest.

Lenin could now claim that the revolutionary struggle for socialism was *more likely to begin in a country like Russia* than in the more advanced countries of Europe. This reversal of what one might have expected might even be facetiously described as "the dialectics of backwardness."[21] The more backward the society the more likely to have a proletarian revolution!

Moreover such a "backward" revolution would have international socialist consequences. An underdeveloped country caught in imperialism was, in Lenin's view, the "weakest link" forged in the global chain by international capitalists, and a revolution in the backward country would break the worldwide chain of imperialism *and spark global revolutions*. The "backward" revolution would cut off superprofits going to the advanced countries. The working classes in developed countries, no longer bribed, would become discontented and revolutionary, and the socialist revolutions, as traditionally expected, would occur. Once that had happened the "backward" proletariat would receive international assistance in constructing a "proper" socialist society.

Impatience with the minimum program had led to the theory of permanent revolution, and Lenin now expanded this notion into the international context. Within an evidently orthodox, revolutionary Marxian framework, Lenin carved out an historically vital role for the "backward" Russian workers and, of course, for his own party.

Lenin's new theories did not mean that he was now confident of an *immediate* revolutionary outbreak in Russia. As a matter of fact, in January 1917, a month before the revolution actually occurred in Russia, he said that he did not think that another revolution would take place in his generation.[22] He was caught by surprise again when events began that not only ended the reign of Tsar Nicholas II but also terminated the entire Romanov dynasty.

*   *   *

Russia was a backward, feudal autocracy in the nineteenth century that tried to industrialize selectively so as not to disturb the ancient power structure. The state capitalism that emerged, however, created the ambience for a discussion of Marxism with respect to Russian needs, and Georgi Plekhanov began the first effective Marxist organization in 1883. The RSDLP that formed in 1898 contained Plekhanov as well as other leaders such as Lenin. During the Second Congress of the RSDLP, in 1903, the group split into the Bolsheviks and Mensheviks and this division became very clear during the 1905 revolution. The Bolsheviks stood for violent revolution led by a minority party that spoke in the name of the proletariat, whereas the Mensheviks spoke for a less rigid, less elitist, and more reformist position.

In 1916 Lenin developed his theory of imperialism, a theory designed to explain why his own brand of revolutionary rhetoric was the only one to listen to. Imperialism taught that backwardness was almost an advantage in the sense that the initial revolution was more likely to come from the backward areas. This act would quickly break the international chain of imperialism, superprofits would be cut off, and the newly deprived proletariat of advanced countries would soon lead their own revolutions. The industrial nations would then show the socialist backward countries the correct path to follow.

AFTERWORD

If it is true that Lenin adapted Marxism to fit Russian conditions as he saw them, it is equally true that Marxist socialists in the more industrialized countries such as Germany did the same thing—neglected overthrowing their capitalist government in favor of *working within the system* to gain working-class reforms. Was Revisionism right and Imperialism wrong? The question implies that a "correct" position exists. Leaders on both sides of the reform–revolution issue chose to emphasize the side of Marxism that best fit their own areas.

Whether or not Lenin was theoretically correct in applying Marxism to a backward society like Russia, the deed was done in 1917. If one calls what happened in November 1917 a Marxist revolution, does one put the emphasis on the adjective or the noun? Was the Bolshevik coup a success for Marx or merely an indication that a radical revolution of some sort was a most understandable social response to the intolerable conditions of 1917 and the ones who succeeded happened to be Marxists?

The real question, therefore, was *how* the Bolsheviks would implement Marxism now that they had power. Would the ten days that shook the world, to use John Reed's description, be able to change the Russian society in ways recognizable as socialism? Or would this be just another palace coup that merely changed the players at the top of the system?

The story of how Lenin and subsequent Bolshevik leaders, in actual control of state power, blended Marxism and Russian conditions is the subject of the next chapter. It will not be a story that Lenin would have predicted, for events and circumstances over which the Bolsheviks had little control profoundly shaped their attempts to put Marxism into practice.

NOTES

1. See George Lichtheim, *A Short History of Socialism* (New York: Praeger, 1970), pp. 157–173 for a detailed description of the divisions, the people, and the events that surround the formation and brief history of the First International. Also see Chimen Abramsky and Henry Collins, *Karl Marx and the British Labor Movement: Years of the First International* (London: Macmillan, 1965). Marx prepared the First International's statutes, sat on its General Council from the beginning, and led the organization from 1868 to 1872 when he helped move its headquarters to the United States to save it from Bakunin.

2.   The actual termination date of the Second International is a bit vague. In 1914 labor parties in general voted for war credits that permitted their countries to go to war against each other even though workers would be fighting other workers. This naturally ended any pretensions to labor internationalism. After the war, however, efforts were made to pull it back together as though it had not dissolved in 1914. Those postwar efforts failed to recuscitate the organization. Hence the *effective* date of demise was 1914. The termination date of the First International was also a bit unclear. Marx caused the move of the headquarters of the International to the United States in 1872 as a tactical move to prevent a Bakunist takeover, but it was never effective in America and quietly died some four years later in 1876. Thus, it seems that the effective termination date was 1872. Dates for the First International would then read: 1864-1872, and for the Second: 1889-1914, the Third: 1919-1943, and Trotsky's **Fourth International**: 1938–present.

3.   For extensive details on the Second International, see the five volumes by George Douglas Howard Cole, *A History of Socialist Thought* (London: Macmillan, 1953-1960). See also Louis Adamic, *Dynamite: The Story of Class Violence in America* (New York: Viking Press, 1931), Evelyn Anderson, *Hammer or Anvil: The Story of the German Working-Class Movement* (London: Victor Gollancz, 1945), G. D. H. Cole, *A Short History of the British Working-Class Movement 1789-1947* (London: George Allen & Unwin, 1947), Lewis Coser, "Marxist Thought in the First Quarter of the Twentieth Century," *American Journal of Sociology*, 78 (July 1972): 173, and Michael Harrington, *Socialism* (New York: Saturday Review Press, 1970).

4.   G. D. H. Cole, *Socialist Thought, Marxism and Anarchism 1850–1890*, vol. 2 of *A History of Socialist Thought* (London: Macmillan, 1953-1960), pp. 72ff.

5.   Marx's negative comments on the Gotha Program can be found in his "Critique of the Gotha Program" in vol. III of *Marx-Engels Selected Works* (Moscow: Progress Publishers, 1970). This criticism of the 1875 SPD Program did not become generally known in Germany until after 1890. Liebknecht suppressed the "Critique" until then. When the Erfurt Program was written in 1891, Marx's "Critique" was fairly well known, but its comments were at that time some sixteen years out of date and more easily ignored.

6.   In Russia, this practice would be called the minimum and maximum progams. The minimum program involved Marxists working for a bourgeois revolution to establish capitalism so that a proletarian revolution (the maximum program) could occur. This strange approach was necessitated by the existence of Marxist parties in countries that had not yet experienced the bourgeois revolution. Instead of seeing that such a situation invalidated historical materialism's neat stages, or at least made Marx incorrect about where and when his solution to the riddle of history applied, Marxists sought to fit his ideas to the reality of their own countries.

7.   Revisionism with a capital *R* should be reserved exclusively for the ideas of Eduard Bernstein. Obviously the word (with a small *r*) can and has been used frequently to condemn an opponent's ideological position. Lenin was so negative about Revisionism that subsequent followers can call their enemies by that name and feel that they have scored points. Mao Zedong, Chairman of the Chinese Communist party, for example, called Nikita S. Khrushchev, leader of the Soviet Communist party, a revisionist. All the word really means in this usage is that the name-caller does not appreciate the ideology of a perceived enemy. In Christianity the same effect might be achieved by calling another's theology *heresy.*

8.   G. D. H. Cole, *The Second International 1889-1914,* pt. 1 of vol. 3 of *A History of Socialist Thought,* p. 277.

9.   *Ibid.,* pt. 2, p. 946.

10.   Heinz Timmerman, "The Fundamentals of Proletarian Internationalism," in Lawrence Whetten, *The Present State of Communist Internationalism* (Lexington, Mass.: D.C. Heath, 1983). p. 4.

11.   This group could possibly have grown into serious competition for Lenin, but it did not last long enough. The new German government that emerged in 1918 saw the Spartacus group as a definite threat to the rather shaky postwar state. Although Spartacus was weak and ran things democratically, it *was* more militant and stood out from most other groups at the time. To insecure German officials, the group seemed like dangerous German "Bolsheviks." In the confusion, the Spartacus leaders—Karl Liebknecht (Wilhelm's son) and Rosa Luxemburg— were executed in 1919.

12.   Karl Marx, "First Draft of the Reply to V. I. Zasulich's Letter, February-March 1881," *Marx-Engels Selected Works* (Moscow: Progress Publishers, 1970), vol. 3:161.

13.   S. P. Turin, *From Peter the Great to Lenin* (New York: Augustus M. Kelly Reprint, 1968), pp. 36–39, 43. (First published in 1935 by Frank Cass & Co., Ltd.)

14.   S. V. Utechin, *Russian Political Thought* (New York: Praeger, 1964), p. 197. Plekhanov's transition was made simpler by his living in Switzerland and because earlier Russians had tilled the Marxist soil. P. N. Tkachev (1844–1886), who was living in Geneva and Paris between 1873 and 1886, had already become a serious student of Marx by 1865.

15.   Utechin called this rigidity on Plekhanov's part a "geographical determinism." Ibid., p. 198. In the *Principles of Communism,* Engels' preliminary document that Marx revised into the *Communist Manifesto,* Engels had written: "It is in the interests of the Communists to help bring the bourgeoisie to power as soon as possible in order to overthrow them again." This concept did not make it to the *Manifesto* but it lay behind Marx and Engels' newspaper efforts in 1848–1849 to support a united front of all democratic forces with a program of universal suffrage, direct elections, the abolition of all feudal dues and charges, the establishment of a state banking system, and the admission of state responsibility for employment. See David McLellan, *Friedrich Engels* (New York: Viking Press, 1977), p. 64.

16.   Quoted in David Shub, *Lenin* (Baltimore: Penguin Books, 1966), p. 39, as the recollection of a contemporary acquaintance of Lenin.

17.   See Lenin, "Draft and Explanation of a Programme for the Social Democratic Party," *Collected Works* (Moscow: Foreign Languages Publishing House, 1964), vol. 2:93ff, and "Our Immediate Tasks," and "An Urgent Question," ibid., vol. 4:215ff.

18.   Lenin, "Party Discipline and the Fight Against the Pro-Cadet Social Democrats," ibid., vol. 11:320 (1906).

19.   The number of deaths and wounded varies with the report. Robert Goldstein states that perhaps 500 deaths and 3,000 wounded resulted from the massacre on that "bloody Sunday." See Robert J. Goldstein, "Political Repression and Political Development," *Comparative Social Research,* 4 (1981):183.

20.   See Lenin, "The Fifth Congress of the RSDLP," *Collected Works,* vol. 12:457–458 (1907), and "The Discussion of Self-Determination Summed Up," ibid., vol. 22:356 (1916).

21.   Alfred G. Meyer, *Leninism* (New York: Praeger, 1962), pp. 257-273.

22.   Lenin, "Lecture on the 1905 Revolution," *Collected Works,* vol. 23:238–239, 253.

DISCUSSION QUESTIONS

1.   Did Marx's criticism of the Gotha Program have an impact on the developing SPD? What does your answer reveal about the implementation of Marxism?
2.   What large gap did the Erfurt Program reveal for the SPD in the early 1890s?
3.   What were the major differences in implementing Marxist socialism in the period 1870–1917? What appears to have been the principal cause?
4.   What are the dates of the First and Second Internationals?
5.   What was anarchosyndicalism?
6.   Explain Bernstein's Revisionism.
7.   Why were Revisionism and Imperialism necessary theories?
8.   Who was Rosa Luxemburg and how did she fit into the differing elements of the Second International?
9.   What effect did Bismarck's antisocialism legislation have on the evolving SPD between 1878 and 1890?

10. How was Lenin's thinking about spontaneity, class consciousness, the proletariat, and the revolutionary role of the party shaped by events in the 1890s?

11. When does the distinction between Menshevik and Bolshevik begin? Why did it begin?

12. What was the idea of permanent revolution? How could it be applied within a single country and also between countries?

13. Describe Lenin's theory of imperialism, using the following words as an outline: finance-monopoly capitalism, exportation of capital to less developed areas, uneven and combined development in underdeveloped areas, the dialectics of backwardness, the breaking of the international chain, and the full proletarian revolution.

14. What questions was Lenin's imperialism theory designed to answer?

15. What was the minimum-maximum program about? Was this idea based on Marx's theory, his practice, both, or neither?

16. How did the minimum-maximum program idea, which seems to *sharpen* distinctions in historical materialism, actually contribute to a *blurring* of those same distinctions?

17. Describe at least one major difference in the development of capitalism in Great Britain as opposed to Russia. What results did these differences have for Russia?

18. What was "On Agitation" about and why was it actually written?

6

Bolshevism in Practice

In February/March 1917, strikes and demonstrations broke out in Petrograd.[1] World War I (1914–1918) had exacerbated Russian economic problems and the tsarist government was incapable of solving them. The demonstrations and strikes, not led by any particular party or group, gradually escalated into what could be called a revolution because no effective counterforce was able to restore order. Within a few days, the tsarist government toppled before the challenge.

In the absence of political order, a provisional government emerged from the weak Russian parliament. At the same time another, rival government appeared—a new soviet called the Soviet of Workers and Soldiers' Deputies. The new provisional government tried diligently to reestablish order, and it might have succeeded had it not tried to please its allies by continuing the Russian involvement in the unpopular war. Its military efforts led to massive desertions from the Russian army and prolonged the social problems that had led to the revolution. The provisional government also failed to speak authoritatively on the land question, and peasants continued to revolt in rural areas. The Petrograd Soviet, democratic and socialist, was an attractive alternative to the provisional government for many people on the left, but the Soviet had little sense of what direction it should advocate. The Bolsheviks were a minority influence in the beginning and there was too much disunity in the Soviet for any coordinated plan to emerge. The result was extensive confusion in Russian society about who was actually leading the country as well as an awareness that no group was addressing the problems that had led to the collapse of the autocracy. Chaos, therefore, continued and the radicalization of the population deepened in the major cities.

Residing in Switzerland, Lenin became frustrated trying to coordinate Bolshevik activities in revolutionary Russia with hostile Germany in-between. The Germans decided to implement a bit of inexpensive strategy to determine whether adding Lenin to the situation in Petrograd would take Russia out of the war against them. They knew that Lenin was opposed to the war and that he would, if given the chance, cause trouble for the provisional government that was continuing the Russian war effort against them. Thus, the Germans permitted a sealed train carrying Lenin and his entourage from Switzerland to move across Germany to Petrograd.

On arriving at Petrograd's Finland Station in April 1917, Lenin astonished everyone by appearing to know exactly what to do. His slogans were not theoretical but down-to-earth and appealing. "All power to the Soviets" sounded like an appeal for democratic and social rights. For him such a slogan denied power to the old order represented by the provisional government, and it gave power to the Soviet organization that the Bolsheviks did not then control, but *could* if given enough time. His slogan "Peace" meant ending hostilities with Germany. Other slogans, equally popular, were obvious in their intent: "Bread to the Worker," "Land to the Peasant," and "Worker Control of Industry."

As summer faded into autumn, Lenin sensed that the time was ripe for revolutionary action. The autocracy had been overthrown—now was the time for the proletarian revolution. "Doubt is out of the question. We are on the threshold of a world proletarian revolution. And since of all the proletarian internationalists in all countries only we Russian Bolsheviks enjoy a measure of freedom . . . [more is demanded of us].[2] Lenin's theories, which had appeared so abstract only a few weeks before, suddenly seemed practical.

Lenin may not have had any doubts, but his party certainly had them. Even though events and people had become radicalized right before their eyes, other Bolshevik leaders doubted the party's ability to succeed. Lenin was furious. He threatened to resign if the party did not move to take power. Reluctantly, the leaders agreed. On October 25/November 7 they overthrew the Kerensky regime, in the name of the Soviet, which they now controlled. The coup was accomplished with little difficulty. For the first time in history, Marxists were in charge of a state.

EARLY EXPERIMENTATION:
IDEOLOGY MIXES WITH REALITY

Lenin did not imagine that this Bolshevik coup would magically bring about socialism. He himself called the coup an armed rising or an insurrection. This, he wrote, was not a gateway into socialism so much as it was a gateway into the path leading to socialism.[3] At the same time, he wrote, the Bolshevik insurrection was most definitely not carried out for the purpose of consolidating a *bourgeois* victory. Lenin argued in 1917 that the 1905 revolution, culminating in the March 1917 revolution, could be thought of as the bourgeois revolution, and that now, in taking power in October/November 1917, the Bolsheviks were not afraid of stepping beyond the bounds of the bourgeois system. On the contrary, he said, we shall fearlessly march toward socialism.[4]

Did that mean that he thought Russia was ready for socialism? He seemed cautious about claiming too much. The insurrection's success persuaded some of the Bolsheviks that since the old minimum program had been left so far behind, the whole idea could now be dropped. Lenin argued against moving too fast because, he said, "We must first carry out the measures of transition to socialism, we must continue our revolution until the world socialist revolution is victorious, and only then, *'returning from battle,'* may we discard the minimum program as of *no further use.* [We have] . . . not yet realized the basic prerequisites for a transition to socialism."[5] Lenin meant that the Bolsheviks had established a beachhead or forward point for international socialism. Because of Russian peculiarities, the Bolsheviks had temporarily gone beyond other proletarians in more advanced countries. The Bolsheviks must hold on until those other revolutionaries could be successful and then come to the aid of the Russians. Assistance from advanced proletarians was vital, he argued, for otherwise capitalist nations would crush the one country that stood on its own for socialism.[6] The Bolsheviks had shown that Marxism *was* applicable to backward, peasant societies, and the onus was now passed to Marxist parties in the more advanced countries. But what does the beachhead party do in the meantime? Even though Marx had provided a partial guide for taking power, Marxists in actual control of a country had few guidelines. More than they realized in 1917, Lenin and the Bolsheviks were on their own.

The Bolsheviks began governing, as might be expected, with a mixture of Marxist socialism and Russian authoritarianism. The ideology that expected a peaceful, happy, and contented society of unalienated people enjoying equality and affluence was grafted onto a Russian system that had experienced centuries of a rigidly unequal social system in which no intermediate groups between the tsar and people ever reduced the arbitrary powers of the government. The Bolsheviks themselves, like the ideologues they were, had already demonstrated an intolerance of opposition, a conviction of their own rectitude, and a certainty that *they* knew what was best for the working class. Their idea of Marxism was their own interpretation, which reflected the authoritarian soil in which it had grown.

A clear example of this narrowing of what Marxism meant was the separation of the words *socialism* and *Communism.* In the nineteenth century, for the most part, "communism" had been used interchangeably with "socialism." When the two words were used separately by Marxists, communism referred to a higher stage of socialism. Although Marx had used the term "Communist party" in the 1848 *Communist Manifesto* written for the League of Communists, the parties that emerged in the late nineteenth century normally were called social-democratic rather than communist.

Almost as soon as Lenin returned to Russia from Switzerland, he urged his followers to change the name of the Bolshevik party to the Communist party in order to distinguish the Bolsheviks from the Second International tradition of social-democratic parties. In April 1917 he argued that the official leaders of social-democracy had *betrayed* socialism by participating in the imperialist war of 1914. This, Lenin argued, meant that they had deserted to the bourgeoisie. Gradually, the new name was accepted and in March of 1918 the Seventh Party Congress confirmed it. Increasingly thereafter, the word "communism" was interchangeable with "Bolshevism."

The distinction between socialism and communism became even clearer after the beginning of the Third International (1919–1943) in the exciting early years of this first-ever success: socialists in charge of a major country. In 1920 the new International adopted twenty-one conditions for membership that forced socialists in other countries to choose sides: Did they agree with Lenin's interpretations or not? Only Lenin supporters were permitted membership in the Communist International, and they were required to form *new* groups in their own countries called *communist* parties. If a socialist from Brazil wanted to join the new International (Comintern), he or she had to gather some friends together to form a Communist party of Brazil in order to do so. This change split the international movement into "socialists" and "communists." In 1920 the word *socialist* began to be a synonym for reformist social-democrats throughout the world who did not agree with Lenin's pursuit of violent revolution by an elite party, and who had reservations about the Bolshevik coup in backward Russia; the word *communist* began to be a synonym for the Russian Bolsheviks and their followers.

However, even in Russia the word *communism* had not really altered meaning: It still referred to a higher stage of socialism that was coming in the future. By changing the name of the party and forcing groups in other countries to do the same, Lenin desired only to separate from the old Second International socialists and to proclaim to the world that the high road to the future was now occupied by the Bolsheviks. He was not implying that this higher stage of socialism had already been achieved in Russia. Looking at Russian economic conditions and the way some people in Russia interpreted communism, Lenin even suggested that *communism might not arrive at all.* The Russian economy lay in ruins after the chaos of World War I. In addition, some people in Russia badly misunderstood the new communist ideology. They imagined that the new order in Russia permitted a free love that justified rape, or thought that the classlessness of communism meant the freedom to break into the homes of wealthy Russians to steal liquor and get drunk. With this ugly side of things in mind, Lenin wrote that no socialist had ever *promised* that the highest phase of socialism would actually arrive. The great socialists had anticipated that it would come, he said, but they did not assume the current low productivity levels in Russia nor the present "unthinking man on the street capable of spoiling, without reflection, the stores of social wealth and of demanding the impossible."[7]

Although aware of Russian limitations, Lenin felt that he could almost ignore them because he so confidently expected international revolutions to follow the Russian success. Contemplating his theory of imperialism, Lenin believed that the weak link of the imperialist chain had been broken by the Bolsheviks. Next would be the increasing revolutionary fervor in advanced industrial countries that would bring about an international triumph of the proletariat, which would then lift Russia out of its backward difficulties. Although he had changed the name of the party to the Communist party of Russia, he was acutely aware of the *great* distance Russia still had to go before even reaching the *lower* phase of the future—socialism.

> I have no illusions about our having only just entered the period of *transition* to socialism, about not yet having reached socialism. But if you say that our state is a socialist Republic of Soviets, you will be right. You will be as right as those who call many Western bourgeois republics democratic republics although everybody knows that not one of even the most democratic of these republics is completely democratic.
>
> We are far from having completed even the transitional period from capitalism to socialism. We have never cherished the hope that we could finish it without the aid of the international proletariat. We never had any illusions on that score, and we know how difficult is the road that leads from capitalism to socialism.[8]

Lenin had a fairly clear idea of what the future should look like. He saw future Russian socialism as being part of a changed world wherein the whole of society would become one office and one factory with equal work and equal pay. The entire world society would be governed by factory discipline that would eventually become so internalized that observance of simple, fundamental rules of social life would become habitual. Then the door would be wide open for transition from the first phase of communist society to the second, higher level—including a complete withering away of the state. The external coercive apparatus of the state, even of a very democratic one, would no longer be needed.[9]

Along with the disappearance of the state, the distinction between manual and mental work would also disappear. Socialism would become extremely productive because the retarding influences of capitalism would be removed. By utilizing new technology, symbolized by the new power of electricity, the labor of millions of workers would be made easier and their workday would be shortened.[10] Lenin believed that the new form of energy, electricity, would help usher in a new world, an international fresh beginning where oppression, poverty, privileges, and disunity would be banished forever. Socializing the means of production would result in even greater production efficiencies and even shorter working hours. Agriculture and industry would be unified on the basis of collective labor and a redistribution of the population, which would end both rural isolation and urban concentration. Every child's education would combine productive labor with instruction and gymnastics, and this would result in better social producers and more fully developed human beings. In the new society there would be neither rich nor poor, because all would share in the fruits of social labor. The standard of living would increase because people working for themselves would work that much harder. To Lenin, as with Marx, the socialist revolution meant the emancipation of all oppressed humanity.[11] The combination of socialism and technology would guarantee it.

But how to get to that desired goal? After taking power in 1917 Lenin more clearly understood the difficulties. Even though waiting for international support to materialize, time was passing, and the Bolsheviks had to make policy decisions for the society they now controlled. They couldn't continue to make "temporary" decisions as though in the next week or so the European revolutions would occur and show them what to do.[12]

In fact, the expected international socialist revolutions did not materialize—Lenin had been wrong. Instead, a comparatively nonradical "revolution" occurred in Germany as World War I drew to an end, placing moderate, reformist socialists in positions of influence and power. Although Allied soldiers rioted to force a more rapid demobilization after the war, they did not seek revolution. Despite widespread hunger and chaos in Europe, the revolutions expected by the Bolsheviks never arrived.

By August 1918 "the temporary Russian beachhead of world socialism" developed a degree of permanency that gradually generated a feeling of accomplishment among the Bolshevik leaders.[13] As the months passed and they were able to maintain themselves in power, the Bolsheviks began to take some pride in the fact that they had already lasted longer than the ten weeks of the 1871 Paris Commune. Although in March 1918 they had signed a very unequal treaty with Germany to get out of World War I (Treaty of Brest-Litovsk), *they were still in power.* Although civil conflicts erupted in 1918, the newly created Red Army was able to protect them. By the time the Third International (Comintern) was formed in 1919, they had begun thinking that *they* might bring about the victory of the international revolution,[14] that *they* had become the model the rest of the socialist world might well follow. Sympathetic leftists from advanced countries were arriving daily in Soviet Russia to see *their* socialist experiment in actual operation. It was a heady experience. But of *what* were they the models? Because the Bolsheviks who had won power in the Soviet Union called themselves Communists, and because they named their new International the Communist International, they became models of *communism*, a communism they still would not have seventy-five years later. The communism that had been their goal became the word used to describe their efforts to achieve it. They did not even have *socialism* until Stalin decreed in 1936 that socialism had been achieved. Model, then, of what? Successful holding on to power in a country?

As they held on to power, moreover, conditions in the Soviet Union worsened. They took over a backward country weakened by three years of war. In order to get out of the war with Germany, the Bolsheviks had to accept the humiliating Treaty of Brest-Litovsk in March 1918. They lost the eastern Ukraine, Poland, Lithuania, Estonia, and Latvia, and only the Ukraine was returned after the Allied victory in November 1918. The militarily weak Bolsheviks felt compelled to grant independence to Finland, and they could not prevent the loss of Kars, Ardahan, and Batum to the Turks, and Bessarabia to the Romanians. The total of lost territory represented nearly one-third of their arable land and included over one-fourth of their railroads, one-third of their textile factories, and three-fourths of their coal, iron, and steel industries.[15]

As if this were not enough, civil wars erupted. The Bolsheviks had seized power in Russia just a few days before elections had been held for a Constituent Assembly that was scheduled to meet in January of 1918 to draw up a new constitution. Part of the strategy for taking power had been to seize control *before* the elections, which the Bolsheviks lacked the power to stop, in hope of avoiding the constitutional route as the answer to Russia's problems. The Bolsheviks wanted people to think of *them* as the solution rather than a new constitution drawn up by elected delegates. Various parties had participated in the elections, delegates had been chosen, and in January elected delegates met as planned—as though the fact that the Bolsheviks were now in charge of much of the country made no difference. After all, it could be said, the voters had not given the majority of votes to the Bolsheviks. Lenin, however, permitted the Assembly to meet for only one day before shutting it down and sending the delegates home. The cancellation of the Assembly caused strong resentments and within a few months the eruption of civil wars became a serious problem for the Bolsheviks.

These internal wars devastated the already weakened country. Bolshevik opponents gathered armies of peasants led by former tsarist army officers to fight against the hastily created Red Army. Some Western support was given the White armies, as they were called, and some Allied intervention in Russia proved irksome, but by 1921 the Red Army was successful in defeating all military opposition. How were the Bolsheviks holding on to power? Militarily. What else could they do—give up?

The need to fight the civil war and Allied interventions made an already bad Soviet situation worse. The struggle for socialism became a stark struggle for survival. A more unlikely place for the socialist sharing of affluence cannot be imagined. To put it mildly, the wealth that socialism assumed from the capitalist stage of production was clearly not there. *The Bolsheviks would have to build that wealth on their own.* The role played by capitalism in historical materialism, showing labor how to produce great wealth, had to be taken over by the Bolsheviks. What the advanced industrialized countries could take for granted, the Bolsheviks had to create intentionally—an enormous task and a powerful impetus for authoritarianism all by itself.

Even with all these problems, however, the Bolsheviks as a group continued to act as though building socialism was a matter of *legislating* it. In the early days they passed laws that recognized workers' control of industry; that abolished all classes, distinctions, and privileges; that established central planning; that abolished all former legal institutions; that centralized banking; removed ranks and insignias from the army; made marriage civil rather than religious; facilitated divorce and abortion; and destroyed all institutions of the former government in favor of a hierarchy of soviets. Inheritance and property rights in land were abolished, as were large-scale industrial and commercial enterprises. Some of this legislation was temporary, such as the removal of ranks and insignias in the army, but it revealed Bolshevik attempts to implement a kind of socialism. The March 1919 party program adopted by the Eighth Party Congress went even further, calling for the liberation of women; an end to privileges one nationality might have over another; full democracy; the right of former Russian colonies to separate; and for vast improvements in housing. New schools, it was hoped, would regenerate the society. Students would receive free food, clothing, shoes, and school supplies. Industry and agriculture were also, somehow, to be greatly improved. If productivity were high enough and if workers were willing to spend two hours a day studying, they could count on a six-hour workday.

These were the intentions, and they were sincere ones, but the emerging (**war communism**) period, one of continually worsening crises, made these positive efforts meaningless. Tremendous shortages of fuel and raw materials forced many factories and railroads to shut down. The food shortage was acute. Cities looked like wastelands because so many people had gone back to rural villages in search of sustenance. Productivity was down seventy percent; inflation was out of control. The October 1920 ruble bought one percent of what it had purchased in October 1917. Between 1914 and 1921 the population of Soviet Russia had decreased by nearly 26 million people: 15 million living in Finland, Latvia, Estonia, Lithuania, and Poland; 2 million lost in World War I; 7 million killed during the civil wars; and another 2 million through emigration to other countries.[16] The pit out of which the Bolsheviks had to climb was indeed deep.

Right from the start, Bolshevik leaders were intolerant of opposition. Rival newspapers were shut down in November 1917. A few weeks later the Cadet Party was declared counter-revolutionary. On December 20, 1917 the secret police *Cheka* was formed to suppress dissent and opposition. Their intolerance worsened over time. By June 1918 the Bolsheviks had expelled all members of the Socialist Revolutionary and Menshevik parties from the soviets. Bolshevik leaders were even becoming suspicious of the large numbers of people who had recently joined their own party. The ranks of sympathetic workers in Petrograd had been depleted by civil wars and hunger; and Lenin began to feel that many workers remaining in the factories no longer supported the party.[17]

Lenin's precoup optimism, expressed in his August 1917 *State and Revolution,* had been based on unrealistic notions of revolution, expectations of European assistance, an overestimation of the consistency of the Russian working class, and on a simplistic view of what the new dictatorship would involve. In theory, a dictatorship of the proletariat would only suppress capitalists, but in practice it maintained civil order as understood by the leadership—like a police force or an occupying army. Lenin argued that to put down crime, hooliganism, corruption, and profiteering an *iron hand* was needed.[18] By May 1918 he was saying that in a real dictatorship of the proletariat the pressures created by this iron rule would be felt in all corners of the country; all opponents, rich farmers (kulaks), grain monopolists, and wealthy people would be punished by the iron hand of the proletarian dictators.[19] This required physical force. "[W]e shall cast aside with contempt all who fail to understand this, so as not to waste words in talking about the form of socialism."[20] *Cheka,* he said, "is directly exercising the dictatorship of the proletariat. . . ."[21]

The narrowing of significant focus was continuing. Marx had begun the process by substituting the proletariat for humanity and suggesting the party might represent the workers. Lenin insisted on the party, and the dictatorship of the proletariat quickly became a party dictatorship. Counter-revolution was anything that obstructed the progress of the *party.* The same discipline and threats that built the Red Army were also needed on the labor front in order to eliminate factory inefficiency or obstructive subversion. In a telegram to Stalin, one of the trusted Soviet leaders at this point, Lenin told Stalin to threaten to shoot the person who provided bad communications between them.[22] Somehow these dictatorial methods would accomplish the emancipation of humanity. Certain harsh, authoritarian measures had to be taken, it was argued, so that socialism and communism might triumph. Marxists who pointed out that the end result of dictatorial policies was an improved dictatorship were dismissed as "sorry revolutionaries" who lacked the understanding and stamina for the "steady advance of the iron battalions of the proletariat."[23]

"Only the development of state capitalism, only the painstaking establishment of accounting and control, only the strictest organisation and labour discipline, will lead us to socialism. Without this there is no socialism," Lenin argued.[24] Although freely admitting in March 1918 that the "bricks" of socialism had not yet been made,[25] Lenin spoke much more optimistically a year later, *when conditions were even more discouraging*, to a crowd in Red Square. He told them that the majority of those present who were thirty to thirty-five years of age would live to see communism in full bloom, even though it was still remote. The goal, he said, was not a fairy tale or a utopia. It *would* come.[26] All one had to do was believe in the party, accept its decisions, and work very hard. Many did.

What little evidence existed that such thinking was correct was understandably seized on almost in panic. An example was the spontaneous emergence of the *subbotniki* (Saturday workers). A few railroad workers tried to overcome the great transportation problems by working on damaged locomotives without remuneration on their day off. An overjoyed Lenin seized on this as a green shoot of communism—evidence that the future communist society was approaching. He built an entire thatched cottage out of this one blade of grass. More *subbotnikism,* he felt, would mean the emancipation of women from the drudgery of petty housework, the establishment of public catering places, nurseries, and kindergartens! The large gulf between Lenin's great hopes and such a small event can be dismissed as wishful thinking, but his failure to leave a good volunteer program alone was inexcusable. He failed to see that the value of *subbotnikism* was in its *spontaneity;* people were volunteering to work at necessary social tasks without pay! Lenin began to organize *subbotnikism* from the top, which, of course, killed the spontaneity. Within months, he was arranging "volunteer" labor and defining communism as voluntary, unpaid work, thus making it a prerequisite for party membership. The addiction to control from the top was evidently overwhelming even though Lenin simultaneously believed that the principle of this volunteerism would eventually triumph.[27]

Lenin insisted that communism be built through organization (party) and technology (electrification), and channeled through the state-controlled, industrial machine. The task of the small Bolshevik party, he said, was enormous, but it could accomplish its mission. "This tiny nucleus has set itself the task of remaking everything, and it will do so. We have proved that this is no utopia, but a cause which people live by. . . . We must remake things in such a way that the great majority of the masses . . . will say . . . [well done]."[28]

The combination of dictatorial methods and socialist legislation in a rhetorical ambience of emancipation for everyone proved difficult for some people to accept. What people did not then realize was that things were going to get worse. The narrowing was going to become even tighter.

*   *   *

The authoritarian regime that became the Soviet government grew gradually out of the combination of Marxism, Leninism, and Russian conditions. The resulting ideology became known as **Marxism-Leninism.** An authoritarian system evolved out of a revolutionary beginning that saw itself as the *solution* to arbitrary state authority. This development resulted from thousands of decisions during the early crisis years as policy evolved out of needs that were military and survival oriented. Any liberal understanding of Marxism was postponed to the indefinite future. The ideology of Marxism that had inspired its beginning became a distant goal in which many believed.

To describe the transition from an authoritarian *party* prior to the seizure of power in 1917 to the authoritarian *regime* imposed on Russia by the Bolsheviks as automatic, inevitable, and irresistible would be simple but incorrect. All the talk of freeing humanity forever was not merely rhetoric designed to fool listeners. For a time the utopian goals coexisted with ruthlessness. The Bolsheviks thought, and so did many others from abroad, that they were beginning something qualitatively new. It quickly began to look like something very old, however, as power passed from Lenin to Stalin.

THE RISE OF JOSEPH STALIN

In 1921 several dormant issues surfaced all at once. In the midst of a flurry of crucial decisions, the political career of Joseph Vissarionovich Dzhugashvili (1879–1953), or Stalin, was quietly advanced. Hardly anyone noticed.

With the end of the civil wars the pressures of several undecided matters erupted at the Tenth Party Congress early in 1921. The meeting immediately faced several threats. The first was from outside the party. Russian sailors at the Kronstadt garrison near Petrograd (now Leningrad) rebelled against the Bolsheviks in March 1921, calling for reelection of the Soviets by secret ballot; freedom of press, speech, and assembly; release of political prisoners; an end to food rationing; and an end to preferential privileges given to members of the Bolshevik party. The sailors hoped that they could stimulate other Russians to join in their demands for socialism without the Bolsheviks. The party acted decisively, and thousands of protesters were killed.

The second threat came from two groups that had developed *within* the party; not a threat to Bolshevik rule but to the idea of so much power being held by a very few individuals at the top of the party. One group called

"The Workers' Opposition" argued that trade unions should be given more control. They thought that in the economic chaos of the time it made sense to allow industry to be controlled by a central group chosen by the unions, to permit union leaders a greater voice in selecting local union committees, and to end Lenin's policy of paying former capitalists very high wages to run factories. A second group, called "Democratic Centralists," wanted to decentralize decision making within the party so as to eliminate the iron rule of the top levels of the party over the lower levels. Too much power was gathering at the very top of the party, they felt, and this conflicted with democratic centralism. The democracy part of that policy was rapidly disappearing. Both groups wanted the top levels to share power, either with the unions or with the lower membership of the party.

Party leaders felt that the within-party challenges had to be as soundly defeated as the Kronstadt rising because of the danger of sharing power in such critical times. But the challenges from within the party were pointing to a real problem—the concentration of power in very few hands. The narrowing was continuing. The dictatorship of the proletariat, which became the dictatorship of the party, was turning into a dictatorship by four or five people at the top *over the rest of the party.* Lenin referred to this in 1921 when he warned that the small group called the Old Guard, who were determining the policies of the party, had to be protected.[29] If they were not protected, he said, dissent on the floor of the congress might cause conflict within this group and endanger the entire party. The Tenth Congress responded by passing a resolution on party unity that *prohibited the creation or adherence to any faction within the party.* Violators could be demoted in party rank or expelled from the party altogether.[30]

With the passage of this resolution both the Workers' Opposition and the Democratic Centralists quickly disbanded. No challenges were possible from now on unless the challengers were willing to risk being demoted or expelled. In choosing the narrower alternative of blocking all dissent within the party, the Tenth Congress hastened the conversion of Bolshevism into a bureaucratic machine whose chief function was to rubber-stamp top-level decisions and to discourage independent thinking in the membership. Communism now became whatever the top leader said it was. Thus the party itself, while still led by Lenin, Trotsky, and a few others, created the opportunity for Stalin.[31]

The party's New Economic Policy (NEP) was, on the other hand, fairly liberal. Adopted in 1921 in the midst of acute economic chaos, the party had no alternative options visible. With famine stalking the land, swollen bellies provided a ghastly mockery of the high hopes of the new regime. The Bolsheviks had won the civil wars, but the prize, Russia, lay in ruins. The NEP ended the forced requisition of grain from the peasants and substituted instead a ten percent tax to encourage crop production. A free market was re-created and small private enterprises were allowed to flourish. To supplement or provide risk capital, loan associations were set up, wage systems were reintroduced, official sanctions against the flow of money were removed, and foreign investment was again encouraged. Gradually the economic picture began to brighten as the less restricted economy bounded upward. By 1925/1926 the economy was just about back to 1913 levels, and people began asking, "Where do we go from here?" So many choices were possible: Continue the NEP, for example, or gradually introduce more controls, or move directly to total control from the top by reorganizing the countryside and engaging in planned, rapid industrialization. Stalin's position on these options wasn't all that clear in the mid-1920s, but his voice was beginning to stand out from the rest of the top leadership—even though most Bolsheviks probably believed that Grigori Zinoviev or Trotsky would take over after Lenin died in 1924, and **Nikolai I. Bukharin** (1888–1938) *seemed* to be the majority leader on the Politburo from 1925 to 1927. Meanwhile, Stalin was quietly building his control.

Joseph Vissarionovich Dzhugashvili (Stalin) was born in 1879 into a Georgian peasant family that endured a harsh poverty. Stalin's father was a peasant who tried his hand at small businesses and factory work. But he drank too much and was a negative figure in Joseph's life. His mother supported the two of them by working as a laundress and as a maid for the local Russian Orthodox priest. Young Joseph received an education at the local church school and attended the Tiflis Theological Seminary on a small scholarship.

He was expelled from the seminary for illegal political activities in 1899. He joined a Georgian group linked with Plekhanov's RSDLP, and by 1901 he had made the transition from vague Marxism imbued with Georgian nationalism to the international socialism of Lenin and began a long career as an underground Bolshevik revolutionary. By 1917, Joseph, now known by his alias, Stalin ("man of steel"), was an "old Bolshevik" who had paid his dues.[32] Lenin considered him one of the five or six reliable old timers perhaps because Stalin was not a challenging, independent thinker who created problems. He was someone, Lenin believed, to whom important matters could be safely delegated.

Thus Stalin began collecting a great many top-level positions in both the party and government because after 1917 there were more jobs than reliable old comrades. By 1922, when Lenin suffered a stroke, Stalin was a member of everything significant. In 1922 he was assigned another job— one that didn't seem very different from the other positions he held—of keeping party records and overseeing individual assignments in the party. He even received a title for this new position: General Secretary of the Party. Although no one else understood this, Stalin now had the reins of power in his hands. Whoever held the General Secretary (Gensec) position, at least between 1922 and 1990, held considerable power. The Gensec keeps track of the party organization; assigning and reassigning people, promoting or

Joseph Stalin   1879-1953

demoting them, and suggesting whom lower party organs should select to represent them at the next higher party level. This power enabled Stalin to pull together quietly a **cadre** of party members who owed their new party status *entirely to him*. While Lenin was still alive and active, while Trotsky was very much on the scene, while other leaders played roles in the limelight that they thought more important, Stalin was undermining the entire apparatus by building a party loyal to *him* rather than to Lenin or the "revolution." It took time, political maneuvering, and unsuspecting colleagues, but when the cards were finally all played, Stalin took the game.

Stalin strengthened his position in the coalitional politics of the 1920s despite a weak effort by Lenin to reduce Stalin's power.[33] By 1925 Stalin was able to see Trotsky expelled from the party and by 1927 from the Soviet Union itself. By 1928 other rivals such as Zinoviev, Kamenev, and Bukharin had been totally outmaneuvered. Stalin had bested them all.

Immediately Stalin began implementing a policy that he had opposed earlier: the forced **collectivization of agriculture** to convert private farming into collective and state farms, and rapid industrialization according to five-year plans that pushed factory output targets to nearly impossible heights. As with the tsars, the new industrialization was partially financed by the extraction of agricultural "surpluses," whether such surpluses existed or not. To create this repressive system, Stalin needed to control the countryside, and he did so by forced collectivization. Urban workers had to be fed, and imported technology had to be financed regardless of the cost in the rural areas.

The new policies were implemented so rapidly and arbitrarily that great strains were created within the country. Millions of people died in the next few years. Stalin's response was to become even more suspicious of opposition—real and imaginary. When the Politburo failed to support him on the question of capital punishment for party members guilty of plotting against him, he quietly began to plot against his colleagues: He engineered the assassination of Sergei Kirov in December 1934 and inaugurated the terrible purges from 1934 to 1938 in which millions of innocent people were killed. The country's troubles were never blamed on Stalin, but on still-existing remnants of civil war anticommunism, or on a Trotskyist anti-Stalinist underground, or, later, on fascist plots to destroy him. These labels provided the secret police with convenient scapegoats. Thousands were imprisoned on mere suspicion. Although the factories were producing more goods, especially capital goods, and although the collectivization trauma in the rural areas was beginning to abate, Stalin intensified the pattern of arrests and terror.

The drive to modernize the Soviet Union was accompanied by a climate of fear and hysteria that mocked the heroic sacrifices of many Soviet people and fundamentally contradicted the utopian expectations of former revolutionaries. The basis was laid for better living conditions, but side by side with these positive changes, millions of people were forced into labor camps where they mindlessly built roads and settlements as part of the overall plan. This was artfully concealed from foreign observers. A new and liberal constitution was promulgated while groups of children, deprived of parents by the secret police, scrounged like wolves for food and warmth. In 1936 Stalin *declared* that socialism had been attained! Seldom have people borne such a tremendous cost for so small a prize.

Many other leaders *still* did not realize it, but Marxism-Leninism or Bolshevism, as defined by the top party leaders, had now become whatever Stalin said it was. The narrowing had gone about as far as it could go. It had tightened to the space of one man—Stalin—who became the standard-bearer and symbol for Soviet "communism" throughout the world. As if this were not bad enough, his policies of collectivized agriculture and the centralized, command economy were elevated to an ideological significance they did not deserve.

*   *   *

Stalin's rise to power in the Bolshevik party is a study of careful political maneuvering. At the time of Lenin's death in 1924, Stalin already held far too many important positions to be ignored. But he faced formidable opposition from the charismatic Trotsky, who had so successfully led the Red Army during the period of civil wars between 1918 and 1921. Trotsky had joined the party late, in 1917, and had been moved to the top immediately by Lenin. This caused resentment among "old Bolsheviks," feelings made worse by Trotsky's arrogance. After Lenin's death and no longer protected by his closeness to Lenin, Trotsky was outmaneuvered by a careful Stalin—to the point of losing his party positions and his ability to live in the USSR.

By 1928 Stalin held all the power. He now collectivized agriculture and pushed rapid industrialization by means of Five-Year Plans. These policies created great strains on the country. Stalin's response was to create a climate of terror known as the Great Purge, which filled labor camps with innocent people. Stalin, the dictator, came to resemble one of the most cruel tsars of Russia's past, Ivan the Terrible. And Stalin became the symbol of communism. No wonder that people feared it.

RENEWED EXPERIMENTATION: REALITY MIXES WITH IDEOLOGY

The narrowed ideology characteristic of the Stalin era had a limited usefulness. It could achieve a great deal but it could not sustain its success. Reality persistently intruded on ideology and eventually could not be denied. This did not become clear until the late 1980s. Prior to that time of ideological widening associated with the emergence of Mikhail Gorbachev in 1985, the Soviet Union had developed international stature in two major ways: first, by leading and dominating the Third or Communist International (Comintern); second, by constructing a fairly modern industry and a first-rate military power through centralized planning and party control of the society.

The Comintern (1919—1943) began as a deliberate alternative to the still-existing Second International that Lenin considered a traitor to the proletarian cause. Responding to invitations broadcast by radio to an organizing conference in Moscow, the new organization was created in March 1919 as the new expression of revolutionary proletarian internationalism.

The Comintern *Manifesto,* written by Trotsky, called for international workers' revolutions against their governments in order to substitute the new form of organization that had worked in the Soviet Union: workers' soviets. Right from the start this was a different form of internationalism: The stress was on political revolution and a copying of the Bolshevik success. Increasingly, this meant copying Soviet authoritarianism. No one seemed to realize that these tactics suggested strategies for other countries that were inappropriate to countries more economically and politically advanced than the Soviet Union. Nor did anyone realize that the greatest impact would be in other underdeveloped societies.

Thus, from the beginning the Comintern was ill-advised in imagining that its greatest hope for international socialism lay in fomenting revolution in advanced countries such as Germany, or that it did not have to pay attention to small communist parties in backward countries such as China. By not properly understanding what they themselves had actually done, and by exporting that misunderstood success through the Comintern, the leaders of the Third International doomed it from the start as an organization capable of creating revolutions in other countries. This was less a story of Trotsky versus Stalin than it was a description of the difficulties of exporting one country's experiences to another, as Fidel Castro discovered in 1967 when the Cuban-led insurrection in Bolivia was defeated. Nonetheless, the existence of the Comintern organization, the use of it by Soviet leaders to funnel money into other countries for subversion, and periodic meetings where revolutionary rhetoric was openly proclaimed frightened or angered other government leaders who often took retaliatory actions against the Soviet Union.[34]

The subversive activity of the Comintern was one vehicle for Bolshevik leaders to carry on "foreign policy." Another was the use of diplomatic channels—even if the other government were capitalist. In the 1920s the new Soviet government realized that it needed international legitimacy to survive in the community of nations. Thus, in addition to maintaining the Comintern, the Bolsheviks set up a regular government apparatus that included ambassadors to other nations and a ministry of foreign relations. By 1928 the entire operation, including both the Comintern and the regular government, came under the total control of Stalin. The Third International faded as the organization that encouraged international revolution as this function was increasingly performed by the Soviet government, at least until the late 1980s. By 1943, when the Comintern was disbanded, it had long ceased to have any usefulness for Soviet foreign policy.[35]

Centralized planning and narrow party control of the society proved to have a limited shelf life as well. Although both strategies had seemed to be successful prior to the 1970s, it became clear by the late 1980s that a restructuring of the economy through *perestroika* was in order. In the seventy-odd years of communist power, the country had grown from a position of economic and military weakness to one comparable to that of the United States. In spite of great losses during World War II, Soviet accomplishments have largely been the result of the command economy, which seems to have a significant but limited utility for less developed economies. Most Soviet citizens live well compared to their recent past. Although the country needs to import food, people do get enough to eat—even if food is starchy and too high in fats. Store shelves are too often empty of variety and quality, but the Soviet citizen is generally proud of the nation's successes in space programs and in building a modern military force with worldwide response capabilities.

However, the command economy has only a limited utility. It is unfortunate that such a temporary asset became so permanent a fixture in Soviet ideology that a substantial part of the definition of socialism was tied in with it. To change the economy was also to change the understanding or definition of socialism—something that for decades was assumed unassailable. Yet comprehensive economic reform could not be postponed—there were no alternatives. The already stagnating Soviet economy was the result of failure to reform decades earlier; of relying too long on the centrally planned economic model. The point is not that Soviet economists should have known the limits from the beginning; no one knew the limits. The point is that once the limits were reached, one could not simply adjust the part that did not work. The entire system had to be jettisoned, and that involved rethinking everything about the economic system that had been installed in 1928. This was expressed very carefully in 1988 by Leonid I. Abalkin in language reminiscent of that which Marx used with reference to capitalism: "Specific forms of socialist production relations can themselves gradually age, cease to serve as a stimulus, and become a brake on social progress. Outdated socialist production relations can become a drag on the system."[36] But significantly altering the command economy, before this drag became an obvious problem, proved impossible when faced with the ideological defense mechanisms involved with narrow party control of the society—mechanisms that rushed to defend old methods whether they were political, economic, or social.

The from-the-top-down approach seems to work well in the beginning of industrialization when *extensive* industrial growth, stressing output, is desirable, but when economic growth reaches the point where efficiency and quality of production is more important than output, a period of *intensive* growth is necessary. This is apparently true for any command economy anywhere in the world. The new economic imperatives in the Soviet Union demanded a loosening of centralized economic controls, which in turn demanded the loosening of all controls so that *real* decentralization of planning, and a market autonomy in terms of price setting and consumer sovereignty could emerge. No one knew how to do this because it had never been done before. Thus the efforts to change the economy, which became efforts to change the entire system, often were gropings in the dark to see what did or did not work, as though Soviet leaders no longer knew what socialism was.[37]

Naturally there was and is resistance to such a full revision of the society. The obvious source of that opposition is the command economy's extensive and powerful bureaucracy. But that group of about 18 million people may not be the most serious problem faced by reformers.

The Soviet people themselves are perhaps a larger obstacle than the entrenched bureaucracy. For several decades the people have enjoyed social benefits they are reluctant to forego. Economic changes that may benefit them in the long run require short-term sacrifices that do not appear attractive. For example, nonsubsidized prices for bread and meat would reduce waste, increase efficiency of production and use, and encourage competition. But removing the subsidies means substantial price increases. To increase wages to meet the new prices would defeat the purpose. A reformer is thus asking people to accept a pay cut with a smile. It doesn't happen that way anywhere.

It was therefore imperative that the party control of society be altered in some fundamental manner, in the hope that a rise in political efficacy and an increase in openness (*glasnost*) would make people less resistant to necessary short-term economic sacrifice. The party control after Stalin *had* lessened, but not enough. There were no guidelines here either.

After Stalin's death on March 5, 1953, none of his successors were able or willing to maintain his level of autocracy. There was even a repudiation of the Stalinist past. At the Twentieth Party Congress in February 1956, Nikita S. Khrushchev delivered a speech that accused Stalin of criminal tyranny. This speech planted the seeds for later changes, but the seeds took a long time to germinate. Khrushchev was forced to retire in October 1964 and during the next eighteen years Brezhnev reinforced party control by resisting significant reform. The economy began to deteriorate. In 1982, change was begun by Yuri Andropov but his term as Gensec was limited to fifteen months. In early 1984 Konstantin Chernenko returned to the no-change Brezhnev style, and his tenure lasted only thirteen months before he also died. In March 1985 a younger and more vigorous reformer became General Secretary—Mikhail S. Gorbachev. The tight narrowing of the Stalin era, only partially opened up by Khrushchev, widened further under Gorbachev's reforms than anyone had dreamed possible.

TABLE 6.1   Party and Government in the Soviet Union

GOVERNMENT	PARTY
Voters elect	Primary Party Organizations select:
local soviets	District Party Groups that select:
regional soviets	Regional Party Groups that select:
republic soviets	Republican Party Groups that select:
Congress of People's Deputies	Party Congress, which chooses:
Congress of People's Deputies elects	Central Committee, which picks:
President of USSR and	Secretariat and Politburo
USSR Supreme Soviet	
USSR Supreme Soviet elects	
Council of Ministers and	
Supreme Court	

In just a few years the Soviet political system has become far more democratic and open than it has ever been. The CPSU no longer dominates the political scene because so much power has been given to the Congress of People's Deputies and the restructured Supreme Soviet. Table 6.1 illustrates the hierarchy of the Soviet political system.

The two parallel organizations, party and government, are described as though they are separate. They are. Party officials are elected in party elections, increasingly in multicandidate elections. Government officials who may or may not be CPSU members are elected in multicandidate (more candidates than positions to fill) general elections in which all Soviet citizens may participate. Elections to the Congress of People's Deputies are direct, whereas they are indirect with regard to the Supreme Soviet and the Supreme Court. Multicandidate elections were not universal in 1989 and 1990, but new laws passed in 1990 were designed to make multicandidate elections the rule in the future. In addition, the office of president was to be directly elected by the people rather than indirectly by the Congress after the end of Gorbachev's term in 1995.

The presidency is a powerful position, but careful checks were placed on the office in 1990. For example, it was stipulated that the president can declare martial and civil emergencies but must notify the troubled area of contemplated action, and that the Supreme Soviet has oversight powers. Executive orders must conform to existing constitutional law. In addition, although the president can veto legislation, once the Supreme Soviet has overridden that veto with a two-thirds majority, the president cannot appeal to the Congress of People's Deputies for a reconsideration. As a further safeguard, the Committee of Constitutional Control, a substitute for a constitution-guarding Supreme Court, was given power to impeach the president and is appointed by the Chair of the Supreme Soviet rather than by the president. How well these controls work will depend on the will to make them work, and the courage of the Soviet media.

The president is known as the head of state. The chairperson of the Council of Ministers, heading a large group of ministers with responsibilities for agriculture, foreign affairs, defense industry, etc., is called the Prime Minister and is regarded as the head of government.

The Congress of People's Deputies is composed of 2,250 elected delegates that meet once or twice per year. It decides constitutional questions and establishes the agenda for the Supreme Soviet, the standing parliament. The Supreme Soviet is a bicameral (two-house) assembly of 542 members that meets regularly to enact legislation. After the Constitutional amendments of December 1988, the Supreme Soviet became a real parliament, complete with informal opposition. Issues are debated publicly, votes are not unanimous, and high-level officials like the head of the KGB have been intensively grilled. Republican Supreme Soviets are unicameral (one-house) assemblies, as are regional soviets, which serve as local governments for smaller units such as cities and rural districts.

Where is the Communist Party of the Soviet Union in all this democracy? That question was easy to answer in the past. The party quietly controlled the government in two ways: first, every governmental position of any significance was held by a high-ranking party member; second, divisions in the party Secretariat paralleled the divisions in the government's Council of Ministers, which allowed the party to control government decisions all the way down to the local level. But increasing power given to democratic institutions in 1989 and 1990 challenged that earlier party hegemony. In addition, defeats of prominent CPSU members in local elections in 1989, the electoral victories of opposition groups in Moscow, Kiev, and Leningrad in March 1990, and the electoral success of antiestablishment groups in local areas across the USSR increased the general feeling that membership in the CPSU had become a political liability. All this made past answers of doubtful utility in understanding the present and the future. These negative attitudes worried Central Committee members at a plenum in March 1990. Speakers deplored the new unpopularity of local party leaders in various governmental positions and the fact that long-standing members of the CPSU were leaving the party. One speaker predicted an imminent split in the party.[38]

In terms of outward structure, however, the party appeared the same. The 28th Party Congress meeting in the summer of 1990 was composed of nearly five thousand delegates. Party Congresses normally meet every five years to determine policy directions and to select a new Central Committee of about 300 prominent members, many of whom are regional party secretaries. In turn, the Central Committee selects the General Secretary and the Secretariat over which he presides, and the Politburo, composed of ten to twenty-four prominent individuals.

The number of General Secretaries has been few throughout Soviet history. Table 6.2 lists the ten Gensecs and shows the length of their tenure.

TABLE 6.2   Secretaries of the CPSU*

Iakov Sverdlov	1918–1919
Nikolai Krestinsky	1919–1920
Viacheslav Molotov	1921–1922
Joseph Stalin	1922–1953
Georgi Malenkov	1953–1953
Nikita S. Khrushchev	1953–1964
Leonid Brezhnev	1964–1982
Yuri Andropov	1982–1984
Konstantin Chernenko	1984–1985
Mikhail Gorbachev	1985–

*The position was called "Secretary" from 1918 to 1922, "General Secretary" from 1922 to 1953, "First Secretary" from 1953 to 1966, and restored to "General Secretary" in 1966.

The shortest time in office was that of Georgi Malenkov—just a few weeks in March 1953; the longest was that of Stalin.

Despite appearances, however, none of the leading party groups are as important as they once were. The office of General Secretary had been the most powerful individual position since 1922, and the Politburo the most powerful group since 1919. Throughout that history, however, the government was weak in comparison and easily controlled. In 1989 and 1990 all this began to change as power was increasingly given to elected governmental institutions. Criticisms of past and present party members including Gorbachev, and even negative remarks about hitherto sacrosanct Lenin, indicated that a fundamental deideologizing was taking place. The party as a ladder for upwardly mobile Soviet citizens was disappearing, and its loss of power, prestige, and perquisites caused it to begin shrinking in size and influence.

Adaptation to the new, more democratic reality was the party's only hope. Increasingly, multicandidate elections occurred within the party for positions of power. Lower level party members were asked to make their leaders accountable to party rules. The leaders of government, except for Gorbachev, no longer held positions of leadership in the party after the 28th Party Congress in July 1990. The old authoritarian party was well on its way to becoming an artifact, but like the partially reformed command economy, the adapted CPSU could not easily be cast aside. The party still controlled vast amounts of property and remained a cohesive force still needed for some time.

In the wake of these enormous changes what has happened to the ideas of socialism and communism? In 1936 Stalin decreed that socialism had been built, so in theory the Soviet Union from then on was engaged in constructing the material and technical basis of full communism. That was the goal articulated by the Third Party Program adopted in 1961 by the Twenty-

Second Party Congress. That program laid out a 20-year economic plan designed to result in the beginnings of full communism in the early 1980s. The Third Party Program in actuality entailed little more than surpassing the United States in the production of various commodities,[39] but the spirit of the Program was its ultimate goal of the construction of full communism. The Fourth Party Program adopted in early 1986 continued to focus on the same goal—gains vis à vis the United States, but by concentrating exclusively on specific expected achievements through the year 2000 and beyond, it effectively lost sight of the broader goal. One way to postpone a goal—communism—is to stop discussing it.

The result, of course, is that the Soviet Union, over seven decades after the seizure of power in the name of communism, is still not a communist country. Nor is it likely to be in any foreseeable future. Soviet ideologues will agree, claiming instead that their country is a socialist nation still on the way to a distant communist future. But very few believe any longer that they or even their children will see it. The Soviet Union has met with far more success acting in its own nationalist self-interest than it has had in following ideological directions. Because of this, that communist future seems increasingly remote and perhaps impossible, even to very dedicted members of the party.

*   *   *

Initially the Soviet Union followed two contradictory directions simultaneously: subversive activities directed against other governments through the Comintern; and regular diplomatic contacts seeking recognition and legitimacy from these same countries. The first direction gradually faded into the second without diminishing the Soviet interest in and financial support of anti-West "liberation" movements throughout the world.[40] The reduction of that support under Mikhail Gorbachev brought this phase of Soviet foreign policy to an end.

Internally, the Soviet Union is altering its institutionalized despotism toward a parliamentary democracy less dominated by the CPSU. The party itself is still ruled from the top down, but this too is in the process of change. The chief powerholder since Lenin has always been the General Secretary of the party, but the position of power now appears to be the presidency. Control of the party organization in the past gave the General Secretary control of all party affairs, all governmental activities, and the entire centralized economy; this is no longer the case.

Stalin declared in 1936 that socialism had been achieved. In 1961 the Party's Twenty-second Congress approved a 20-year program that would bring about the beginnings of full communism, but in 1986 a revision of that program postponed communism to the indefinite future.

What remains is an exciting system in the process of change from ideological rigidity to pragmatic ambivalence. The USSR's main problem is its stagnant economy and its own citizens who not only are reluctant to, but are actually resistant to, change. Comprehensive economic reform, nonetheless, is sorely needed.

AFTERWORD

Marxist socialism/communism was implemented in other areas of the world outside the Soviet Union, but this expansion did not occur until after World War II (1945). Prior to that time many communist or Comintern parties had existed in various countries but none held governmental power. This lengthy time period, from 1917 to 1945, gave the CPSU time to solidify into a model of "successful communism" that was ready to be exported into other areas. But just as the concept of Marxism was earlier adapted, interpreted and changed by implementation, so too was the Soviet model altered by being applied in other countries at later times.

The changes and alterations would have been greater and more immediate, had not the initial expansion of communism outside of the Soviet Union into Eastern Europe been reinforced by the presence of the Soviet army. Even so, challenges and changes have occurred and are occurring in all parts of the communist world. Considering these events in the next three chapters rounds out one's understanding of the implementation of Marxism.

NOTES

1. The three units of time: day, month, and year, do not reconcile well. For example, a solar year is 365.242199 days, and the lunar month is 29.53059 days. Every calendar, therefore, has built-in errors that cause a periodic need for adjustment. In 1582, when Pope Gregory XIII introduced a new calendar called the Gregorian calendar, replacing the Julian calendar that had been in use since about 50BC, ten days were skipped so as to correct errors that had built up over that long period of time. October 4 was followed by October 15. Not all countries used the new calendar in the next few centuries because so many people resisted changing the day on which they celebrated religious holidays. By the time of Peter the Great many countries used the Gregorian, but some still used the older one—the Julian.

Peter adopted the *Julian* calendar on January 1, 1700, and slowly the gap between the two calendars grew. By 1917 the Julian calendar in use in Russia was thirteen days behind the Gregorian calendar used in the West. The October 25, 1917, "Great October Socialist Revolution" (the Bolshevik coup) actually took place on November 7 in other areas of the world. Because the Bolsheviks changed to the Gregorian calendar on February 14, 1918, the revolutionary holiday has always been celebrated by Soviet citizens on November 7.

2. V. Lenin, "The Crisis Has Matured" (September 1917), in *Collected Works*, vol. 26:77.

3. V. Lenin, "Speech to the First All-Russia Congress of Soviets" (June 1917), in *Collected Works*, vol. 25:17–42. Similar references are located in nearly all his writings of the time period surrounding the November coup.

4. V. Lenin, "Revision of the Party Programme" (October 1917), in *Collected Works*, vol. 26:170.

5. Ibid., p. 171.

6. V. Lenin, "The Principles Involved in the War Issue" (December 1916), in *Collected Works,* vol. 23:158.

7. Lenin, *State and Revolution* (New York: Vanguard, 1929), p. 201.

8. Lenin, "Third All-Russian Congress of Soviets," *Collected Works* (Moscow: Foreign Languages Publishing House, 1964), vol. 26:464–465 (January 24, 1918).

9. Lenin, *State and Revolution,* op. cit., pp. 205–206. Also see pp. 155, 189, 193, 194.

10. Lenin, "A Great Technical Achievement," *Collected Works,* vol. 19:62 (April 1913).

11. See Lenin, "The Working Class and the National Questions," ibid., p. 92 (May 1913) and many other selections.

12. Lenin, "Theses on the Question of a Separate Peace," ibid., vol. 26:443–444 (January 1918).

13. Lenin, "Speech at a Meeting of Sokolniki District," ibid., vol. 28:53 (August 1918).

14. Lenin, "Resolution of the Joint Session of the All-Russian CEC," ibid., vol. 28:130 (October 1918).

15. Basil Dmytryshyn, *A History of Russia* (Englewood Cliffs: Prentice Hall, 1977), p. 488.

16. Ibid., p. 505.

17. Lenin, "Fourth Conference of Trade Unions," *Collected Works,* vol. 27:466 (June 1918).

18. Lenin, "The Immediate Tasks of the Soviet Government," ibid., vol. 27:264 (March–April 1918).

19. Lenin, "Report on Foreign Policy, ibid., vol. 27:379 (May 1918).

20. Lenin, "Session of the Central Executive Council, Moscow Soviet, Red Army, and the Trade Unions," ibid., vol. 27:435 (June 1918).

21. Lenin, "Speech at a Rally and Concert for the All-Russia Extraordinary Commission Staff," ibid., vol. 28:170 (November 1918).

22. Lenin, "Telegram to J. V. Stalin," ibid., vol. 30:363 (February 1920).

23. Lenin, "Left Wing Childishness and the Petty-Bourgeois Mentality," ibid., vol. 27:276–277 (May 1918).

24. Lenin, "Session of the All-Russia CEC," ibid., vol. 27:297 (April 1918).

25. Lenin, "Extraordinary Seventh Congress of the RCP (B)," ibid., vol. 27:148 (March 1918).

26. Lenin, "Three Speeches Delivered in Red Square," ibid., vol. 29:330 (May 1919).

27. See Lenin, "A Great Beginning," ibid., vol. 29:427, 429 (July 1919); "The Fight to Overcome the Fuel Crisis," ibid., vol. 30:141 (November 1919); and "Political Report of the Central Committee," ibid., vol. 30:186 (December 1919). For a glimpse of how this idea was viewed in 1990, see Francis X. Clines, "Leninist Zeal is Overtaken by Humbugs," *The New York Times,* April 22, 1990, p. 1.

28. Lenin, "Speech at a Plenary Session of the Moscow Soviet," ibid., vol. 33:442 (November 1922).

29. Lenin, "The Conditions for Admitting New Members to the Party," ibid., vol. 33:257 (March 1922).

30. See Lenin, "Tenth Congress of the RCP (B), Preliminary Draft Resolution of the Tenth Congress of the RCP on Party Unity," ibid., vol. 32:244 (March 1921); and Robert V. Daniels, *A Documentary History of Communism* (New York: Vintage Books, 1960), pp. 206–216.

31. See Svetozar Stojanovic, *Between Ideals and Reality: A Critique of Socialism and Its Future,* trans. Gerson Sher (New York: Oxford University Press, 1973), pp. 55–56; and Leonard Schapiro, *The Communist Party of the Soviet Union* (New York: Random House–Vintage Books, 1971), pp. 201ff.

32. The designation "old Bolshevik" did not refer to the age of the individual but to long-standing party membership as opposed to all of the newcomers in the 1917–1921 time period. The phrase refers to the group of Bolsheviks that had been involved with Lenin for some years prior to 1917. This category would definitely not include Trotsky, a former opponent of Lenin, who had joined the Bolsheviks only in July 1917.

33. Lenin's main effort to remove Stalin was a memorandum he dictated on December 25, 1922, after Lenin's stroke. This became known as Lenin's "Testament." On January 4, 1923, Lenin dictated a Postscript. In the Testament he expressed fear that rivalry between Trotsky and Stalin would split the party, adding: "Comrade Stalin, having become General Secretary, has concentrated an enormous power in his hands; and I am not sure that he always knows how to use that power with sufficient caution." As for Trotsky, the Testament praised his "exceptional abilities" but faulted his "too far-reaching self-confidence and a disposition to be too much attracted by the purely administrative side of affairs." But this too was dictated because of a feared split more than to get rid of one or the other of them.

The Postscript is clearer, but still weak. "Stalin is too rude, and this fault, entirely supportable in relations among us Communists, becomes insupportable in the office of General Secretary. Therefore, I propose to the comrades to find a way to remove Stalin from that position and appoint to it another man who in all respects differs from Stalin only in superiority— namely, more patient, more loyal, more polite, and more attentive to comrades, less capricious, etc."

But again this was put in the context of avoiding a split. Stalin's maneuvers against Trotsky, supported by others on the Politburo, rendered that fear meaningless. If Lenin had said in early 1923 "Get rid of Stalin now or I will resign" it would probably have been done. But the cautious attempts, noted above, followed by Lenin's incapacitation for almost all of 1923, precluded that stronger possibility. See Samuel Hendel, ed., *The Soviet Crucible: The Soviet System in Theory and Practice* (Princeton, N.J.: D. Van Nostrand, 1963), pp. 280–282.

34. One example of such a backlash was the trouble Stalin had with Great Britain, particularly from 1927 to 1929, over the issue of Soviet subversive activities against the British government. One description of these events is Franz Borkenau, *European Communism* (New York: Harper & Bros., 1953), pp. 63ff. A book describing the revolutionary atmosphere when the Comintern was founded is F. L. Carsten, *Revolution in Central Europe, 1918–1919* (Berkeley: University of California Press, 1972). Other books include Helmut Gruber, ed., *International Communism in the Era of Lenin* (New York: Doubleday Anchor Books, 1972) and Kermit McKensie, *Comintern and World Revolution* (New York: Columbia University Press, 1964).

35. Although the organization did not appear to be useful from the Soviet perspective, it certainly was used by the Soviets to influence public policy in the 1930s. Stalin, frightened by the rise of Hitler's fascism in Germany, used the organization to develop anti-fascist attitudes in Western countries. Communists throughout the world organized antifascist "fronts." In 1939 when the Soviet Union signed the nonaggression pact with the Nazi government, the Comintern abruptly changed tactics. Now members were supposed to change their antifascist fronts to peace fronts to prevent war from developing. In the summer of 1941, when Hitler's Germany invaded the Soviet Union, this again changed. Now, once more, communists became antifascists. How intelligent people in the organization could go through these abrupt switches in policy is a mystery. Perhaps Comintern membership for an American communist, for example, was so valued that remaining a member and serving the "motherland of socialism" took precedence over any other consideration, including the needs of one's own country. Although the Comintern activities sometimes appeared similar to an old Keystone Kops' movie, it was taken *very seriously* by most members.

36. Leonid I. Abalkin, "Restructuring the Management of the Economy is a Continuation of the October Revolution's Work," *Economic Questions*, republished in *The USSR Today* (Columbus, Ohio: Current Digest of the Soviet Press, 1988), p. 16.

37. For a comprehensive look at this complicated problem, see Edward A. Hewett, *Reforming the Soviet Economy* (Washington, D.C.: The Brookings Institution, 1988).

38. "Speeches at the Plenary Session of the CPSU Central Committee, March 16–20, 1990," *Current Digest of the Soviet Press*, vol. 42:12 (April 25, 1990), pp. 11–12.

39. For more information on the Third Party Program, see Theodore Denno, *The Communist Millenium: The Soviet View* (The Hague: Martinus Nijhoff, 1964), and James R. Ozinga, *The Relevance of Marx and Lenin to the Soviet Transition to Communism*, unpublished Ph.D. dissertation, University Microfilms, Ann Arbor, Michigan.

40. Roberta Goren, *The Soviet Union and Terrorism* (London: George Allen & Unwin, 1984).

DISCUSSION QUESTIONS

1. Name the secretary generals of the CPSU since the position was formed in 1922. Does it make any difference who is in charge?
2. What would real economic reform entail for the Soviet Union?
3. Was the Comintern as radical and revolutionary as Western political leaders feared? Why or why not?
4. What was the Comintern Popular Front in the 1930s? Why did it begin in 1935 and end in 1939?
5. Describe how Stalin managed to take over the CPSU.
6. Was Bolshevism in its early days only an authoritarian system or was it almost a dialectic of authoritarianism combined with socialist liberalism?
7. What is a *subbotnik?* How did this arise? How did Lenin both welcome and damage the movement?
8. What was the importance of the prohibition on factionalism in 1921 at the Tenth Party Congress?
9. Did Lenin believe that the Bolsheviks had led a proletarian revolution? Did he believe they had entered into socialism or communism?
10. What decisive impact on the Bolsheviks did the failure of other "proletarian" revolutions have?
11. When do the words *socialism* and *communism* really begin to mean different things? Why is this distinction still confusing?
12. What are some of the barriers to comprehensive economic reform in the Soviet Union?
13. Is communism still expected as a final phase of socialism? When?
14. What are the reforms associated with the name of Gorbachev?

7

Eastern Europe
From Monolithic Orthodoxy to Real Diversity

Eastern Europe became the "Soviet Bloc" as a consequence of World War II. The Red Army's success in pushing Hitler's forces westward, away from the USSR and back to Germany, created two opportunities. First, the Red Army occupied the areas of Eastern Europe that were crossed in pushing the Germans back to Berlin. Second, in countries where the Red Army was not significantly involved, as in Yugoslavia and Albania, indigenous communist forces led by Josef Broz (Tito) and Enver Hoxha, which for years had been fighting first the Italians and then the Germans, came into power as Germany was defeated. A significant area—involving not only Yugoslavia and Albania but also Poland, Hungary, Bulgaria, and Romania—was pulled under Soviet control, with Czechoslovakia joining the bloc in 1948. The accompanying maps show the result.

Various ideas about restoring independence to Eastern European nations and the right of the Soviet Union to have friendly nations on its borders were discussed at the Yalta (February) and Potsdam (July) conferences in 1945 when Germany was obviously defeated. Western leaders at these meetings decided to believe that Stalin's willingness to allow elections in Eastern European countries would solve the problem of Soviet occupation, in part because the United States still needed Soviet intervention in 1945 against Japan so as to reduce the large number of anticipated American

Map 4 Europe between the wars

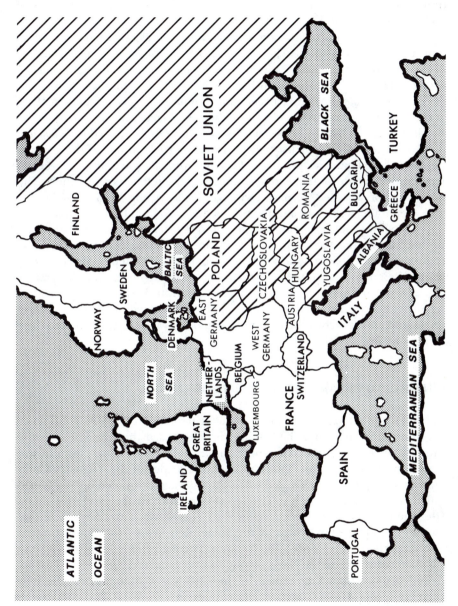

Map 5 Europe 1950

127

casualties. In August, however, after atomic bombs were dropped on Hiroshima and Nagasaki, Japan surrendered. Why then did the trust in Stalin's kind of elections continue? Because the end of the war released a great desire among many people to resume their day-to-day lives, particularly in the United States, and unfortunately, Eastern Europe was not an area of prime concern. As a result, the earlier trust in Stalin's promise of elections for Eastern European countries was not rescinded despite the beginnings of strong anti-Soviet rhetoric from leaders in Western capitals.

Yugoslavia and Albania already had communist governments in 1945. In the remaining countries, elections did take place, but the choice given the electorate was usually between right-wing parties associated with fascism and liberal-sounding socialist parties. Covert Soviet control of the governments of these countries gradually became overt. By the end of 1948 even democratic Czechoslovakia had become a Soviet satellite like the others. The Soviet zone of occupied Germany, which in 1949 became the German Democratic Republic, swelled the number of obedient satellites from seven to eight.

Thus by 1948/49, in the absence of Western interference, Stalin had imposed a "barracks communism"[1] on the area; each country, including Yugoslavia and Albania, was expected to march in lockstep to Stalin's every whim. The communism of Eastern Europe was, of course, Stalin's version. Diversity was not permitted. East European nations became appendages of the Soviet Union, occupied by Soviet soldiers, infiltrated by the Soviet secret police, and governed by local communists more loyal to Moscow than to their own countries.

ATTEMPTS TO BREAK FREE OF THE SOVIET MODEL

The first major attempt by a communist state to break free of Soviet influence was unusual in the sense that Stalin himself caused the rift. This was the interesting case of Yugoslavia where the dictator, Josef Broz Tito, did not owe his position to Stalin. Tito had been the leader of the Yugoslav Communist party since the 1930s, and when Yugoslavia was invaded during World War II by Italy and Germany, Tito led the partisan struggles against them. After the war ended, he was in control of Yugoslavia. Tito and his cohorts had not been placed in power by the Soviet Red Army—they had won that power on their own. Moreover, because Tito had helped coordinate the Albanian resistance to the Nazis through Enver Hoxha (1908–1985), Tito actually led more than Yugoslavia. In the early years after the war the new Albanian leader, Hoxha, seemed subordinate to Tito. What Tito and Hoxha imposed on both Yugoslavia and Albania in 1945 was Stalin's version of communism.

By 1947 it was obvious that Tito had larger plans than even Yugoslavia and Albania: a Balkan federation that included Bulgaria and Romania. This activity did not have Stalin's approval, and a meeting held in Moscow in February 1948 made his opposition to Tito's ambitions quite clear. The Soviet Union declined to renew the trade agreement with Yugoslavia and withdrew all Soviet civilian and military personnel in March 1948. Hostility was manifest.

Stalin's problem with Yugoslavia was not ideological, but a matter of control. Tito acted like a colleague rather than a subordinate, and Stalin found that he could only control Yugoslavia through Tito's party organization. In the context of Stalin's increasingly tight and direct control of the rest of Eastern Europe, this Yugoslav independence was a decided irritant. In Stalin's mind, Tito became an enemy that had to be deposed.

But how? Sending in Soviet troops was not a good idea because there was no common border,[2] because of the mountainous terrain in Yugoslavia, and because of the 1944 percentages agreement between Stalin and Winston Churchill that gave Britain and the USSR equal influence in Yugoslavia. Stalin did not wish to alarm the Western powers. The method by which Tito was handled had to be devious so as to make removing Tito look like the desire of other Eastern European leaders rather than the result of Stalin's mania for control. Thus, Stalin used an organization that had been created in 1947 to coordinate Eastern European affairs called the Communist Information Bureau (**Cominform**). An ironic touch was that the new organization's headquarters were initially in Belgrade, Yugoslavia. In June 1948 when Mikhail A. Suslov, acting for Stalin, invited the Yugoslav Central Committee to the Cominform meeting, Tito blocked the obvious strategy by rejecting the invitation. The Cominform responded by ousting Yugoslavia from the new organization. All trade between Yugoslavia and socialist countries was forbidden so as to force the Yugoslav Central Committee to choose another leader in order to get back into the fold.

Stalin's plan stopped the Baltic federation in its tracks, and it succeeded in gaining Albanian separation from Yugoslavia. However, it failed to dislodge Tito. After the shock of the Cominform's action wore off, Tito and other Yugoslav leaders accepted the isolation and developed a different brand of communism in the 1950s. Stalin's actions stimulated Yugoslavian anger, nationalism, pride, and the conviction that Stalin's kind of communism was not worth emulating. Rural collectivization was abandoned in favor of cooperatives, free enterprise was permitted in the economy, and much more democracy began to characterize Yugoslav political and economic life. Elections to public office became real elections, and **workers' councils** were given real decision-making powers in the economy. Yugoslavia became a "middle ground" between Soviet communism and the West. When Tito began getting economic and military aid from the United States, Yugoslavian survival was assured.

The second major attempt of a communist country to free itself from Soviet control was the case of Hungary in 1956. Yugoslavia's continued viability was a significant part of the background to Hungary's efforts in 1956, because Stalin's irritation with Tito forced other Eastern European leaders to emulate Stalin's hostility in order to demonstrate their orthodoxy. That meant suppressing and branding all nationalist sentiments as "Titoism" and a continued glorification of Stalin. The charge of nationalism became a serious one, resulting in purges and, in some cases, executions of alleged nationalists. To suggest that there could be such a thing as a Polish or Hungarian road to socialism was dangerous, and few tried.

Even after Stalin's death in March 1953, the power base of each of the East European leaders, the test of their orthodoxy, remained anti-Tito and pro-Stalin. Orthodoxy changed, however, when Nikita S. Khrushchev tried to bring Yugoslavia back into the "socialist camp" in 1955. In February 1956 Khrushchev gave his famous "secret speech" at the Twentieth Party Congress in which he denounced Stalin as a criminal. In this attempt to place the Soviet Union at the head of *all* communist countries (including Yugoslavia) and to enhance his own political power within the Soviet Union by distancing himself from Stalin, Khrushchev unwittingly created a novel situation in which Eastern European leaders were suddenly advocating the wrong things. Pro-Stalin and anti-Tito policies had to switch to become anti-Stalin and pro-Tito policies. Some of these leaders couldn't easily make the abrupt change that the new circumstances dictated or remain quiet long enough to see if this change were real.

Why? Because their economies were in trouble. More than anything else, communist leaders had become managers of their country's economy and *their executive success was measured in the economic growth of their nation.* For those leaders who headed countries that had not yet developed problems with the Stalinist economic model of central planning and emphasis on heavy industry, the abrupt change was possible without too much fuss. But in countries like Poland and Hungary in the mid-1950s where national economies faced problems, party leaders were already in trouble. What was saving them was their tremendous loyalty to the Stalinist economic model and the strength of their support from Moscow. When Khrushchev began flirting with economic reform in the Soviet Union, their power base really fell apart. Within their own parties such leaders were already seen as unsuccessful but protected by Moscow from open criticism. Taking away the Soviet Union's approval of their base of power—loyalty to Stalin, dislike of Tito, and slavish acceptance of the central planning economic model—withdrew that protection and permitted open criticism from within the parties.

The formerly subdued discussion of alternative economic directions became public. Perhaps Tito did have some good ideas. Perhaps Stalin was not always correct. Perhaps there were other ways to improve the economy. Khrushchev had not intended to give so much creative room to Eastern European countries, but it happened nonetheless. And with the discussion of alternative economic reforms came a sense of the possibility of liberalizing the

Soviet model in other areas besides the economy. One opening led to the seeking of other openings for the simple reason that economic reforms would make the economy less centrally controlled, less rigid, and more flexible. If that occurred in an area of life as important to communists as the economy, liberalizations in other dimensions of social life were seen as not far behind. In this way economic liberalization led to ideas of political liberalization as well. For example, was it possible that the path to socialism in Poland could be a Polish rather than a Soviet path?

Such ideas even seemed in harmony with Khrushchev's more liberal regime in the Soviet Union and with *Pravda* editorials that suggested the new flexible attitudes toward the economy were solidly based on Leninist principles.[3] Additionally, the organization that bound Eastern European countries together, the Cominform, was quietly dissolved in 1956. All this suggested the possibility of developing *separate national paths* within the common framework of Marxism-Leninism.[4] The 1955 military alliance, the Warsaw Treaty Organization (**Warsaw Pact**), still tied Eastern Europe to the Soviet Union for military matters and overall foreign policy, and socialism was still the goal, but the *path* to that goal appeared more flexible.

How flexible was the question. Even "liberal" Khrushchev still wanted to dominate the area—that is why he wanted Tito back in the fold. Eastern Europe was still expected to remain subordinate to the Soviet Union[5] and the populations of East European countries to remain subordinate to their own country's communist parties.[6] The construction of socialism meant, therefore, moving out of backwardness by following the Soviet example in building heavy industry under the leadership of the individual nation's Communist party. The degree of variance from the Soviet model was smaller by far than that anticipated, but the door to *some* deviation had been opened. Two nations stepped through that opening in 1956: Poland and Hungary.

The Polish situation in 1956 differed from the Hungarian crisis in that the Polish Communist party, called the Polish United Workers Party (PUWP), never lost control of the country. When Polish workers demonstrated in Poznan in 1956, the *Polish* army restored order. Although the party itself was in crisis, it never lost its ability to hold Poland in line. Soviet forces were not needed to maintain control. Wladyslaw Gomulka (1905–1982), an alleged liberal who had been under house arrest as a nationalist, was placed in charge in Warsaw and the country quieted down.

In Hungary in 1956, however, that same control of the crisis was not demonstrated by the party. The top leadership of the Hungarian Communist party was split between liberals and conservatives, and this split was exacerbated both by Soviet interference and by Tito's clumsy attempts to guide what he saw as "national communism." Neither side of the Hungarian dispute had any tolerance for the other. Matyas Rakosi, the Hungarian leader who was a conservative Stalinist, was replaced in 1953 by Imre Nagy, a liberal. Rakosi, although ousted, kept trying to discredit the Nagy government, which only added to the uncompromising hostility between the two major factions. Soviet leaders kept Nagy in power but failed to discourage Rakosi's challenges that undermined Nagy's control.

Conservative changes in the ideological atmosphere in the USSR in 1955, and the illness of Imre Nagy were successfully utilized by Rakosi to regain power in Hungary during the spring of 1955. Soviet leaders did not interfere as Nagy was removed from all leadership positions and in November from the party as well. But the liberal period from 1953 to 1955 had created sufficient expectations of change in Hungary that the renewed Stalinism of Rakosi was not well received. Opposition mounted within the party and focused around the name of Imre Nagy. After Khrushchev's anti-Stalin speech in February 1956 at the Twentieth Party Congress, Rakosi had even less support within Hungary. When Rakosi responded to the political threat of the growing opposition by seeking to destroy it, the Central Committee appealed to the Soviet Union. Soviet intervention was half-hearted and satisfied no one. A compromise leader named Erno Gëro was chosen in July, but he satisfied very few. Tensions increased in both the party and the population in general.

In October, the news of Gomulka's reinstatement in Poland suggested to Hungarians that the Soviet leaders were not interested in using force to combat new liberal directions. To a great many people that meant a new possibility for Imre Nagy, but Gëro was unwilling to resign. Violence broke out in Budapest that the Hungarian army did not control. The secret police opened fire on the demonstrators, causing the protests to become even more widespread. At this point, on October 23, 1956, two simultaneous events occurred: Soviet military assistance was requested by Gyorgy Marosan, a member of the Politburo, and Imre Nagy was named premier by the Central Committee. When Soviet troops came to defend the Hungarian government, ironically, they were protecting the government that revolutionaries desired. Nagy negotiated an end to this confusing situation on October 28, and Soviet troops began to withdraw.

At this point, however, events quickly deteriorated from the Soviet Union's perspective; the Hungarians moved too far too fast. On October 30 a multiparty system was reinstituted. The next day Nagy stated that *he* had not invited the Soviet troops into Hungary to restore order, and he began negotiations to withdraw from the Warsaw Pact. One day later the Nagy government proclaimed neutrality.[7] Such activities in 1956 made Soviet leaders nervous because Nagy's positions would move Hungary away from the status of a friendly satellite to an independent and suspicious "neutrality" that seemed dangerous to Soviet interests.[8] Soviet troops and tanks returned a few days later, and a bloody repression ensued.

This time there were no liberal "experiments." The rigid Soviet model was reimposed on Hungary by the new leader Janos Kadar. Nagy was executed for his "crimes" on June 30, 1958 as a lesson to others who might be tempted to emulate him. Eastern Europe settled down again in dull conformity to Soviet definitions of orthodoxy.

The third example came twelve years later when conflict erupted in Czechoslovakia. Under the leadership of conservatives, the country did not deviate from the Stalin model until well into the 1960s when the Czech economy began unraveling. At this point political stability was threatened by a lack of economic growth, and reforms were introduced in 1966. Again, the signals from Moscow seemed supportive for such changes in the economy: Alexei Kosygin, the Soviet Prime Minister and Politburo member, had introduced in 1965 what appeared to be substantial reforms in the Soviet Union, based in part on the Liberman proposals of 1962.[9] The Czech reforms were not that different: selective decentralization of the economy and a stronger emphasis on the profitability of individual enterprises in the state-run system.

These necessary reforms, however, were resisted by those whose power depended on central planning. Defenders of the old orthodoxy were the conservatives who classed the reformers as heretical liberals, once again demonstrating the tight connection between ideology and central planning. In the Soviet Union, at least until the 1990s, this battle was always won by conservatives.[10] And so it turned out for Czechoslovakia as well. But, for a time, the Czechoslovak debate created the same greater sense of freedom that had been released in Hungary a dozen years earlier. In January 1968, liberals were successful in naming one of their own to lead the party—a young Slovak named Alexander Dubcek. Within a few months Czechoslovak Stalinism eroded within the party itself and a clamor for liberal reform quickly spread throughout the general population.[11]

Dramatic changes appeared in the April (1968) Action Program of the party, changes that would reappear in many of the later Gorbachev reforms. The Czechoslovak party now *denied* that it was a group that could dictate to the population at large. Party members should lead, the Action Program stated, not by authoritarian direction, but by service, by example, by earning the right to lead. Instead of prohibiting factions within the party, different ideas should honestly confront each other. The Action Program called for complete democracy and a free flow of information. Newspapers began to be less censored and then not censored at all. People in the factories began talking about establishing their own workers' councils to represent them rather than party-controlled unions, and questions were publicly raised about people previously executed or imprisoned for political heresy.

This debate could not be kept within party ranks; it soon spread to the general population. The demand for "socialism with a human face" became demands by demonstrators for opposition political parties in a new political system. Nervous Soviet observers, unwilling to consider such expectations in the USSR, began to feel that the Czechoslovak party was losing control of the situation—meaning that the party in Czechoslovakia was not following Moscow's cues so much as it was writing a new play while on stage.

When Czechoslovakia extended diplomatic recognition to Israel it seemed like a rude gesture toward the Soviet policy of backing militant Arab states against Israel.[12] Dubcek began to look to Soviet leaders like a new Imre Nagy, and an alarmed Leonid Brezhnev summoned Dubcek to Moscow. When Dubcek returned to Prague, he did not reestablish party control of the escalating developments. This can be considered bravery, but it was more likely a mistaken judgment that assumed continued nonintervention by the Soviet Union.[13]

In August 1968, however, Warsaw Pact forces entered Czechoslovakia to put down this potentially contagious reform. The streets rumbled with tanks, visible symbols of both Soviet power and Czech impotence. Thousands of people were imprisoned, thousands exiled, and hundreds of intellectuals were forced into manual labor or unemployment. Dubcek disappeared under secret arrest in Slovakia. Soviet, East German, Polish, Hungarian, and Bulgarian soldiers had come to "liberate" their friends in Czechoslovakia, to "free" them from the "counterrevolutionary" forces that had seized control of the country. It helped, a little, to paint swastikas on Soviet tanks and "Ivan Go Home" on walls, but gradually resistance, hatred, and fear had to be suppressed.[14]

Czechoslovakia was forcibly dragged back into rigid conformity to Brezhnev's concept of socialism. The fearful economic reforms were scuttled in favor of the old central planning and heavy industry model with which Soviet ideologues were more comfortable. Soviet leaders appointed a more reliable head of the purged party, Gustav Husak, who remained the Czech party leader for the next nineteen years! The operating principle in Czechoslovakia became *ad hoc* crisis management of an inflexible economic system.

*   *   *

Overt resistance occurred in Yugoslavia, Poland, Hungary, and Czechoslovakia. These different efforts to remove tight Soviet control began within the communist parties of these nations and expressed a desire for greater liberty and a more national approach to the socialist goal.

Yugoslavia's break with the Soviet Union was caused by Stalin's desire to bring Tito into a more acceptable conformity, while the crises in Poland and Hungary in 1956 appeared to result from Khrushchev's pro-Tito and anti-Stalin position, which undercut the power base of Eastern European leaders in countries experiencing economic distress and opened up the possibility of significant reforms. Czechoslovakia in 1968 was a similar reaction to the limits of the command economy. In Yugoslavia the result was a mixed economic and political system. In Poland the advent of Gomulka promised far more liberalism than he delivered, and the necessary reforms were postponed. In Hungary and Czechoslovakia, military intervention reimposed the command economy and the rigid political system.

ADAPTING THE MODEL: POLAND'S SOLIDARITY
AND HUNGARY'S NEW ECONOMIC MECHANISM

The name *Solidarity* refers to the Polish workers' movement that began in 1980 and was suppressed by the Polish government in December 1981. From 1982 to 1989 Solidarity led an underground, harassed, and truncated existence. From the beginning, moreover, it was a different kind of workers' movement. Solidarity in 1980/81 was neither an outright rejection of the existing communist regime, with its brutal and inefficient economic system, nor an attempt to achieve "true socialism" like the revisionist movements during the earlier Gomulka years.[15]

In Poland after 1956, Gomulka initially took steps that maintained hopes that real changes might occur. He decollectivized agriculture and permitted private farming, granted the Roman Catholic Church in Poland more freedom, allowed the publication of a weekly newspaper (titled *To Put It Plainly* in English) that addressed critical issues, and permitted the growth of workers' councils in factories and enterprises. These changes were thought only the beginning of more decentralization and worker control. In a short time, however, the pendulum shifted back again as Gomulka recentralized and diluted the effectiveness of the workers' councils. In 1964 the two authors of *An Open Letter to the Party,* Jacek Kuron and Karol Modzelewski, who called party bureaucrats the real exploiters of the working class, were imprisoned.[16] By 1968 the overt repression of a student protest and an officially sanctioned anti-Semitic campaign suggested a full return to a **totalitarian** focus by the party. One of the prominent revisionists who had been hopeful earlier, Leszek Kolakowski, began to liken the idea of nontotalitarian communism to boiling ice.[17]

Economic difficulties in the unreformed system continued to multiply. In 1970 to relieve the pressure of government subsidies, retail food prices were raised considerably. The move was badly timed and resulted in a general strike that began in Gdansk. Gomulka was removed from office and replaced by Edward Gierek, but very little changed. A similar attempt to raise food prices in 1976 resulted in another strike in the tractor factory at Ursus. In both 1970 and 1976 the price increases were rescinded by an embarrassed government. The workers, sensing their latent power, continued labor activities outside government control.

For example, workers formed the Committee for the Defense of the Workers (KOR), and by mid-1977 it had won the right to exist and freedom for those jailed in the 1976 strike. KOR helped publish material not authorized by party-controlled writers' unions, helped to set up a "flying university" where students were taught unscheduled subjects (classes were held in people's apartments), and published a regularly appearing newsletter that was passed out in factories.[18] In 1978 a Baltic Free Trade Union was founded by worker activists such as Lech Walesa, Andrzej Gwiazda, and Anna Walentynowicz.

Thus, by 1980 Polish workers already had a history of organizing and demanding explanations and changes in government policies. By August 1980 there was an existing informal labor structure when Anna Walentynowicz, a crane operator at the Gdansk shipyards, was unfairly prevented from working. She had been active in radical politics since 1970 and was one of the organizers of an underground newspaper (titled *Workers of the Coast* in English). On February 1, 1980, many people involved in the trade union, including Anna, were laid off at the Gdansk shipyards. Anna fought her layoff in Polish labor courts and won her case, but her job was not given back to her.[19] Other Gdansk workers rallied to support her reinstatement and this demand was supplemented by a demand for pay raises. Someone mentioned "strike," and Lech Walesa, a former electrician at the Gdansk shipyards, joined the protesting workers. In short order Walesa was leading the strike. When the Gdansk managers capitulated, the Gdansk workers voted to continue the strike in "solidarity" with workers in other factories to force the *government* to grant a more general pay increase. They initiated an Inter-factory Strike Committee (MKS), and by the end of the first week some 200 factories were involved.

The momentum swiftly mounted. Two graphic artists in Gdansk, J. and K. Janiszowski, turned the Polish word *Solidarnosc* (Solidarity) into a logo with each letter leaning on the other and a Polish flag arising from the letter *n*.

Quickly the logo and Solidarity became a symbol of far more than wage demands. The strike committee became the focus of a new demand for a free trade union to represent the legitimate interests of the workers—a goal practically inseparable from the struggle for more general freedoms in noneconomic areas. As a result, Solidarity went further than previous movements. It sought free trade unions first of all, but it also tried to force party awareness of the need for more independence in key areas such as workers' self-management and freedom of the press.[20] Intellectuals rallied around. The Catholic Church, from the new Polish Pope on down, seemed supportive.

There was more joy than ideology in the movement. Lech Walesa rejected the words, the labels, and the slogans—even the notion of political right and left. "I express myself with my words: good, bad, better, worse. And I say: If it serves the people it is good. If it doesn't serve the people, it is bad."[21] Confrontation with authorities was *not* sought; it was *avoided* in order to protect what Solidarity had gained. In Walesa's view, a view not necessarily shared by more impatient workers, freedom was a food that must be carefully administered when people are too hungry for it.[22] Although Walesa insisted on more overall free trade union responsibility in the society, he pulled that goal—radical for Poland—into an evolutionary, not a revolutionary, strategy.

Government representatives and Solidarity leaders negotiated an agreement, which was signed on August 31, 1980.[23] It was an astonishing document that went well beyond a communist country agreeing to legalize a free, representative union, or a union agreement in the West. For example, Solidarity agreed it would not become a political party, that it would honor the socialism of Poland, the leadership of the communist Polish United Workers' Party (PUWP), as well as Poland's existing system of international alliances, including the Warsaw Pact. Issues that had caused Soviet intervention in both Hungary and Czechoslovakia, the lack of party control and failure to recognize Soviet hegemony, were carefully avoided in the agreement. In return, the government agreed that Solidarity had the right to strike without fear of government retaliation.

Part of the reason for Solidarity's rapid growth and acceptance by the authorities was Poland's continuing economic troubles. And, in part, those troubles were caused by the Soviet-imposed military-industrial emphasis, which was draining the economy.[24] But a large part came also from bad planning by incompetent administrators. Thus, a portion of the Gdansk agreement included the union's commitment to set up a research committee to determine ways in which workers could become more involved in economic decisions. The agreement encouraged union participation in economic reforms, workers' self-management, workers' councils, and self-governing rural cooperatives. The workers, in other words, would participate in management. In addition, the state agreed to allow freedom of expression in the media and grant the media access to government planning documents. For the first time since World War II, Sunday Mass could be broadcast over the radio.

Previously jailed or disadvantaged strikers and student supporters from 1970 and 1976 were to have their rights reestablished. All political prisoners were to be freed. Repressions against people for their opinions would cease. Past cases were to be reopened and reinvestigated, and full liberty of expression was guaranteed in public and professional life. The full text of the Gdansk agreement would be published by the national news media so that all citizens would know what rights they had. Special stores serving the privileged would no longer sell commodities that were in short supply in stores elsewhere.

The Gdansk agreement attacked the tightly controlled party *nomenklatura* system for selecting key personnel, and the government agreed that cadre selection should be on the basis of individual qualifications rather than membership in a particular party. The government and Solidarity agreed that certain issues, such as raising pensions and the wages of health professionals, improving working conditions for everyone, ensuring sufficient day-care centers, and improving maternity leave compensation, would be implemented or consulted about in the near future. Problems of housing and long waiting lists for apartments would be discussed in local areas with competent organizations involved, not just party representatives. The workweek should be shortened by making Saturdays a free day as soon as possible.

The Gdansk agreement laid the basis for a legally chartered, free union involved in important decision making. If implemented in any sincere manner, the inefficient Polish system would have been changed in a fundamental way. But it was not implemented sincerely. Wherever the language in the agreement was somewhat ambiguous, government leaders waffled and postponed action. Any opportunity to delay implementation was seized upon. This put Solidarity in the position of pushing for what had already been successfully negotiated. Workers seeking greater involvement in the planning process were made to feel that they were obstacles rather than participants. Sharing economic planning power with workers was very difficult for party leaders who saw their primary function as managers of the economy, even if they managed badly. Doing without the *nomenklatura* was also difficult for a party that had followed that system for thirty-five years.

The PUWP needed the help of the Solidarity union but could not admit this. Since 1975 Poland's economic problems had clearly been created by inept managers, poor investment decisions, irrational price structures, and excessive foreign borrowing to smooth out problems. Moreover, for this kind of performance the party expected privileges denied to common citizens. Solidarity did not pretend to be perfect, but it represented honesty against corruption, openness against secrecy, frankness against dissembling, and conviction against cynicism. In attempting to ignore, dilute, or combat Solidarity, the party refused what it should have welcomed.

The new union filled a void in Polish life, the moral gap between the official government and the Polish people. Solidarity was *Polish* in a sense that the party could not be. Not that the PUWP represented the Soviet Union more than Poland, but that the party, in representing itself and elite interests over the years, had ceased to speak a language that Polish people heard as meaningful. The population of Poland adopted Solidarity as its own, as the keeper of order in the society. Cases of theft and rape and disputes of all kinds were brought to the union for consideration and handling. Solidarity became an extension of the people in general, a genuine expression of their desire for honest self-rule.

In March 1981 at Bydgoszcz, outright government provocation of Solidarity radicalized the Polish temperament, seriously undermining Solidarity's moderation and Lech Walesa's leadership. After Walesa cancelled a planned general strike for March 31, a more militant mood developed in Solidarity and this, however understandable, made the government's attempt to portray Solidarity as a threat to the system more credible. The summer and autumn of 1981 grew tense. In October the program adopted by the union's National Congress called for a pluralist society, genuine workers' self-management, an end to the *nomenklatura* system, and representative government at the highest levels.[25] Workers also began speaking of a new strategy called the "active strike." This meant continuing to work during the "strike" but seizing economic power at the same time. Workers' councils would run things on the principle of workers' self-management. Stefan Bratkowski summed up the active strike as follows: "The factories will work during the strike, trade will go on. Only the authorities will have nothing to do."[26] To protect the "active strikers" it was proposed that a workers' guard be established to defend both industrial enterprises and distribution networks against retaliation from the authorities. Preparations began in some areas to implement these ideas. This sounded enough like revolutionary strategy for the government not only to justify the imposition of martial law on December 13 but also to outlaw Solidarity.

Was Solidarity becoming revolutionary? Adam Michnik insisted later that this was not true,[27] but Andrzej Slowik argued that Solidarity had no choice but to offer a revolutionary solution to the Polish people.[28] However one interprets Solidarity's intentions (because both Michnik and Slowik were correct), the preparations for martial law had been underway for some time. The Soviet Union pressed General Wojciech Jaruzelski, the PUWP leader, for action to contain Solidarity because they feared a Solidarity "spillover" into the Soviet Baltic republics.[29]

Solidarity was contained by martial law. Its leaders were imprisoned and the organization was outlawed. Aspirations were again smothered, and, except for the brief excitement of the papal visit in 1983, Polish citizens settled back into sullen obedience, an unhappy acceptance of the status quo, and a renewed bifurcation of life. This kind of change could not, it seemed, come from within the subordinate nations of Eastern Europe.

The death of Leonid Brezhnev in November 1982 did not alter this situation. There were modest changes in the USSR but the situation in Poland continued to be bleak. The murder of pro-Solidarity priest Jerzy Popieluszko in October 1984 followed reports of earlier kidnappings and beatings of Solidarity members by hard-liners in PUWP. Polish courts convicted three security police officers for the abduction and murder of Father Jerzy Popieluszko, and the head of the ministry involved was forced to resign. These swift government actions partially defused the tense situation, but the explosive potential remained under the surface. It seemed that any real change had to await alterations in the model itself—significant changes in the Soviet Union. Throughout most of the 1980s that seemed a forlorn hope.

And yet Solidarity had existed long enough to develop a history and sense of mission. Although this would later be important, in the mid-1980s Solidarity seemed like many other earlier hopes in Eastern Europe—buried before it had a chance to breathe.

However, a different attempt to adapt the Soviet model had been going on for some time in Hungary, hardly attracting any attention at all because the attempted changes were modest, limited to the economy, and were initiated by the party leader, Janos Kadar, the very man installed by the Soviet Union after crushing the brief Hungarian revolt. Although Kadar had Imre Nagy arrested in November 1956, conspired in Nagy's later execution, and dissolved workers' councils above the factory level, he moved against conservatives in the party as well. In the months after October 1956 he rebuilt the party from "the large corps of functionaries who had never sided with Nagy and who had never been rigid conservatives."[30] Reconstruction, repair, and consolidation were slow,[31] but already in December 1956 Kadar put together a team of 200 experts to study the economy and make recommendations. In 1957 the group published its report calling for a rational and decentralized economic system. But in 1957 Khrushchev was fighting colleagues in his own Politburo who disliked his de-Stalinization campaign and his overtures to Tito. So this was not a time to move in liberal directions. With Khrushchev seeking to demonstrate his own orthodoxy at home, Kadar would have been foolish to move in unorthodox directions. The experts' report was therefore shelved and Kadar conformed to the new pressures emanating from the Soviet Union to recollectivize Hungarian farmers. By 1961, rural Hungary again followed the collectivist model,[32] and the command economy remained in place until 1968.

As noted above (pp. 115–116), the centralized economic model (the command economy), fits periods of *extensive* growth but not those demanding *intensive* growth.[33] In the first period, massive introductions of capital and labor produce a rapid growth of basic industries, while postponing production in light industry and in consumer goods. The need to adapt becomes critical when labor reserves are exhausted and the return rate on investment begins to decline. These events signal a need to increase efficiency and productivity through a more sophisticated mechanization and to pay far more attention to the quality of what is produced. At the point where the economy becomes more sophisticated, central planning breaks down because the planners are too distant from the arena of economic action—like driving a car from the back seat—not impossible but certainly clumsy. Central decision making begins to exacerbate rather than ease economic problems.

By the mid-1960s Hungary was at that intensive stage, and it was easily recognized since so much of Hungary's national product was exported to the more quality-conscious Western markets. The quality disadvantages of the old central model were thus noticed more quickly. In the 1960s about one-third of Hungary's exports went to the West, and by the 1980s this figure had grown to about one-half. Any economy of scale in a small country like Hungary meant building factories that had export potential. Dependence on exports, a greater emphasis on quality, and the need for a high-technology production persuaded Janos Kadar to consider radical economic reforms more seriously than they were considered in the Soviet Union at this time. Brezhnev did not have the necessary vision to see the future need for such economic reform both because high oil prices that brought substantial hard currency revenues to the USSR obscured economic difficulties, and because the much larger domestic Soviet market shielded Soviet planners from the negative consequences of shoddy production.[34]

Three basic reform ideas surfaced in Hungary: (1) Leave the model intact and strengthen centralized planning; (2) leave the model intact and improve an incentives system; and (3) change the model by decentralizing as much as necessary. The Hungarian reforms began with the first and second ideas, and ended up rather quickly with a full commitment to the third; seeking reforms that would not be easily reversed and that would confer substantial long-term benefits on the society.[35] These reforms were called the New Economic Mechanism and were ready to be implemented by 1968. The results have been positive, even though problems emerged. The reforms were no sooner implemented than the quadrupling of oil prices hit Hungary. This severely depressed the growth rate of the economy even though much of Hungary's oil came from the Soviet Union at prices below world rates. Hungary's growth in gross industrial output went from 6.4 percent between 1971 and 1975 to 3.4 percent between 1976 and 1980, and 2.4 percent between 1980 and 1985, compared to figures for Eastern Europe as a whole of 8.7, 5.7, and 2.1 percent, respectively.[36] The rise in imported oil costs caused panic and a partial return to centralized subsidies, thus damaging Hungary's international balance of payments position and causing the government to borrow extensively from Western banks.

To extricate itself from this situation, further decentralization rather than recentralization was instituted in 1978. Subsidies were again lowered and central investments reduced. These actions sacrificed short-term growth so that long-term growth would be more firmly based. This was a courageous approach that recognized the futility of retreating back into a command economy and earned Hungary an international reputation for prudent money management.

One key to the success of the plan in Hungary during those years was that political power relationships were not altered. Obviously, economic ministries were disadvantaged by the reduction in responsibility, but competing interest groups were taken care of through compromises right at the beginning. With the political power structure relatively unaltered and unchallenged, Soviet leaders had little concern as long as the reforms worked.

Keeping the overall domestic and international ideological framework intact permitted Hungary to abolish the compulsory indicators from the central planning agencies. As a result, enterprises began responding to market signals through the price system, so as to maximize profits instead of meeting output criteria. Wage determinations were decentralized as were almost all investment decisions. New sharing funds for bonuses, pay increases, and development were created.

New economic freedoms, even in the absence of political change, spilled over into other related areas. In 1979 the frontier with neighboring Austria became an open border without visa restrictions, although still guarded and marked by barbed wire (until 1989). In 1983, for example, over a half million Hungarians visited the West and over forty percent of them went to Austria, while a million and a half Austrians visited Hungary. Economic cooperation between the two countries rose steadily in the period between 1979 and 1985. Some 600 Austrian firms developed business links with Hungary and more than a hundred active industrial cooperation arrangements were signed—some for joint projects in Third World countries. Trade between Hungary and Austria more than doubled. Austrian firms made direct sales to Hungarian department stores and other consumer outlets. People from either side of the Danube moved up and down the river without concern about straying too far toward the other side.[37] This border freedom was possible because the Hungarians who left, with few exceptions, returned.

In January 1984 price increases averaging twenty percent went into effect as part of the subsidy reduction and market-oriented pricing plan. There was no organized protest as there would have been in Poland. Although at this point Hungarian citizens had few political rights, and many felt the need to work at more than one job in order to make ends meet, the lack of social protest indicated some confidence that the economic decision-makers knew what they were doing. Even when there was a bad harvest, as in 1983, Hungarian shops were full of goods—somewhat like supermarkets in the West. The general availability of Western goods also contributed to consumer satisfaction. Prices were high, but goods moved rapidly.

Despite new reform efforts in 1985 to protect state-owned enterprises from interference by government ministries, however, this interference continued because government subsidies were still manipulated from the center, which made it difficult to determine the profitability of an enterprise. In addition, the very high taxes paid by successful enterprises reduced incentives to succeed. This combination of central decision making along with a partial market economy proved unfortunate. The reform left too much unchanged that should have been removed. No political change, and too much central planning interference, at first seen positively as reducing the potential of Soviet interference, eventually created a problem for Hungarian citizens that seemed to worsen with time: an increasing cost of living, double-digit inflation, personal income taxes, and the highest per capita foreign indebtedness in Eastern Europe, which demanded more rather than less austerity. Many Hungarians now began to hold three rather than two jobs to make ends meet.

The New Economic Mechanism was curiously a success and a failure at the same time. An example of this was the rhetoric about full employment under socialism while insisting on the need to allow bankruptcy, which, of course, creates the ideologically denied unemployment.[38] Many sound economic ideas emerged and were implemented, but economic reform cannot accomplish much unless it is accompanied by social, particularly political, reforms. In the absence of these reforms, Hungary began to stagnate, but in economic terms, Hungary certainly led the way toward comprehensive reform, and even its mistakes proved educational for other nations, especially the Soviet Union. Party leaders who called for political reform were thought of as radicals despite the fact that the general deterioration of life in Hungary by 1987 was sufficient to warrant a very depressing assessment from Prime Minister Karoly Grosz (who replaced Kadar as party leader in May 1988): The public mood is deteriorating, he said, while living standards have either stagnated or decreased. As a result, confidence in the leadership has dwindled, and "sometimes the viability of socialism is put in doubt."[39]

The new leadership in 1988 did not make major changes despite the overwhelming need. The alterations called for were seen as too dramatic, too strong by far to introduce, and yet promises of great change appeared in the offing. In the meantime the Communist party waffled backward and forward, trying without success to find the right combination that would allow the party to remain in power and simultaneously lead the society to affluence. But confidence in the party deteriorated.

Like Solidarity in Poland, the New Economic Mechanism could only go so far with the existing structures then prevailing in Eastern Europe. Like Solidarity, the New Economic Mechanism went deeper and further than was anticipated. But both attempts to adapt the Soviet model without outright defiance ran into substantial obstacles that could only be removed if the model itself—the Soviet system—began to lead the way. Slowly, and with many creaking joints, that is what began to happen in 1989.

*   *   *

Solidarity arose in an almost accidental fashion over the failure to reinstate Anna Walentynowicz, a respected labor activist who worked in the Gdansk shipyards as a crane operator. A wage increase was added to the demand for her reinstatement, then the strike broadened to include workers' interests in other Polish factories. The Gdansk agreement, if it had been followed, might have altered Poland a step at a time, but government hostility triggered a greater radicalism in Solidarity that gave General Jaruzelski a strong motive for the repression of Solidarity in December 1981. The crisis that spawned Solidarity in August 1980, however, was not resolved, and Poland remained a sleeping bear waiting for the spring.[40]

Hungary chose a different path of adaptation, leading the way to the comprehensive economic reform that all other East European nations, including the Soviet Union, had to face. Hungary's reforms were designed to implicate only the economic sphere of society, leaving the Hungarian Communist party in control and loyalty to the Soviet Union unquestioned. Hungary's economic miracle, however, was of brief duration, and it was impeded by the stagnation of the rest of the society. Further reforms were required.

THE FRACTURING OF THE MODEL—1989–1990

The strongest constraint on any real political evolution in Eastern Europe prior to 1989 was the combination of two factors: stagnating political systems, which stifled criticism and constructive change, and the tendency of the Soviet Union to intervene militarily (the Brezhnev Doctrine) whenever it appeared as though change was threatening Soviet hegemony in the area.

Stagnation can be measured in a variety of ways. One way is to consider the turnover of personnel in the top ruling body—the Politburo of the Communist party. Considering only the full, voting members of the Politburos of the eight countries of Eastern Europe, it became obvious that the stability of the region was threatened by either of two extremes: too rapid a turnover indicating party crisis, and far too slow a turnover indicating turgidity and stagnation. Table 7.1 summarizes this data.[41]

TABLE 7.1   **Politburo Full-Member Expected Tenures Since 1953 in Eastern Europe (ranked from lowest to highest in years)**

Czechoslovakia (prior to 1968)	5.39
Poland	6.97
Hungary	7.13
Bulgaria	10.28
Romania	12.47
German Democratic Republic	13.77
Albania	15.50
Czechoslovakia (after 1968)	25.00 +

Note: Czechoslovakia is included twice in this table because of the remarkable changes occurring after 1968. To average the figures would be misleading. Yugoslavia is not included here because, after 1967, electoral reforms made tenures nonexponential in character. This table should be used with caution and serves to illustrate a possible operationalization of the concepts of crisis and stagnation.

Expectations of tenure in the Soviet Politburo since 1919 hovered around the ten-year mark. Taking this as a benchmark of stability over time suggests that numbers less than ten move toward crisis and those greater than ten point to stagnation. The countries on the low side of this division—Czechoslovakia prior to 1968, Poland, and Hungary—were countries that experienced crises in the ruling parties themselves and were consequently more open to change in order to resolve those crises. Countries on the high side (see Table 7.1)—Bulgaria, Romania, the German Democratic Republic, Albania, and Czechoslovakia after 1968—were countries that not only exhibited extensive stagnation but also resisted change far beyond the actual need for it. The greater the stagnation, the more profound and rapid the change when it came.[42] Those countries experiencing crisis in their parties, namely Poland and Hungary, gradually underwent profound changes in government in 1988–89, changes that demonstrated to the more stagnant countries that there really was an alteration in the Brezhnev doctrine.

The Brezhnev doctrine had underscored a Soviet hegemony in the area that was understood as ideological orthodoxy. If a country were not entirely within the parameters of ideological correctness, the "heretic" was considered to be leaning to the "other" enemy side. Until repeal of the Brezhnev Doctrine was *seen to be real,* the stagnant countries continued in the inertial rigidity that had characterized them for decades. However, even when Poland opened up its government to Solidarity in 1989, and Poland became the first country to be ruled by a coalition government composed of both communists and Solidarity delegates, and even when the leaders of the Hungarian Communist party changed the party's name and orientation away from communism to social democracy, party leaders in the stagnant countries still needed a push from their own people *and Mikhail Gorbachev* before they would open the door to significant change.

The change began slowly in 1988. Cracks in the monolithic dam, seen more clearly through hindsight, became visible in Poland in late 1988, when Solidarity was encouraged to participate in roundtable discussions with the communist government about various reform proposals. When it became clear that the government needed the cooperation of Solidarity, the union pushed for relegalization. A significant aspect of the debate included discussions of Solidarity participation in democratic elections in which the PUWP would face real opposition at the polls for the first time. Legalization of Solidarity occurred in April 1989 and free elections were held in June, with Solidarity the very clear winner over an embarrassed PUWP. Negotiations about the new government that would be formed from Poland's revitalized Parliament ended with a compromise: Power would be shared between the PUWP and Solidarity, with a PUWP president and a Solidarity prime minister installed at the head of the government.

The coalition government worked. Not everyone in Poland is delighted with the directions this new government has taken, particularly after comprehensive and rapid economic reform was introduced on January 1, 1990. Solidarity was no longer the opposition, but a responsible part of the government of Poland, occasionally generating hostility from its own people.[43] Nonetheless, Poland's clear move to democracy was an important step in opening up not only Poland but the rest of Eastern Europe to significant political and economic reform. The possibility of *real* reform, not simply cosmetic changes, became evident for the rest of the area.

Hungarian changes began slowly in 1989, with dramatic results in 1990. The Communist Party changed its name, and presumably its orientation, to the new Hungarian Socialist Party. The intention was to focus on social democracy rather than communism as the goal, and to facilitate that transfer of focus the parliament amended the Hungarian constitution to delete all traces of Stalinism and to clear the way for a freer society. The party militia, a para-military group of some 60,000, which had been formed in 1956 to protect the Communist Party faithful, was dissolved.

The 1989 changes in Hungary appeared initially to be cosmetic because the new Socialist party was led by former leaders of the Communist Party, and it was still in charge of the state. However, an early clue to what was destined to happen in the March 1990 elections was the fact that most of the former members of the Communist Party failed to register with the newly-named Socialist Party. This harbinger of change was confirmed in the March elections in which former communists were soundly defeated. What emerged from the second round of voting in April was a coalition government dominated by the Hungarian Democratic Forum and the Free Democrats—somewhat to the right of center and decidedly anticommunist. The accelerated economic reform and the new democracy in Hungary go well beyond the aspirations of Imre Nagy thirty-four years earlier.

Bulgaria also underwent a series of changes in 1989 as a result of pressure by the people and of prompting by Gorbachev in the Soviet Union. The old ruler who stood for uncompromising communist supremacy, Todor I. Zhivkov, was removed from office in November 1989. A factor facilitating this was the growing popular support for an environmental group called Eco-glasnost. The reforms that followed in Bulgaria were significant but initially modest in comparison to Poland, Hungary, and the German Democratic Republic. For example, the Bulgarian Communist party was given an opportunity to reform itself, and in the process began to split. The article in the constitution giving the party supremacy was suspended by parliamentary action in April 1990, and democratic elections occurred in mid-1990. The renamed Communist party, now called the Bulgarian Socialist party, distancing itself from what it called the mistakes of the past, did better in the June elections than might have been anticipated. Many noncommunist voters following the May lead of the Romanian electorate evidently felt that stability in Bulgaria had a better chance if change were as gradual as possible.

One former country that Table 7.1 identifies as decidedly resistant to change (indicated by stagnating politburo tenures) was the German Democratic Republic (GDR). What happened in that country in 1989 became a frightening specter for hardliners in other Eastern European countries where tumultuous events and rapid changes were about to result from rapidly deteriorating economies,[44] inflexible leadership, and very strong popular pressure. A strong desire to leave the GDR infected thousands of East German citizens in the summer of 1989, particularly after Hungary removed the barbed-wire barriers on its frontier with Austria. A mass migration occurred, first through Hungary and then through Czechoslovakia. In the full glare of international publicity, the dam (the Berlin Wall) was holding, but the river of popular pressure was circumventing it. The GDR leadership contemplated a military crackdown that did *not* have Soviet support. Gorbachev did not want a European repetition of the Chinese government's June suppression of student demonstrators in Tiananmen Square. The GDR leadership therefore first chose to do nothing, but the mass exodus of people continued. What had to give way was not the people's push for changes already achieved in the Soviet Union, but the inflexible leadership of Erich Honecker, who had led the GDR since May 1971. The celebration of the fortieth anniversary of the GDR in early October 1989 sparked widespread protests, with demonstrators shouting "Gorby, Gorby!" to voice their dissatisfaction with their own government and their support for the kind of economic and political reforms associated with the name of Gorbachev. These demonstrations, aided by Protestant churches and later joined by Roman Catholics, were suppressed by police and security forces, but the end of the Honecker regime was near.

Eleven days after the anniversary celebration Honecker resigned, and was replaced by Egon Krenz, who quickly demonstrated the bankruptcy of the hard-liner position by opening the Berlin Wall and permitting free emigration to East German citizens. The Berlin Wall had stood since August 1961 as a symbol of repression, but its opening on November 9, 1989, did not stop emigration nor the internal pressure for change. Citizen marches and demonstrations continued to demand further, lasting reforms, and the stagnant communist regime crumbled. Elections in March 1990 repudiated the communist past and supported democratic parties in the GDR that were similar to the Christian Democrats and Social Democrats in West Germany. The stagnant regime of the past 40 years had fallen, and attention immediately turned to a rapid reunification of the two Germanies.

Czechoslovakia's stagnating leadership, also illustrated by Table 7.1's very high figures for expected length of tenure since 1968, similarly fought both a worsening economy and unrelenting pressure from the populace and from the Soviet Union in 1989. Change was long overdue in Czechoslovakia, and the longer the party resisted the change the more extensive it was when it came. The removal of Gustav Husak as party leader in 1987 had not initiated a solution, because in 1987 internal pressures as well as the signals from the Soviet Union were not strong enough. The post-1987 administration of Milos Jakes represented a new administration but not a reform-minded one. The difficulty for hard-liners in Czechoslovakia was that their power had been justified for over twenty years by their opposition to the "errors" of the "Prague Spring" of 1968. The reform movements in 1989 appeared to represent similar, if not even more liberal sentiments than those which had been suppressed in 1968. To give in to the demands for change would have the appearance of proving Alexander Dubcek to have been right all along, an idea that had been resisted as long as possible. Like logs jamming a river, the hard-liners' recalcitrance had to be pushed aside. Only great pressure, suddenly applied, could trigger the change.

The beginnings of that popular pressure, encouraged by what had happened in the GDR, can be traced to a speech by Jakes on November 12, 1989, in which he told a youth conference that the party would not tolerate street protests or relax its control of the country. Thus was evidenced the continuation of the same old rigidity, the same failure to sense the momentum of change. Five days later, tens of thousands of demonstrators rallied in Prague and were promptly crushed by the police. A stalemate ensued. Two days later, however, the courage of the people was shown in another demonstration as thousands protested the brutality of the police. These protests were not crushed, and widespread participation of all elements of the Czechoslovakian population swelled the size of further demonstrations, which began to occur on a daily basis.

By November 24, pressure was sufficient to force Milos Jakes and many other hard-liners to resign, but this did not satisfy the demonstrators. Pressure continued until the two-hour general strike of November 27 revealed an almost total involvement of the populace, especially in the cities. Alexander Dubcek returned to Prague to speak to cheering demonstrators. Vaclav Havel, the dissident playwright who had become the voice of protest, was named leader of the new opposition political group called Civic Forum, and by the end of November the Czechoslovakian Communist party was in full retreat. A coalition government emerged, dominated by the Civic Forum but containing many reform-minded communists. A slow pace of economic reform and divisions within the Civic Forum, however, led to a return of political apathy in 1990. The democracy that emerged after the June elections was, therefore, not as exciting as events in late 1989 appeared to promise.

Romania was another fiefdom with a long history of ignoring changes in Moscow. The Romanians lived under a system that, like Albania, resembled the Stalinist era in the Soviet Union: The glorification of the country's leader, Nicolae Ceausescu, was in inverse relationship to the amount of freedom enjoyed by the people. Romania, however, was unlike Albania in that changes were occurring all around it, making the continued power of Ceausescu the main barrier to significant change. As was the case with the removal of Erich Honecker in the German Democratic Republic and Todor Zhivkov in

Bulgaria, the overthrow of Ceausescu in Romania brought significant change. This unexpectedly occurred in December 1989, the last dramatic event in that very significant year.

The cause of the upheaval was mixed and the specific spark uncertain. The Romanian persecution of a Hungarian minority within Romania, which earlier had drawn protests from Hungary, focused on the attempted deportation of a clergyman from Timisoara, some 250 miles northwest of Bucharest. The clergyman, Laszlo Toekes of the Reformed Church in Timisoara, had defended the rights of Hungarians in Romania, and the Ceausescu regime wanted to expel him. Hundreds of ethnic Hungarians and Romanian citizens formed a human chain around his residence to protect him. After several days, the incident escalated. When security forces arrived on December 16, the human chain turned into an anti-Ceausescu demonstration. Thousands of people in Timisoara were fired on and hundreds were buried in mass graves. The bloodbath enraged the entire Romanian population and public order disintegrated. When Ceausescu quickly returned to Bucharest from a state visit to Iran, the crowd that assembled to hear his speech drowned out his words with shouts of protest. A visibly distraught Nicolae Ceausescu and his wife Elena quickly departed by helicopter, but they were arrested by the army, tried for past crimes, and executed on December 25, 1989. Battles between the army and the Securitate, the security forces still loyal to Ceausescu, continued for the next few days.

The interim government, called the Council of National Salvation, contained many former members of the Communist Party who had lost favor under the Ceausescu regime. This fact enraged many who had participated in the December anticommunist revolution, and it polarized the Romanian people. Popular demonstrations for or against the National Salvation Front, the political party that coalesced from the new governing body, continued through early 1990, largely displacing political campaigning for the May elections. The results, a resounding victory for the Front and its leader, Ion Iliescu, signaled the first time in history that a government dominated by former communists had been freely chosen by a major Eastern European electorate.

One of the Eastern European countries would not allow its population to demonstrate dissent and would not respond positively to Gorbachev's push to change. This was isolated Albania, which had been going its own way since the events of 1948 had freed the tiny nation from Yugoslavia. Albania's status as a loyal Soviet satellite deteriorated shortly after Khrushchev's secret speech in 1956 in which he condemned Stalin as a criminal. At that point the more Stalinist Albania became less friendly to the Soviet Union, became instead the European ally of Maoist China, and dropped out of the Warsaw Treaty Organization. When China began to liberalize in the late 1970s, Albania again withdrew into itself and continued in its isolation to exhibit an astonishing stagnation unrelieved by popular demonstrations of dissatisfaction or by any intention of following the post-1985 liberalizing trends in the Soviet Union. Albania, therefore, which had forbidden religious observance of any kind since 1967, continued to practice its own "religion": authoritarian control of its backward society in the name of a communism that had lost any real meaning. Multicandidate elections were promised, but within a one-party framework. This very poor and backward country is the last Eastern European nation to loosen its authoritarian constraints. But even there the reform process has begun. The hostility against public expressions of religious belief and travel abroad lessened in 1990. The pressure not to change comes from Stalinist conservatives, while democratic alternatives are pushed by a small group of politically active liberals. A small elite maintains the authoritarian control, but defensively, and the walls it had created around itself to shield Albania from outside influence are now being penetrated.

This fracturing of the monolith in Eastern Europe in 1989–90 fundamentally altered the European scene. Confrontation between West and East was replaced with cautious cooperation, and the almost unilateral Soviet aid was replaced by multilateral Western assistance in Eastern economies that had been badly managed. Revitalizing the economies and the workers used to "iron rice bowls" will take years. This transition is a political nightmare. Communism might be ending, but political problems continue, especially in Poland, Bulgaria, and Romania, where the break with communism was insufficiently complete. In addition, successful anticommunist coalitions tend to break apart into rival groups, allowing ethnic rivalries and nationalism to rise to the surface. These are serious problems for the area that will take decades to solve.

*   *   *

Eastern Europe, with the exception of Albania, experienced significant change in 1989, which was reinforced by new political structures in 1990. The rapid evolution was from the barracks communism of enforced orthodoxy and rigid authoritarianism to a much looser, democratic, and open society. Europe, once again, appeared to be a reality, even though Eastern Europe continued to have a long way to go—economically and politically.

AFTERWORD

This chapter has concentrated on resistance to the armed imposition of Soviet communism on Eastern Europe, and the changes that have occurred in several Eastern European nations as a result of internal pressures (populist and economic) and/or external influence from a reforming Soviet Union. The next chapter describes a very different scenario: the coming to power of a communist party in China that, even more than in Yugoslavia, gained its victory through its own efforts, against some opposition from the Soviet Union. The story of modern China must be simplified to make it fit into one chapter, but it is far better to simplify than to ignore altogether.

NOTES

1. The phrase "barracks communism" came from *Magyar Hirlap,* (August 8, 1976) cited in Bennet Kovrig, "Hungary," in Teresa Rakowska-Harmstone and Andrew Gyorgy, eds., *Communism in Eastern Europe* (Bloomington: Indiana University Press, 1981), p. 90.

2. Khrushchev later stated that if Yugoslavia and the USSR had had a common border, troops would have been sent. See Strobe Talbott (trans. & ed.), *Khrushchev Remembers: The Last Testament* (Boston: Little Brown & Co., 1974), p. 181.

3. The editorial seemed to approve of different roads to socialism—even giving the idea a Leninist ambiance. But a critical clause should not have been missed: ". . . given unity in the chief fundamental matter of ensuring the victory of socialism. . . ," different paths were possible. It does not take a lawyer to comprehend that that clause should have created great caution because its very ambiguity in an otherwise clear editorial should have raised suspicions. Excerpt taken from *Pravda,* (July 16, 1955) trans. in *The Current Digest of the Soviet Press,* 7, (August 10, 1955):3; also cited in Paul E. Zinner, ed., *National Communism and Popular Revolt in Eastern Europe: A Selection of Documents on Events in Poland and Hungary, February–November 1956* (New York: Columbia University Press, 1956), p. 8.

4. From "Announcement of the Dissolution of the Information Bureau of the Communist and Workers Parties, April 17, 1956," *Pravda,* April 18, 1956); cited in ibid., p. 11.

5. Consider the nuances in the following sentence of a *Pravda* editorial in 1956: "The communist construction in the Soviet Union and the socialist construction in the people's democracies form a unified process of the movement of peoples toward a new life." Such jargon was not difficult to understand for East European leaders skilled in reading between *Pravda*'s lines. First, the phrase "people's democracies" referred to East European countries. Second, what was happening in the Soviet Union? The construction of *communism.* What was occurring in Eastern Europe? The construction of *socialism.* Using Marx's separation of the two with respect to the future society, what the Soviet Union was doing was of a higher order because communism was a higher, second, or final phase of the future. Socialism's construction was thus subordinate, like someone in college describing someone else still in high school. Third, what moves people to the new life was not greater amounts of liberation or freedom, but *construction* or economic growth. From "The International Forces of Peace, Democracy, and Socialism Are Growing and Gaining in Strength," *Pravda* (July 16, 1956); cited in ibid., p. 20.

6. Ibid., p. 19.

7. Zbigniew K. Brzezinski, *The Soviet Bloc, Unity and Conflict* (New York: Frederick A. Praeger, 1965), pp. 216–229.

8. Think of how U.S. leaders of both political parties frequently view South and Central American countries: within the United States' sphere of influence, and expected to be responsive to U.S. economic imperatives. In the 1980s this view was particularly visible in U.S. President Ronald Reagan's reactions to Nicaragua: The Sandinista government was evil because it was Marxist, and those opposed to it (the contras) were seen as patriotic freedom fighters. Both the United States and the Soviet Union define the world according to their own parochial interests.

9. For a summary of the Liberman ideas and the Kosygin reforms, see Edward A. Hewett, *Reforming the Soviet Economy* (Washington, D.C.: The Brookings Institution 1988), pp. 228–240.

10. Prior to Gorbachev, liberals had a difficult time in Soviet politics because the authoritarian regime was conditioned to view any challenge to the total power of the top party leadership as a life-and-death struggle. Little actual room existed to debate such things as economic reforms. Despite the overwhelming need to decentralize, too many top leaders or

their friends were involved in the central planning system and they resisted any weakening of their power. The military and the KGB were also advocates of heavy industry emphasis and weapons production. In addition, leaders were understandably reluctant to dismantle the Stalinist economic system that brought power and prestige to the Soviet Union and raised the standard of living for Soviet citizens. A person wanting to produce more consumer goods and introduce more consumer sovereignty in the marketplace, therefore, had a difficult time.

11.   Much has been written on this subject that merits attention. For example: H. Gordon Skilling, *Czechoslovakia's Interrupted Revolution* (Princeton, N.J.: Princeton University Press, 1976); Galia Golan, *The Czechoslovak Reform Movement: Communism in Crisis, 1962–1968* (Cambridge: Cambridge University Press, 1971); Galia Golan, *Reform Rule in Czechoslovakia: The Dubcek Era, 1968–1969* (Cambridge: Cambridge University Press, 1973); and Vladimir V. Kusin, *The Czechoslovak Reform Movement, 1968* (London: International Research Documents, 1973). Events were also covered extensively and intensively by journal articles.

12.   Keep in mind that the year was 1968—just one year after the Six Day War in the Middle East when Israel's military totally dominated the Soviet-backed Egyptian forces. Soviet foreign-policy makers were frantically seeking to demonstrate to the Palestine Liberation Front, for example, that their backing of Arab causes was meaningful in the anti-Israeli context. The Czech recognition of Israel was more of a slap in the face to the Soviet interests in the region than it at first appeared to be.

13.   Jiri Valenta, *Soviet Intervention in Czechoslovakia, 1968* (Baltimore: The Johns Hopkins University Press, 1979), pp. ix–xii. Some did predict the invasion that occurred in August—I did myself in May of 1968. My prediction, however, appeared in a local newspaper and was largely unnoticed.

14.   The resistance of top government officials, particularly President Svoboda, and the existence of radio stations that made these facts known contributed to the sparing of Alexander Dubcek's life. The resistance made it very difficult for the Soviet leaders to argue that they had been invited into Czechoslovakia by the government of that nation. See Harry Schwartz, *Prague's 200 Days* (New York: Praeger, 1969), pp. 211ff.

15.   Alain Touraine, Francois Dubet, Michel Wieviorka, and Jan Strzelecki, *Solidarity* (Cambridge: Cambridge University Press, 1983), pp. 19, 26.

16.   Daniel Singer, *The Road to Gdansk, Poland and the USSR* (New York: Monthly Review Press, 1981), pp. 161–162.

17.   Cited in ibid., p. 246.

18.   Ibid., pp. 183ff.

19.   Gail Russell Chaddock, "Sounding an Alarm on Poland," *Christian Science Monitor* (November 16, 1989), p. 14. This interview with Anna Walentynowicz provides a less enthusiastic perspective on the 1989 success of Lech Walesa and Solidarity.

20.   Touraine, et al., *Solidarity*, p. 20.

21.   Oriana Fallaci, "Interview with Lech Walesa" (excerpts) (March 1981), in Stan Persky and Henry Flam, eds., *The Solidarity Sourcebook* (Vancouver, New Star Books, 1982), p. 103.

22.   Ibid., p. 104.

23.   "The Gdansk Agreement" (sometimes referred to as the Gdansk, Szczecin and Jastrzebie Agreement), in Persky and Flam, *Solidarity Sourcebook*, pp. 93–99.

24.   Michael Checinski, "Poland's Military Burden," *Problems of Communism*, 32 (May–June 1983):31–44.

25.   "The Solidarity Program," Persky and Flam, *op. cit.*, pp. 213–215.

26.   Ibid., p. 234.

27.   Adam Michnik, "We Are All Hostages," ibid., pp. 248, 250.

28.   Zbigniew Kowalewski, "Solidarity on the Eve," ibid., pp. 236–237.

29.   V. Stanley Vardys, "Polish Echoes in the Baltic", *Problems of Communism*, 32 (July–August 1983):21–34.

30.   Paul Zinner, *Revolution in Hungary* (New York: Columbia University Press, 1962), p. 353.

31.   Bennett Kovrig, *Communism in Hungary: From Kun to Kadar* (Stanford, Calif.: Hoover Press, 1979), p. 319.

32.   Ibid., p. 340.

33.   Paul Hare, Hugo Radice, and Nigel Swain, eds., *Hungary: A Decade of Economic Reform* (London: George Allen & Unwin, 1981), pp. 5–6.

34.   These reasons for delay in reforming the Soviet economy are certainly no longer true, which helps to explain the attractiveness of comprehensive reforms.

35.   Hare et al., *Hungary: A Decade of Economic Reform*, p. 12.

36.   Han Vanous, "East Europe Economic Slowdown," *Problems of Communism*, 31 (July–August, 1982):3.

37.   Eric Bourne, "Austria and Hungary Find Their Open Border Serves them Well," *Christian Science Monitor*, (February 6, 1984), p. 16.

38.   See the curious example of Hungary's only maker of bathtubs, cast-iron bathtubs at that, which was bailed out of economic difficulties in 1987 mainly to prevent unemployment. Details are provided by William Echikson, "Why East-bloc bathtub maker didn't go down the drain," *Christian Science Monitor*, (October 19, 1987), p. 1.

39.   Henry Kamm, "Hungarians Told to Tighten Belts Indefinitely," *The New York Times*, (September 17, 1987), p. 2.

40.   Casmir Garnysz, "Polish Stalemate," *Problems of Communism*, 33 (May–June 1984):59.

41.   Table 7.1 is derived from an unpublished essay by James R. Ozinga and Harold T. Casstevens III, "The Circulation of Elites: Politburo Turnover and Tenure in the Soviet Union and Eastern Europe," presented at the Annual Meeting of the Midwest Political Science Association, Chicago, April 1988. The data for Eastern Europe were derived from Radio Free Europe (RFE) files in Munich with RFE staff assistance. The reference to caution in using Table 7.1 is because whenever one churns large clumps of numbers several times, both rounding and assumption errors can distort the data. The table is included here for illustrative purposes only.

42.   This prediction was made in an unpublished version of the above paper by James R. Ozinga, Thomas W. Casstevens, and Harold T. Casstevens III, "The Circulation of Elites: Comparative Analyses of Warsaw Pact Politburos 1953–1985," copies of which are available from the author.

43.   The inflation rate in Poland at the end of 1989 was 900 percent. Money was relatively useless and clearly something had to be done—and quickly. The problem was not the goal—that was the free market system. The problem was the pace of reaching that goal. Should the bandage be removed quickly to minimize the duration of the pain or should it be removed slowly, thus causing less pain over a longer period? If pain is inevitable, then quick is always better, but there must be intelligence behind the implementation. Not everything needs to be done at once, but some things must occur together. See, for example, Edward A. Hewett, *Reforming the Soviet Economy, Equality vs Efficiency* (Washington, D.C.: The Brookings Institution, 1988), pp. 356–357.

44.   David Binder, "Grim State of East Germany's Economy Is Disclosed to Parliament," *The New York Times* (November 16, 1989), p. 8.

DISCUSSION QUESTIONS

1.   In what two ways did Nikita Khrushchev undercut the power base of East European party leaders in the 1950s?

2.   Were Soviet leaders really willing to tolerate different roads to socialism? What were the very important limits?

3.   Did the 1944 Allied invasion of Europe at Normandy or the Yalta Agreements in 1945 contribute to the Soviet occupation of Eastern Europe? How?

4. What was the major reason why Soviet military forces did not intervene in Poland in either 1956 or 1981? Does the reverse of that reason explain the invasion of Hungary in 1956 or Czechoslovakia in 1968?

5. Why was Tito's Yugoslavia merely expelled from a communist organization instead of invaded?

6. Was U.S. President Harry Truman's decision to assist Yugoslavia with economic and military aid a good decision? Did this decision conflict with the Truman Doctrine?

7. Why did Solidarity form? What happened to the movement in early 1981?

8. What was Hungary's New Economic Mechanism? How was such deviation possible in an East European country?

9. Why was Czechoslovakia's "socialism with a human face" seen as such a threat?

10. Describe how Poland's changes in June 1989 helped considerably to stimulate subsequent changes in East Europe.

11. Should credit for reform movements in Eastern Europe be given exclusively to Mikhail Gorbachev? Explain.

12. Why was it significant that so few former communists in Hungary signed up for the re-named Socialist Party in 1989?

13. Who and what caused the openings in the Berlin Wall in 1989?

14. What factors brought about the downfall of Nikolae Ceausescu?

15. Describe the sequence of changes in Bulgaria during 1989–1990.

16. Why has Albania been so slow to change?

8

China
Theory and Practice

Communism officially came to power throughout China in 1949 when the Chinese Red Army defeated the Nationalist (Guomindang) forces and took over the country. Like other sites for the implementations of Marxism, China seems a strange place to apply Marx's ideas, but Marx was wrong about where his ideas would have their greatest effect. Underdeveloped societies facing a crisis of modernization have implemented Marxism (and Marxism-Leninism) far more than advanced capitalist countries.

Throughout most of its very long history, China followed the precepts of Confucianism. Through more than twenty imperial dynasties, Confucianism maintained the Chinese hierarchy as a part of the cosmic and eternal order and supported China's sense of being the center of the world—of superiority over "barbarian" cultures on the edges of its empire. The Chinese empire was the whole of the world that mattered; areas and regions beyond that world were either unknown or unimportant. The emperor represented the center of the cosmos.

Most of China's large and growing population[1] were peasant farmers engaged in subsistence agriculture. The few people at the top of society were court favorites, intellectuals, and bureaucrats. In rural settings, landlords and warlords were the upper class. Life was ruled by the iron hand of tradition and custom. The centuries' old sense of superior isolation remained undisturbed even when Jesuit missionaries and Portuguese sailors arrived from Europe, or when Russians began probing the Amur River area in the northeast region of China.

Contacts with foreigners were ritualized by a tribute system that included an exchange of gifts and the *kowtow*. Visitors to Beijing[2] normally received more valuable gifts from the emperor than they had presented, so the exchange was not a system of extracting wealth from foreigners; rather, it was a polite and courteous way of showing respect for each other. The kowtow ceremony showed the great deference of the visitors to the emperor; they were expected to kneel and bang their foreheads on the floor in the emperor's presence. The tribute system endured for centuries.

Why did anyone in China ever imagine that Marxism fit their country? Two reasons. First, the Western world destroyed "old" China in the nineteenth century, creating a very deep crisis of modernization. Second, the Russian Bolsheviks demonstrated in 1917 that Marxism–*Leninism* did fit a backward society hungry for a modernizing revolution. Thus, the first reason led to the second, and China was profoundly changed.

THE HUMILIATING NINETEENTH CENTURY

The nineteenth century was a terrible period for China. Western nations came to China to make profits from trade whether the Chinese wanted to trade or not. Both Chinese isolation and their sense of superiority were destroyed.

Britain provides the best example of the Western impact on China. British trade, conducted through the East India Company, had created a strong English market for Chinese tea. Because China did not value the goods British merchant ships brought to exchange for the tea, the British began to purchase the tea with silver. Soon a serious silver drain from England worried British merchants and government officials. The British needed to find a product the Chinese wanted to exchange for tea so as to stop the flow of silver out of Britain. The product that put British-Chinese trade on a more sound economic basis was opium.

From the British economic perspective the advantage of opium was that it was addictive. Its Chinese users would demand more and more of the drug. Although the Chinese government made opium importation illegal, British merchant-men smuggled the drug into China with the help of Chinese profiteers. Soon so many Chinese became addicted that the high demand for opium reversed the silver drain—silver now began to flow out of China along with tea to Britain. Concerned Chinese officials tried to negotiate a solution but they failed. For twenty-one humiliating years (1839–1860) China fought unsuccessfully against Britain in what were loosely called the Opium Wars.[3]

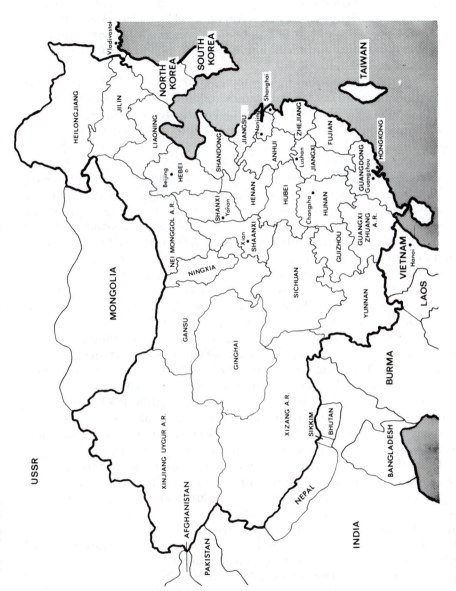

Map 6 China

In the 1842 Treaty of Nanjing, Britain won the right to sell opium in China as well as other concessions. Hong Kong was ceded outright to Britain, and five other areas were named open ports: Guangzhou (Canton), Xiamen (Amoy), Fuzhou (Fuchow), Ningbo (Ningpo), and Shanghai. Queen Victoria declared Hong Kong to be a British Crown Colony in April 1843.[4] (In 1997, after nearly a century and a half of possession, Britain will finally cede Hong Kong back to China.)

Other Western nations quickly forced concessions as well. In the Treaty of Wangxia in 1844 the United States won the same privileges as Britain, and in the 1844 Treaty of Whampoa, the French also won trade agreements and the right to send Catholic missionaries to China to evangelize the population.

The right to send missionaries was more important than it may appear on casual reading. Christianity appealed to some Chinese, but to most the new religion was a foreign intrusion and violated Chinese tradition. The Chinese stoutly resisted it and often feared it. The violent incidents in the nineteenth century involving missionaries, church schools, orphanages, and hospitals reflected China's humiliating inability to rid herself of these aliens and their ideas. When Chinese people were kidnapped and forcibly taken to Central, South, and North America for use as laborers, the Chinese often indiscriminately blamed *all* foreign devils—many of whom professed to be Christian. Thus the anti-Christian violence was also due to the inhuman and exploitative activities by Westerners, seen as a totality.

In turn, anti-Christian violence on the part of some Chinese provided excuses for more gunboat diplomacy, more concessions, and more aggressive proselytizing. The treaties following the Opium Wars set the stage for a nineteenth-century Western imperialism that turned China into a pawn, pushed about at will by the greater military strength of the industrialized nations. The Western world took advantage of this weakness: Sea merchants seeking profits and missionaries seeking souls often arrived on the same vessel to a China that welcomed neither. Beginning in the 1860s China tried to fend off the growing number of exploiting Western nations through "self-strengthening" reforms designed to develop a defense against Western weapons. The reforms, however, were too little and too late. A sheep faced a pack of wolves and the results were predictable. China the cosmic center? Both the pride and the belief evaporated.

In addition to foreign exploitation, the nineteenth century witnessed natural and internal dislocations. Floods, famines, and plagues affected millions of people while frequent internal rebellions challenged the right of the central government to rule. From 1850 to 1864 the Taiping rebels posed a serious threat. Their leader, Hong Xiuquan, believed that he was a special emissary of the Christian God and declared himself the Heavenly King in charge of the Heavenly Kingdom of Great Peace, with its capital at Nanjing. The Taiping rebels desired more than the overthrow of the central government—they wanted a social revolution that would drive out the alien Manchu rulers of China, end private ownership of land, improve the status of women,[5] end the opium traffic, and set up a communal society. When they introduced land reform in areas under their control, they gained many new adherents from the Chinese peasantry.[6]

Western nations took advantage of the confusion created by the Taiping uprisings and increased their holdings, often at gunpoint. Russia began to devour the northeast of China and in 1850 established a military base at Nikolaievsk. Ten years later, in 1860, Russia set up a new city in the northeast called Vladivostok, which meant, unhappily for China, "Rule of the East." In the same year (1860), British and French forces temporarily occupied Beijing and spent several days looting and burning the old summer palace outside the city.[7]

Conditions continued to worsen. China suffered Moslem rebellions, Russian incursions into western China and the northeast, more violent incidents involving missionaries, and frequent military reprisals against Chinese citizens. In addition, China lost former satellites on the periphery of its empire: France took Vietnam; and Japan moved against Taiwan, the Ryukyus (Okinawa), and Korea. The Sino-Japanese War was disastrous for China. Germany and Italy made new demands, and the United States introduced an "Open Door" policy to reduce Western competition and regularize the exploitation of China.

Out of the humiliation emerged the 1899 Boxer Rebellion. The anti-foreign and anti-Christian Boxer movement was an understandable phenomenon, but it weakened China even further. In a complex and confusing situation, the central government declared war on the Western powers. Western countries responded by sending in troops, which looted without fear of punishment. While all this was taking place, a confrontation on the Amur River gave Tsarist Russia a pretext for invading Manchuria.[8]

One of the proudest and oldest and most stable of countries was visibly reduced to futile ineffectiveness. Anyone who wished to push at it did so. Anyone wanting another concession from a proud people received one. China's humiliation was profound. This was China's crisis of modernization, long in the making, a crisis that caused intellectuals to look for revolutionary solutions. The best-known of these revolutionaries was Sun Yat-sen, one of the founders of the Nationalist party (Guomindang). By 1911 the revolutionaries had been successful in establishing a Republic of China (ROC) with a temporary capital at Nanjing. The emperor abdicated in 1912, but China remained divided into feudal feifdoms held by warlords and/or foreign interests. Even though the Western powers recognized a new nominal government in Beijing, they still retained their old privileges and ambitions. Japan was particularly aggressive toward China. The strains, the humiliating and subordinate status, and the domestic unrest continued. This "revolution" had changed little.

Frustrations increased during and after World War I when the Versailles Treaty awarded former German holdings *in China* to Japan rather than to China. In protest, on May 4, 1919, students, intellectuals, merchants, and workers demonstrated against the West that had betrayed China and the weak Chinese government that commanded no international respect. Conditions in China were radicalized, worsening the modernization crisis.

Revolutionary Marxism developed in this context. Although a few Chinese intellectuals had previously read Marx, they assumed that his writings did not apply to China because he expected full capitalist relations of production before socialism was implemented. But with the 1917 Bolshevik seizure of power in Russia, which demonstrated that Marxism *could be applied* to a backward society hungry for an anti-West model of modernization, Marxism began to make sense to the Chinese. Marxism was a revolutionary ideology that did not imitate Western capitalism so much as *transcend* it—a notion that fit the Chinese sense of superiority.

Chinese Marxists identified with the Bolsheviks because Western powers so disliked and feared the Lenin government. "Whom my enemy hates must be my friend" underlay their thinking. Besides, the Lenin government seemed willing to give up some of the old tsarist claims on Chinese territory. But the Chinese did not understand that the revolutionary change in the Soviet Union did not necessarily mean a change in the old imperialist attitudes toward China.[9] When the truth finally became clear to the Chinese, China would regard the Soviets as "social imperialists." But in the beginning the Chinese Marxist radicals could appreciate what they heard of Lenin's analysis of Western imperialism. China had suffered that imperialism throughout the previous century. In this climate of greater openness toward Russia and an appreciation of Bolshevik power, as well as the logical force of Marxism–Leninism, revolutionary Chinese Marxists increased in numbers. In 1921, after the Comintern was established, the Chinese formed the Chinese Communist Party (CCP) and soon joined the Communist International.

The CCP fit into old Chinese traditions in a number of ways.[10] Chinese intellectuals tended to see things as a whole rather than as parts and appreciated a programmatic approach aimed at solving all the problems of China at once. They were also drawn to historical materialism because of its use of the past and present to predict a future that broke out of the traditional cycle of history and moved to a new, higher plateau. The dialectic of Hegel and Marx even seemed to some Chinese as a Western counterpart of the Taoist belief in the two interrelated and interdependent but opposing forces, Yin and Yang, that characterize all of life. Although China did not have a sizable proletariat, Russia in 1917 had not had one either. Besides, Lenin said that the party carried the revolutionary consciousness of the working class. In a way, the party replaced the proletariat, and this made the lack of a large working class less important.

Hence, the humiliations of the nineteenth century, the radicalizing circumstances after World War I, and the Bolshevik success in 1917 all increased the attractiveness of revolutionary Marxism, even though joining the Communist International meant accepting the Soviet Union as the leader of world socialism and following Soviet directions. This, it was imagined, was the route to success in one's own country. In China's case, however, revolutionary agitation was *discouraged* by the Comintern. Lenin and, later, Stalin believed that China was still feudal and had not passed through the bourgeois revolution. Thus, following the minimum program guidelines, the Comintern directed the CCP to form a coalition with the Guomindang to help bring about the bourgeois revolution. Nationalist (Guomindang) leader Sun Yat-sen accepted this idea, and after Sun's death in 1925, so did his successor Chiang Kai-shek. With this coalition the USSR achieved a friendly Guomindang government on its long eastern border even if the idea proved disastrous for the CCP.

When the CCP was small and weak, going along with the Comintern directions made sense. But by 1927 the CCP had grown to nearly 58,000 members, and Chiang Kai-shek saw them as a growing threat to his own power in the Guomindang. In April 1927 Chiang's troops attacked Shanghai labor unions and workers' organizations, and, within the next six months, almost destroyed the CCP. The scattered CCP survivors of Chiang's military actions were without geographical base or consistent leadership.

During the next ten years, attempts by the Comintern to regain some control of general Chinese developments proved very difficult, and it was nearly impossible to coordinate activities within the scattered CCP. Ironically, this lack of control by the Comintern created an opportunity for the splintered party to develop more independently and to adapt Marxism more completely to the Chinese situation.

*   *   *

China experienced raw imperialism in the nineteenth century by more powerful Western nations. One example was the British opium trade and another was the unequal treaty system imposed on China by the foreign powers. After Britain exposed Chinese vulnerability, other Western nations joined in the rape of China, creating an enormous sense of humiliation to a proud people.

Internal rebellions unsuccessfully attempted to throw out the foreigners and establish a stronger Chinese government. Sun Yat-sen and others helped create a revolution in 1911 and the emperor abdicated a year later. But the new China was still divided among warlords and foreigners.

The Bolshevik seizure of power in Russia in 1917 and the 1919 frustrations over the Versailles Treaty spurred the formation of the CCP as part of the Comintern. Soviet advice to link CCP fortunes with the Guomindang led by Chiang Kai-shek proved disastrous in 1927. The party was almost exterminated by Chiang's military actions against it.

MAO ZEDONG AND REVOLUTIONARY CHINA

Mao Zedong was born on December 26, 1893, to a reasonably well-off peasant family in Hunan province. He was relatively well educated, and grew up in the atmosphere of China's humiliation and weakness. As a young man in his twenties, Mao was a revolutionary without a specific ideology to guide his thinking. His move to Beijing in 1918, to take a minor post in the university library, provided an ideological focus for his revolutionary feelings. Mao's superior in the library was a Marxist named Li Dazhao, who had organized a Young China Study Society in 1917 that Mao Zedong joined. This group discussed Marxism with reference to China, a topic of particular excitement after Lenin's success in November 1917. Mao read the *Communist Manifesto* and other available Marxist literature in a Chinese context: namely, the need for a social revolution to rid China of foreigners and warlords. The Marxist ideas were within a framework of Leninism: the need for a strong party to guide the total revolution China required. From this point on Mao was involved with the development of the Chinese Communist party, but he brought to it the peasant orientation he had acquired in Hunan province as a young man. In 1921, for example, he organized a Hunan branch of the CCP.

Mao Zedong became a part of the CCP–Guomindang coalition (1924–1927): an alternate member of the Nationalist Party's Central Executive Committee and deputy chief of the propaganda department.[11] These government positions disappeared when Chiang Kai-shek began his purge of the CCP. Mao's party positions suffered as well in 1927 because he was blamed for the failure of a Hunan peasant demonstration called the "Autumn Harvest Uprising." He lost both his leadership of the Hunan branch of the party and his status as alternate on the central party's Politburo.

At this point Mao seemed to be on his way out of the CCP, but the party organization was shattered, dispersed, and lacked direction. Mao Zedong moved south, set up a military headquarters in the Jinggang Mountains (Jiangxi province), and recruited a small army of peasants. Mao was not the only party member to set up a peasant force; several others did as well. Later these groups would form the Chinese Red Army. For example, in November 1927 another party member, Peng Pai, established the first Chinese "soviet," or rural, military communist settlement in Haifeng to the south of where Mao's small band was located. This new soviet lasted until the following February when Guomindang forces overran Haifeng. Elsewhere, the Red Army was born during the Nanchang Uprising in August 1927. Survivors of that battle linked up with Mao's band in April 1928. Mao Zedong was not the only significant leader.

This Jinggang Mountain group became the Fourth Red Army and was led by Mao Zedong and Zhu De. In early 1929 they were joined by the Fifth Red Army, led by Peng Dehuai. This combination became the nucleus of the Red Army that would eventually triumph in 1949. In the late 1920s and early 1930s, however, they established some six soviet regions in the south of China against which Chiang Kai-shek threw his "bandit-suppression" military campaigns for the next few years.

Comintern directives enforced by the CCP leadership created a problem for the guerrillas. The comintern and their proteges in the CCP wanted the peasant armies to seize cities so as to gain a proletarian base of operations. But taking cities and holding them exposed the Red forces to attacks from Chiang's troops. The policy was foolish. Mao's reluctance to follow these suicidal orders did not please the CCP leadership. On February 9, 1929, for example, the Central Committee (dominated by Li Lisan—a strong Comintern follower) issued a letter critical of Mao and directed him to disperse his troops. The next day, however, Mao's forces were successful against nationalist troops at Dabaidi (Jiangxi province), which gave them a base for the establishment of a new headquarters. Mao rebutted the letter and then ignored it.

In 1930, until that Comintern policy was repudiated, other attempts to seize key cities resulted in costly and temporary successes. For example, when Peng Dehuai's army took Changsha it faced opposition from Western military forces that were helping the Guomindang: Japanese, American, and other foreign warships in the Xiang River opened fire on the city and communist forces were only able to hold it for ten days.[12] On September 15, 1930, Red Army troops returned to secure rural bases and abandoned the idea of capturing and holding cities. Mao Zedong made the decision to do this independently of either the CCP or the Comintern leadership. Some other leaders objected, a mutiny resulted, and between two and three thousand people were killed before the rebellion was controlled.[13]

The willingness to develop an independent policy based on Chinese conditions led to Mao's focus on organizing *rural* soviets. That, in turn, led to a military strategy, called guerrilla warfare, based on those rural strongholds. This strategy emphasized hitting the enemy at weak points, retreating frequently so as to attack from another angle, relying on the local population for cover, and avoiding pitched battles until total victory was near.

The headquarters of the CCP, in Shanghai until 1933, tried to control and coordinate the rural soviets—a difficult task in the circumstances. Mao Zedong and Zhu De's soviet was especially troublesome to headquarters because of Mao's growing power and occasional defiance of the central office. To Chiang Kai-shek these soviets were alarming successes, and he threw five extermination campaigns at them, each more extensive than the preceding one.

By October 1934 the southern positions could no longer be maintained by the Chinese soviets and they broke through enemy lines to begin the move to the northwest that has become known as the "Long March." During the year-long struggle to reach the secure areas in Shaanxi province in the northwest, the whole character of the situation changed. First, there was an enormous attrition of party members. Between 1933 and 1937 the number of party members plummeted from 300,000 to 40,000. Much of that decline can be attributed to the Long March. Second, Mao Zedong and his faction became dominant in the restructured CCP. Third, communist elements relocated and reassembled in the northwest after having been scattered all across China since 1927. Fourth, the Long March marked the end of Comintern control over the CCP. Fifth, the Long March became a symbol of heroism and victorious survival against great odds and set the stage for the decade of desperate struggle and impressive successes known as the Ya'nan Period (1935–1945). In turn, this decade dramatically influenced the policies and leadership of China after 1949.

The nature of the military struggle changed with Japan's invasion of China in 1937. The civil war between the Guomindang and the Red Army was postponed so that both could fight against the Japanese.[14] But the moment Japan was defeated in 1945, civil conflict resumed. Mao's rural orientation, however, never changed; the mutual sacrifice and strong sense of brotherhood forged through these years of struggle were strengths Mao Zedong cherished all of his life. After the CCP victory in 1949, as he confronted one problem after another, he expected the population as a whole to adopt those same revolutionary, self-sacrificing strengths. This is why Mao appeared to be "throwing ideology" at every problem. He was convinced that any long-term solution to China's problems required the revolutionizing of the population. This approach placed Mao to the left of more pragmatic Chinese leaders.

Take production incentives as an example. If workers needed to raise productivity, the pragmatic leaders might think of paying higher wages. Mao, however, pushed nonmaterial moral incentives: Produce more because you then help the whole of China, not because it helps you alone. Mao's approach was actually a pragmatism in ideological dress. For a poor country like China, low wages meant rapid *social* accumulation of wealth. This goal was necessary and desirable. In addition, China could not afford higher wages for workers and there was little to buy with the money. So underneath the ideological words and moral incentives with which Mao Zedong became identified there was a strong degree of common sense—especially during the period of initial economic growth.

Mao also believed that putting revolutionary theory into practice was critically significant in guiding expected social contradictions in the right directions. Dialectical confrontations, Mao believed, did not end with the triumph of the political revolution. The confrontations continued into socialism and communism. Just because the long civil war was over did not mean the struggle had ended. Earlier, he said, the country faced enemies with guns, but now China encountered enemies without guns, and they must not be taken lightly.[15]

He did not mean that class war would continue. Class *antagonisms* would disappear, but *contradictions* would continue to characterize all life in the future as did the Yin and Yang of Taoism: an opposition occurring within a unity. Contradictions, unless they were allowed to grow unchecked, would not tear the system apart the way class antagonisms could. In the Chinese society ruled by the CCP, the conflict that developed out of social contradictions would force *adaptations* rather than dramatic *upheavals* like revolutions because the primary part of the contradiction would be proletarian, and the bourgeois part would be secondary. In other words, the proletarian side of the conflict was dominant in China after 1949, and that meant that contradictions were a valued mechanism for adaptive change, a force for evolutionary development. Pragmatists took the easy way out by seeking to reduce contradictions by common-sense policies. An ideologue like Mao expected and valued continuing social contradictions, and he was not reluctant to *push* Chinese society in an effort to revolutionize it.

Mao Zedong's independence was facilitated by the lack of help received from the Soviet Union. During the civil war period such assistance was minimal to nonexistent, and, after 1949, such help was miserly and demeaning.[16] Helping China succeed was never high on any Soviet list. Just because they were both run by communist parties did not mean a comradely relationship. Too much divided the two countries: very different histories, racism, and disputed territories. In addition, China believed that Soviet imperialism and arrogance made the USSR resemble the West, while the Chinese belief in their own superior ability to lead the Third World angered Soviet leaders. The two nations competed more than cooperated. In the 1960s a complete break would become known as the Sino-Soviet split, leading to actual military battles in 1969.

Mao Zedong's theory of contradictions could also fit international relations. China followed the Stalinist economic model of rural collectivization and rapid industrialization according to five-year plans (except for the "Great Leap Forward") but the context was one of intense ideological or moral incentives that emphasized *rural* strength. Nuclear weapons were not ignored nor was the army neglected, but Chinese socialism was understood as a rural socialism. Contradictions between China and the West could be expected, but conflicts (class antagonisms) could also occur between China and a socialist nation like the Soviet Union that acted like the West. In any expected conflict, Mao felt, whether with the Soviet Union or the United States, the Chinese rural side was primary—it was the side that would continue into the future. Here Mao did not emphasize "proletarian" but "peasant-rural," believing that *rural communism*, a communism of the people, would become the ideology of the Third World, gradually triumphing over the urban worlds of both the Soviet Union and the West. China would lead Third World communist movements and eventually regain the status of world "center" that had been lost in the terrible nineteenth century. The future, in other words, belonged to the rural world led by China, triumphing over the urban world

Mao Zedong   1893–1976

represented by Moscow and Washington as two poles of an imperialist continuum.[17]

Mao Zedong was not the undisputed leader of China that he appeared to be. He was frequently blocked by other leaders and sometimes out of favor—not really in charge at all. His emphasis on moral or ideological incentives to get people to work, and his desire to recreate the Ya'nan revolutionary experience for the Chinese people as a whole, made Mao Zedong a consistent leftist in a party replete with pragmatic administrators. Revolutionaries are normally left of center *before* the revolution, but afterward, when society has to be pulled back together, revolutionaries are usually interested in protecting the new state. So Mao's leftism was often out of step with the attitudes of other leaders. Even so, a **cult of the personality** was allowed to develop, portraying him as the revolution's father figure, the symbol of the new China. Once begun, the cult grew rapidly. Two Chinese songs illustrate just how far that cult could grow in only ten years. The first song heard in 1949 called Mao Zedong the great hero who appeared on China's horizon, the savior of the people. This was, evidently, not enough. The second song, in 1959, described Mao's infinite kindness and argued that ten thousand songs could not sufficiently praise him even if trees were used as pens to write on the sky with an ocean of ink![18]

Despite or perhaps because of this adulation, struggles for power and influence were continuing below the surface of the Mao worship, even though Mao's thought became the official line, the authoritative word on everything from growing watermelons to fixing a jet aircraft. Chinese citizens carried little red books containing the precious thoughts of Mao Zedong. Even the courtship of a woman by a man was influenced by Mao's "thought." The existence of such adulation allowed Mao Zedong greater influence than his political position otherwise warranted.

In 1956, for example, he declared that socialism had been achieved. That in itself was harmless rhetoric, but it led to a mistake—an eagerness to bring the future communism into existence. Mao Zedong pushed the pace of change between socialism and communism, feeling that increased ideological pressure on society would cause a rapid economic development toward communism. These attitudes underlay planning for what came to be known as the Great Leap Forward, begun in 1958.

This thinking was not unique to China. Both Yugoslavia and the Soviet Union were toying with twenty-year plans that supposedly would create the basis for full communism.[19] China rushed into the building of communism, however, in its own way—Mao's way. Communism would emerge from the people engaged together in the heroic struggle to move China from one stage to the other. The Great Leap Forward involved an intensive effort to build agricultural communes on a widespread scale. Peasants were discouraged from moving to the cities by ideological lectures and by checkpoints along main transportation lines. Although the first commune was named *Sputnik* in a flattering reference to the first orbiting Soviet space object, the claims made for the new communes easily outdistanced anything that the USSR possessed on either its collective or state farms. The *socialist* phase in the countryside was going to be bypassed—the move would be directly to full communism. The new communes, prototypes for others to follow, would manage within their borders all industrial and agricultural production; cultural and educational work; trade; and political affairs. Within the context of an overall central plan, decentralized communes would consolidate the social system and energetically create the conditions for gradual transition to communism, while eradicating differences between town and country and between mental and manual labor.[20] This was a heavy philosophical load for the new communes to carry.

The Great Leap Forward also tried to bypass stages of industrial growth through a massive mobilization of the productive energies of the population. Chinese leaders intended to show the world: Liu Shaoqi announced in December 1957 China's intention of overtaking Britain in gross heavy industry output by 1972.[21] Enormous production gains would be made, they felt, through intensive five-year plans and a strong decentralization of production that included innovations such as backyard steel plants.

Expectations were too high and the economy was pushed too hard. Extraordinarily bad weather made things worse for the new agricultural communes. A critical factor in the failure of the Great Leap Forward occurred when Nikita Khrushchev, angry with Chinese independence, withdrew all Soviet technicians and cancelled most Soviet economic aid in 1960. The Great Leap Forward collapsed as the evolving Sino-Soviet conflict erupted violently into the open. Two factors underlay the timing of this eruption.

First, the Chinese claim to be able to develop communism directly from the rural communes threatened Soviet leadership of the socialist camp. The Soviet mother hen wanted to stay in front of her chicks, even if she had not "hatched" the Chinese "chick." Mao had not agreed with Khrushchev's de-Stalinization speech in 1956 and had called him a "revisionist," a dirty word ever since it was used to describe Eduard Bernstein in 1899, meaning "betrayer of the socialist cause." Khrushchev resented Mao's criticisms.

Second, Chinese leaders had been pushing Khrushchev to give China the nuclear weapons he had earlier promised to share. China would acquire more prestige and clout if it possessed nuclear weapons, and China would be able to counter the U.S. Seventh Fleet that was protecting nearby Taiwan—where Chiang Kai-shek's Guomindang had fled in 1949. Taiwan (Formosa), traditionally a Chinese possession, was occupied by an army considered an enemy. Khrushchev, however, with Soviet interests paramount, was advocating detente rather than confrontation with the United States and refused to give China nuclear assistance.

The break in relations between the two countries quickly became intensely vituperative. Both sides developed ideological justifications for their position, meaning that one side was totally right and the other all wrong. Compromise became extremely difficult.

Mao Zedong learned that China would have to do everything on its own. Khrushchev and the Soviet Union were now on the enemy side and represented, in his mind, a dictatorship of the bourgeoisie rather than the proletariat.[22] Mao turned again to remolding the Chinese people into sharers of the Ya'nan revolutionary experience. Internalizing the revolutionary spirit became even more important to Mao Zedong in the shattering aftermath of the failure of the Great Leap Forward and the famines resulting from natural disasters in the early 1960s. Even though the original revolution had been successful, it was not enough. Success, Mao felt, brought about a corresponding loss of revolutionary vision and drive to reach the real goal of Marx's communism that would surpass both the West and the Soviets. The achievements of the CCP so far had to be risked in order to redeem the failure of the Great Leap Foward, to re-create that spirit of social self-sacrifice, and to leave a revolutionary legacy behind him. He therefore encouraged an ideological revival called the "Cultural Revolution," which lasted, on and off, for ten years.

Beginning in 1966, the Cultural Revolution was both a purge of high party leaders who, Mao felt, had become bureaucratic and too far from the revolutionary vision, and an attempt to create an atmosphere of revolutionary revival. Adolescents were organized into Red Guards and given the authority to criticize and shame party leaders. Some of the sharpest critics of political leaders were children under the age of twelve.

The Red Guard youth were often too destructive, and the army had to be called in to restore order. Millions of people in and out of the party were affected during this period of civil war and party genocide. Party members, including those with high positions like Deng Xiaoping (b. 1904), were often demoted and forced to apologize to the people for their "crimes." Bourgeois influences were seen everywhere and ruthlessly uprooted. Material goals were discouraged in favor of more intense moral incentives. The people, particularly the youth, were urged to learn from Wang Je, a young soldier who saved his group by altruistically throwing himself on an explosive device, or from the example of Lei Feng, another selfless proletarian soldier.

Some of the force of the Cultural Revolution was felt by the Soviet Union. The Soviet ambassador and his family were beaten and spat upon during riots in Tiananmen Square in Beijing, before being expelled from China. Chinese students in the Soviet Union, asked to leave the country, seized their passenger train and went on a rampage. It was a wild time. Soviet leaders were concerned that the entire Chinese nation had gone mad and the "word war" between the two countries became ferocious. They even stopped cooperating with aid for Vietnam against the United States.

The Cultural Revolution also attacked educational institutions and intellectuals. Being "red" became much more important than being "expert." As late as 1973, when many of the excesses of the Cultural Revolution were long over, the *Liaoning Daily* approvingly published a letter from a student named Zhang Tiesheng that denounced people who were against practical knowledge as "bookworms." Zhang Tiesheng justified his handing in a blank examination paper because he had been working too hard on his commune. His letter was reprinted by the *People's Daily* three weeks later.[23] The predictable result was the near destruction of the educational system in favor of "union" or "oneness" with the masses. Proper "study" in China became learning from the common people, the peasants, and spending time at what were called May Seventh Cadre Schools where manual labor was the major learning device created for intellectuals and bureaucrats. Student Red Guards were sent to the countryside to learn from peasants who often saw only more mouths to feed. Some of those relocated students were still in rural areas in 1985 when they protested their inability to come back to the cities of China.

While all this upheaval was occurring domestically, China successfully faced hostilities with other nations. A border conflict with India ended well for China. And not even the Soviets could nibble at China any longer. In 1969 armed conflict with the USSR developed over the Zhenbao (Damansky) Islands in the Ussuri River, followed by fighting on the Sino-Soviet border at Yumin, and armed battles on an island in the Amur River near Khabarovsk. These clashes demonstrated the extent of the Sino-Soviet split and China's ability to hold its own. With the explosion of China's first hydrogen bomb in 1967, China gained a place among the major nuclear powers, even though its missile capacity was limited.

Because of China's positive accomplishments and the border struggles with the Soviet Union in 1969, China's negative attitudes toward the United States gradually thawed. These same factors weakened American hostility toward China and encouraged the *realpolitik* of American Secretary of State Henry Kissinger, who traveled to China to establish relations between the two nations. Despite an ongoing Vietnam War and basic ideological hostility toward the leading example of bourgeois power in the world, the Chinese leaders welcomed American President Richard M. Nixon in 1972 in a surprise visit arranged by Kissinger. This visit culminated in diplomatic relations being established between China and the United States, and China taking its seat in the United Nations' Security Council. Within a few years formerly isolated China became the China able to influence superpower relations by leaning toward one side or the other. If China acted as though it might patch up its quarrel with the Soviet Union, the United States became nervous and more friendly. If China was very friendly with the United States, the USSR became concerned and less hostile. In addition, the presence of the China side of the triangle presented both the United States and the Soviet Union with a "China card" that could be played in the international game of strategy between the two cold-war enemies. The Kissinger-Nixon initiative in 1972 created, at least temporarily, a tripolar world that raised China to great-power status and reduced the direct confrontational cold war between the United States and the Soviet Union both by making it more complicated and by raising the threat level of China toward the Soviet Union. Soviet leaders felt compelled to increase their already expensive troop strength along the Chinese frontier.

Even with this much pragmatism, as long as Mao Zedong dominated China it was an ideological period. The ideology was a leftist, populist variant of Marxism that applied a revolutionary, nearly anarchic version of the advanced, anti-West, antibourgeois ideology of Marxism. Even though China appeared to be *outside* historical materialism and was a country whose people did not exhibit the alienation Marx sought to overcome, in the 1960s and 1970s some Western leftists thought Mao Zedong was *more* Marxist than other communist leaders because of his stress on revolutionary brotherhood and sacrifice. Often this was said approvingly, in a context of a romantic identification with revolution by the oppressed against their oppressors, without considering who the oppressors were in this instance or whether the people of China benefited from such ideological leadership.

At just the point where the cultural revolution appeared to gather new life, the leftists around Mao Zedong made a critical mistake. On January 1, 1976, editorials in the *People's Daily, Red Flag,* and *Liberation Army Daily* signaled that a new form of class struggle was once again starting against the alleged restoration of capitalism in China. Mao Zedong reportedly insisted that China's recent stability and unity did not mean the end of the class struggle, the key element on which everything else depended.[24] Vice-Premier Deng Xiaoping, a noted pragmatist who had suffered embarrassing demotions during the Cultural Revolution, began to be criticized again as though a campaign were underway to discredit him. Moreover, the death of Foreign Minister Zhou Enlai, a pragmatist, on January 8, 1976, apparently freed the leftists behind Mao Zedong to become more open. Here was where the mistake was made, because the leftists became identified with instability at the critical juncture in Chinese politics when Mao Zedong died.

Resenting the adulation being given to Zhou Enlai who had been their ideological opponent in Chinese politics, the leftists arranged for the removal of wreaths and placards that mourning demonstrators had erected in Zhou's memory. This angered the crowds. Demonstrations increased in size and frequency in the capital city as well as in several others, and the tone of the crowds in the streets began to sound political, as though the leftists were seeking to manipulate the party through the demonstrators and wall posters. Support for moderate party leader Hua Guofeng became visible, as did the criticism of Deng Xiaoping. Just before the death of Mao Zedong on September 9, 1976, the demonstrations became more violent. In the minds of party leaders the enemy of Chinese stability was not Deng Xiaoping but the leftist "Gang of Four" (Mao's widow Jiang Qing, Zhang Chunqiao, Yao Wenyvan, and Wang Hongwen) and the revolutionary turmoil they were creating. Without Mao Zedong to protect them, the Gang of Four were vulnerable, and they were summarily swept from the stage of Chinese politics. With the radical left isolated under house arrest, Deng Xiaoping was rehabilitated. New wall posters sang his praises, and new directions opened up for China that would have appeared ludicrous a year before.

*   *   *

China was not always led by Mao Zedong, but as long as he lived China was affected by his charisma. The period between 1949 and 1976 can be described as a time of heightened ideology, of an intense revolutionary emphasis presented as a moral force. The disruptions caused by such an approach served to confirm Mao's expection of continuing contradictions both in socialism and in communism.

The Cultural Revolution followed the breakdown of the Great Leap Forward and kept China in turmoil. The power struggle after Mao's death resulted in the triumph of the pragmatists, particularly Deng Xiaoping, over the leftist Gang of Four. China was ready for new roads.

DENG XIAOPING AND THE LIMITS OF PRAGMATISM

The chaotic beginnings of change in 1976 resulted from a stiffening of resistance to any more revolutionary leftism in the CCP Politburo. It was as though other leaders said to each other: "We have had enough of the confusion of the Cultural Revolution. We have seen enough of forcing moral platitudes and the Ya'nan experience on the population of China. This does not accomplish what we wish China to become: a self-sufficient power in its own right."

On July 21, 1977, an important meeting of the CCP established two new directions. The first was to acknowledge the overall leadership of Deng Xiaoping. His new rehabilitation involved membership on the Central Committee, Politburo, and the Standing Committee of the CCP, becoming the Deputy Chairman of the Central Committee and its very powerful Military Affairs Committee, Vice-Premier of the State Council, and Chief of the General Staff of the People's Liberation Army. The second direction was the way deliberately *not* taken by the CCP in its 1977 meeting, a mirror image of the first direction. If Deng was again in favor, then those who had earlier condemned him were in trouble. The Gang of Four was expelled from the party and dismissed from all posts. This action officially confirmed the group's disgrace; they had already been arrested and imprisoned on October 6, 1976, less than thirty days after Mao's death. The detention, of course, continued.

These two decisions marked the end of the Cultural Revolution and cleared the way for new party goals.[25] The direction Deng moved China after 1977 was a combination of Adam Smith and Karl Marx: Leave the people alone to make money for themselves and as though guided by an invisible hand they will also produce the social wealth that was the goal of the central plan. This new pragmatism moved China a long way from the ideological levels under Mao Zedong and fundamentally transformed the nation, but the pragmatism was restricted to the economic sphere. There were no political changes to accompany the economic transformation, which meant that political efficacy, the belief that one's personal involvement made a difference, remained very low.

This limited pragmatism, nonetheless, produced real changes—at least for a time. Private enterprise was introduced into Chinese economic life, and it took root in both the countryside and in the cities. Communes were replaced by administrative townships. Small business people flourished and prospered. Ideological change was visible in the media. In April 1978, for example, an editorial in *People's Daily* praised material rewards along with moral ones. Deng Xiaoping was quoted as arguing that what people ought to do was to seek truth from facts rather than from continually talking about the "thought of Mao Zedong." On September 29, 1978, Ye Jianying, head of the National People's Congress Standing Committee (see table 8.1), declared that the ten-year Cultural Revolution was the work of the *counterrevolutionary* Gang of Four, and was not only totally unnecessary, but also brought calamity and disaster to China.[26]

The same approach was visible in 1980. Hu Yaobang, the party's Secretary General and a Deng Xiaoping supporter, said on December 14: "Nothing was correct or positive during those ten years. The whole thing was negative. Tremendous damage was done to our economy, culture, education, political thinking and Party organization."[27] Actually Hu's statement was more rhetoric against the Cultural Revolution than fact. The Chinese economy grew at an annual average of about six percent during 1966 to 1976; not spectacular but hardly evidence of "tremendous damage."

Mao Zedong began to be described as a man who could and did occasionally make mistakes, like the Cultural Revolution, rather than as a god who could not err. The new leaders of China enjoyed a greater freedom than Khrushchev possessed after Stalin's death, permitting them to talk about

TABLE 8.1 Party and Government in China

MAJOR GROUPS	
GOVERNMENT	PARTY
National People's Congress (2,900)*	National Party Congress (1,936)
Standing Committee of NPC (23)	Central Advisory Commission (172)
State Council (54)	Central Committee (348)
Inner Cabinet (15)	Politburo (18—including 5 below)
President	Standing Committee of Politburo (5)
Premier	Central Military Affairs Commission (5)
	Secretariat (5)
	General Secretary

*Numbers in parentheses refer to the approximate size of membership, which changes over time. For details on the selection and significance of each group and other, less significant groups, see Alan P. L. Liu, *How China Is Ruled* (Englewood Cliffs, N.J.: Prentice-Hall, 1986), pp. 57–99.

rebuilding China in concrete rather than spiritual terms. The goal changed from internalizing the revolutionary spirit to quadrupling China's per capita national income by the year 2000. The Maoist "let's all be poor together" was rejected in favor of "let's all be rich together," even if some became rich faster than others.[28]

Military ranks, abolished in the early years of the Cultural Revolution, were restored. Although the restoration of ranks was antiegalitarian, it won the support of military leaders who already felt disadvantaged when they looked at their country's list of priorities. The military was fourth on that list after agriculture, industry, and science. Defense spending as a percentage of gross national product (GNP) was kept at lower levels than in either the United States or the Soviet Union.

On the former communes the land was contracted into households, and families now planted, harvested, marketed, and profited from their own crops on the allotted land. Although they didn't own the land, after 1980/81 they could buy tractors and hire laborers. Some families benefited more than others, perhaps because they had more adults to work the land, or because they guessed correctly about profitable activities. Also the commune/ cooperatives near cities usually generated more income than those more isolated where transportation costs ate into profits. The resulting differences in wealth triggered resentments. The presence of factories or other collective enterprises on the cooperative frequently meant that only a small percentage of the commune labor force was consistently engaged in agriculture. The seasonal nature of some tasks allowed laborers to do other things for much of the year. On some communes only women who wanted part-time work were actively involved in agriculture. On the Lusha commune near Fuzhou the peasants became wealthy. From an average income of 132 yuan, or about $66 per year back in 1978, the new average in 1983 was nearly 700 percent higher at 909 yuan ($454.50). Only about 10 percent of the total income for the commune came from agriculture and only about twenty percent of the people were directly involved in farming. The rest of the income and work was in local industry and related sidelines.[29] The statistics on incomes for the country as a whole were almost as startling. Using 1980 dollars, the World Bank estimated in 1989 that per capita income in China steadily rose during the 1980s, from about $290 in 1980 to over $500 in 1987.[30]

Social egalitarianism, exemplified by the model Dazhai commune during Mao Zedong's lifetime, had to be discredited in favor of what was called the "responsibility system." Farmers signed contracts specifying what and how much they would produce, what the government would pay them, and what bonuses would be paid for producing over quota. Peasants were also encouraged to spend time on private plots after finishing their common duties. Within this system, farmers were encouraged to become key households concentrating on high-yield grains, cash crops, and other agricultural pursuits. This emphasis stimulated the growth of capitalized agriculture and resulted in farm surpluses for sale. Assistance was available from local governments that were given more decision-making power. Aggregates of households produced the food that the population needed, even though gains in food production were frequently offset by population growth. Even with stringent birth controls, the population base of one billion people created sufficient new children each year that the *per capita* food production in 1984 was only a little better than it was two thousand years earlier.[31]

Within the context of central planning goals, industrial concerns in the cities and towns began to feel the effects of the market in terms of the reward for efficiency and the punishments for inefficiency and failure. Beginning in 1981, workers contracted to run their own concerns. Sometimes the enterprises paid taxes rather than deliver goods to the state. Similar enterprise systems, coordinated since 1979, allowed for more efficient purchases of raw material and research and development.

In the middle of the 1980s some pitfalls still existed: overproduction, overspending for construction, overemphasis on heavy industry as in the Stalin model, and depreciating, aged equipment. Even so, the prospects for initiative seemed boundless as private individuals were allowed to hire up to eleven employees, and incomes rose. A new income tax in 1980 that began to penalize very high incomes over $480 per month made the Chinese economy appear even more Western and being taxed seem like a status symbol.

How capitalist or how much like Adam Smith was all of this really? Material rewards, market incentives, worker choice of occupation, personal income taxes, economic zones to attract foreign investors, maids in demand in Beijing, active government involvement in purchasing Western technology and arms, and enticements to overseas Chinese to come back home and invest their money—all of this sounded more like New York than Beijing. But underneath the evident growth and ideological relaxation two interrelating factors ticked like time bombs waiting to explode.

The first factor was the negative side of this economic miracle, and this negative side had many dimensions. Widespread corruption undermined the reported efficiency of the new economy. Double-digit inflation not only erased gains made by wage increases but it also forced the government to retreat from its policy of removing controls from prices in 1988. The wavering between economic liberalism and central planning meant not only insecurity among the leadership, but also confused signals sent to the economic decision makers. The low levels of cash held by the government often meant it could pay farmers only in paper IOUs. Investment in education was very low, and this was particularly acute in rural areas. The gap between rich and poor widened considerably, and the increased discontent among the poorer segments of society fueled a spontaneous re-deification of Mao Zedong. Confusion was evident when Mao loyalists reappeared in the media and were very critical of the new China while at the same time official descriptions of the Maoist period called it an historic tragedy.[32]

In addition, there was regional defiance of central political authority, and the center (represented by Deng Xiaoping) appeared unable to keep the conservative and liberal factions apart. The struggle between the two major wings in the party resulted in a haphazard adoption of economic reforms that mixed badly with state planning agencies. The result was chaos, more inflation, more corruption, and economic losses. Indecision at the top meant that political dissent could not be handled. Even in the National Peoples' Congress this dissent began to be seen in negative or abstaining votes on issues formerly adopted unanimously.

The second related factor ticking away was the absence of political reforms, which would have placed significant issues on a wider, more open stage where compromise and progress could have been made. The absence of democracy led to a continued struggle at top party levels between a liberal, less ideological approach and a conservative, much more ideological one. Democracy would not have been a panacea for China, but the future of China could have been openly determined by millions of citizens rather than secretly by a few old men. Signals of the strain, actually a preview of the summer of 1989, were exhibited by the result of student demonstrations in early January 1987. What was that result? The forced resignation of liberal Hu Yaobang on January 16, 1987, replaced by Zhao Ziyang, who had been Prime Minister. Zhao was also a liberal, but the new Premier was Li Peng, a conservative. Hu had advocated loosening the political system, and his ouster signalled that economic freedoms were not to be matched in the political sphere. This fear of political reform strengthened the hard-line ideological stance favored by party leaders. The liberalism of Zhao Ziyang, the new General Secretary, therefore, faced a resurgent conservatism that Deng Xiaoping had previously restrained but had not quelled.

To people in the CCP who took the older ideology seriously, Deng's reforms had threatened the theoretical foundations of the party and world socialism. To them the reforms undermined the sacrifices made during the pre-revolutionary and Maoist periods. "Did we struggle so hard so that people could make money?" they asked. Unaware that they were begging the question about why they had struggled so hard if not to increase people's affluence, the hard-liners helped maintain China as a communist country run by a dictatorial party that had not—definitely not—relinquished its hold on the nation.

Even though China had moved a great distance from the ideological period under Mao, some of the change was more apparent than real. The four principles of the ruling CCP were never changed and remain in effect. Those principles, articulated in the first section of the 1978 constitution, can be summarized as follows:

1. China is a socialist state under the dictatorship of the proletariat. The notion of the "state of the whole people," a euphemism Khrushchev introduced in the Soviet Union, was specifically condemned.

2. Under the banner of Marxism-Leninism-Maoism, the Communist party of China is the leadership core of the whole Chinese people. Democracy is considered in the context of a CCP in control.

3. The state protects and develops the socialist basis of public ownership of the means of production. Chinese capitalism, in other words, is seen as a *socialist* variant—a kind of socialism rather than a kind of capitalism, if it is assumed that state capitalism is still socialism. In China, capitalism depends on the state. In the United States the reverse seems to be true.

4. The Chinese people are the masters of the country because all power in the People's Republic belongs to the people. The party and the state represent the interests of the people in a people's democratic dictatorship.[33]

The continuing political authoritarianism meant that what was granted in the more pragmatic modern period could be taken away again. The ideology surrounding the Four Principles outlined above remained all along a controlling factor that worked two ways: reminding people that only limited powers had been granted to the marketplace, and reminding party liberals that traditional verities still remained. The result was stasis when there should have been motion.

The death of liberal Hu Yaobang on April 15, 1989, triggered student demonstrations. Several thousand young people chanting democratic slogans and singing revolutionary songs began a process that ended in tragedy in Tiananmen Square in early June. But on April 22, over 100,000 students illegally occupied the square and began camping overnight. The students wanted to talk but the government refused. On May 13 several thousand students began a hunger strike, and the Politburo responded by advocating discussions with the students. At this point Soviet President Mikhail S. Gorbachev arrived in Beijing on a state visit to celebrate the end of the Sino-Soviet rift. Hunger strikers, sensing the opportunity and increased publicity Gorbachev's visit gave to their cause, became more adamant about continuing their strike. On May 19, Premier Li Peng and General Secretary Zhao Ziyang met with students in a nationally televised meeting in which Zhao tearfully told student leaders that their goals were good and the issues they had raised would eventually be resolved. Li Peng, on the other hand, was moved in the opposite direction. The next day troops were summoned to enforce martial law, but thousands of people blocked the troops off from Tiananmen Square, and a reported million people took to the streets to defy the martial law. Zhao Ziyang was ousted as General Secretary and replaced by Jiang Zemin, the 62-year-old former leader of Shanghai. The stalemate continued for several days.

If history's camera can be stopped at this point it offers the possibility of sober analysis. The stalemated struggle could have been avoided, of course, and it should have been avoided—again, of course. But at the point where the stalemate is present, what does a political leader do? Capitulate? Seek to restore order at any cost? What did the students want? Democracy and political pluralism, evidently, but there were very few specifics. What the students accomplished, other than the sympathy of millions of observers inside and outside of China, was the creation of the crisis rationale that the hard-liners needed to rally more party support to their side of the factional struggle. On May 27 the students demanded the ouster of Li Peng, but this was not to be. On June 3 and June 4, troops and tanks cleared Tiananmen Square by opening fire on crowds of people and destroying the barricades that had been erected. Demonstrations now were needed from student supporters, to once again flood the square with protest. That did not occur, as it would a few months later in Czechoslovakia. Conservatives appeared the winners in what turned out to be a very unequal struggle. If the confrontation in Tiananmen Square had occurred only seven months later, it might have turned out differently. In December 1989 many East European examples of people power existed. In May 1989 not even the elections in Poland had yet been held, and no examples existed. China could have led the democracy movement, but it was not able to do so.

Nonetheless, what happened in China in 1989 was very instructive to other leaders of communist systems intent on necessary reforms. The lesson that could be learned was that the command economy's utility, while limited, is nonetheless long enough to become entrenched in the official ideology. From thence it can only be dislodged by a process of de-ideologizing that moves well beyond the desanctification of the former, charismatic leader (Mao). The de-ideologizing process is a lengthy and painful one, which can best be accomplished slowly. An indispensable ingredient is political reform, real political reform, which runs the risk of political pluralism in order to encourage latent political efficacy. The goal of the reform, therefore, is not so much the democratic one on the surface but the more subtle one of moving unavoidable economic and political discontent into safer channels and avoiding the all-or-nothing confrontations that characterized Tiananmen Square in 1989.

Until this is understood in China, there can be economic reforms and even significant changes, but the low levels of political efficacy will once again create avoidable confrontations that result in a no-win situation for the Chinese people. And it is those people, those seldom considered people, that Marxism and Marxists sought to help decades before. The future for China is not clear. China in this most recent pragmatic period has had a chance to achieve a standard of wealth for its people sufficient to lessen the ideological strictures required for building socialism and grant greater personal freedom for the Chinese. But ideologues afraid to change stand in the way.

They were even afraid to describe the tragedy properly. All the blame for Tiananmen Square was given to Zhao Ziyang, the ousted party chief, who was accused of having been a counter-revolutionary for some time.[34] This political hypocrisy attempted to paper over the real political and economic problems that had brought about the confrontation. In 1990 stability was preferred even to the point of strengthening central economic planning. State controls were reimposed over nearly all parts of the economy. State planning and management of major firms and investment decisions were reintroduced or firmed up and centrally set prices continued. Agriculture faced the prospect of new collectivization. Liberalization in 1990 was thought of negatively: something to resist or avoid.[35]

Meanwhile the gap between the rich and the poor widened. Not only had liberty been denied, but also the egalitarianism that was supposedly the communist goal. China had come far, but it still had a very, very long way to go.

*   *   *

The pragmatic period beginning in 1977 marks the efforts of Deng Xiaoping and his supporters to modernize China, and it appeared in the early 1980s as though this could be accomplished by reducing the ideological connections with the planned economy. This reforming goal was sought through a reintroduction of free enterprise socialism that rather rapidly increased the wealth of the Chinese nation.

Along with those successes came failures—the chief of which was deliberately to avoid a political reform that would have increased people's sense of political efficacy. The result of that failure was the confrontational situation in Tiananmen Square in the spring of 1989. In consequence, China became more conservative and less reformist. Subsequent changes require new faces, more patience, and greater willingness to tolerate dissent. Otherwise a return to provincial autonomy, warlordism, and political weakness will make a mockery of the high aspirations of early Chinese Marxists.

AFTERWORD

The major implementations of the ideas of Marxist communism have now been covered. But the story cannot stop here, for another whole topic has yet to be considered. The minor chords of communism, described in the next chapter, are minor only in the sense that the nations involved are not large and powerful. In two other ways, however, they are not minor.

First, the mere existence of Marxist governments in these small countries is irritating to the United States and expensive for the Soviet Union to maintain. Thus their effect on the superpowers is not minor. Second, these smaller countries have the capacity to continue the adaptations of the Stalin model of Marxism in such a way that the future may see an astonishing variety of socialist-communist states—a variety that has already helped the Soviet Union itself to change. This actual and potential role is not minor.

NOTES

1. China's population was fairly stable until 1750. The introduction of new crops, especially maize and sweet potatoes that would grow on marginal land, and a wider use of early ripening rice that led to double cropping, created a larger food base. This period was also one of peace and many public works. From 1750 to 1850 the population grew from about 150 million to 450 million, exacerbating the modernization crisis.

2. The *pinyin* system of romanization of Chinese names and places, officially in effect since January 1, 1979, has been followed in this chapter with very few exceptions, like Sun Yat-sen and Chiang Kai-shek. In this system "Peking" becomes "Beijing," and "Mao Tse-tung" becomes "Mao Zedong."

3. The *morality* of the opium struggle between China and Britain is not discussed here. The view of Chinese that most Westerners seem to have had in the nineteenth century is similar to views American settlers had of Indian tribes to whom whisky was freely traded, or American attitudes about blacks before and after slavery: subhuman in the sense that normal moral standards did not apply to them. Christian missionaries and opium cargoes arriving on the same ships led to a Chinese identification of Western exploitation and Christianity, but it did not sufficiently bother Westerners to alter the practice. The practices of Christianity and of capitalism have not always been honorable.

4. Colin Macherras, *Modern China: A Chronology from 1842 to the Present* (San Francisco: W. H. Freeman & Co., 1982), pp. 24, 25.

5. See Kay Ann Johnson, *Women, the Family, and Peasant Revolution in China* (Chicago: University of Chicago Press, 1982).

6. O. Edmund Clubb, *Twentieth-Century China* (New York: Columbia University Press, 1972), p. 13.

7. Macherras, *Modern China*, pp. 81, 82.

8. Ibid., p. 198.

9. Mark Mancall, *China at the Center: Three Hundred Years of Foreign Policy* (New York: The Free Press, 1984), p. 263.

10. For a fuller description of the relationship between Chinese tradition and Marxism-Leninism, see James Chieh Hsiung, *Ideology and Practice: The Evolution of Chinese Communism* (New York: Praeger, 1970), pp. 34–37. Also see John K. Fairbank, *The United States and China* (Cambridge: Harvard University Press, 1959), pp. 291–296; Edward E. Rice, "A Radical Break With the Past," *Problems of Communism*, 23 (September-October 1974): 16–20; Krishna P. Gupta, "Continuities in Change," ibid., pp. 33–38; and W. Dobson, "China as a World Power," unpublished Centennial lecture delivered at the University of Toronto by Professor Dobson on March 6, 1973.

11. Macherras, *Modern China*, pp. 295, 307.

12. Ibid., p. 330.

13. Ibid., p. 332. Mao Zedong *claimed* that the rebels were followers of Li Lisan, a party leader loyal to the Comintern line. In two months, by November 1930, the Comintern itself, in a change of direction, attacked the CCP's "take cities strategy," and the CCP quickly changed the policy. However, Mao's *independent* change, even though only two months early, was not appreciated by other more loyal followers of the Comintern organization—hence the mutiny.

14. Chiang Kai-shek was reluctant to resist the Japanese invasion of China despite clear efforts by the Comintern and by the CCP to gain a temporary truce and military coalition against Japan. Chiang, after being arrested and held captive by his own officers in the 1937 X'ian Incident, agreed to postpone the civil war so as to fight Japan, but his agreement proved temporary. Throughout the years of the Sino-Japanese struggle Chiang manifested far more willingness to fight against the Chinese Red Army than against Japan, despite extensive Soviet military, economic, and personnel assistance provided to the Guomindang from 1937 to 1940 (prior to the Russo-Japanese Nonaggression Treaty in 1941), and extensive economic assistance provided by the United States to Chiang Kai-shek to fight Japan. See Mancall, *China at the Center*, pp. 280–284, for details.

15. Mao Zedong, *Selected Works* (New York: International Publishers, n.d.), vol. 5:364, cited in David E. Powell, "Mao and Stalin's Mantle," *Problems of Communism*, 17 (March-April 1968):25.

16. Mao Zedong, cited in Arthur A. Cohen, *The Communism of Mao Tse-tung* (Chicago: University of Chicago Press, 1964), p. 21. Also see Stuart Schram, *The Political Thought of Mao Tse-Tung* (New York: Praeger, 1969), pp. 84–110 and 194–201.

17. In Mao Zedong's view, Mark Mancall wrote, the world consisted of three zones that corresponded to Western concepts of the first, second, and third worlds: first, the United States and its sphere of influence; second, the Soviet Union and its sphere of influence; and, third, an intermediate third world area that included China but belonged to neither power's sphere of influence. The implication in Mao's analysis was that the third zone was led by China, or that perhaps China constituted a fourth zone that represented the political and spiritual power of the third zone and to some extent the better side of the first and second as well. Both Western imperialists (first zone) and the social imperialists (second zone) were, in Mao's judgment, paper tigers because of the superiority of political and spiritual power represented by China. In a way, China was seen against the world as Lenin saw the Bolshevik party, as representing the "proper" consciousness for others not yet capable of it. See Mancall, *China at the Center*, pp. 352–354 and 402.

18. Songs quoted from James T. Myers, "The Political Dynamics of the Cult of Mao Tse-tung," in Yung Wei, ed., *Communist China: A System-Functional Reader* (Columbus, Ohio: Charles E. Merrill, 1972), pp. 83, 89.

19. James R. Ozinga, *Marxism and Leninism in the Soviet Transition to Communism*, unpublished doctoral dissertation, Michigan State University, 1968, available on microfilm from the University of Michigan collection.

20. See "Tentative Regulations (Draft) of the Weishung (Sputnik) People's Commune," *People's Daily* (September 4, 1958), cited in Theodore H. E. Chen, *The Chinese Communist Regime, Documents and Commentary* (New York: Praeger, 1967), p. 240.

21. Cited in Harold C. Hinton, *Communist China in World Politics* (Boston: Houghton, Mifflin, 1966), p. 36.

22. "On Khrushchev's Phoney Communism and Its Historical Lessons for the World," cited in A. Doak Barnett, *China After Mao* (Princeton, N.J.: Princeton University Press, 1967), p. 131.

23. Macherras, *Modern China*, p. 573.

24. Ibid., p. 588.

25. With a CCP of nearly 40 million members, most of whom had entered the party under Mao, and some 10 to 15 million of whom had joined *during the Cultural Revolution*, the change in direction at the top did not mean that it would necessarily be followed by the middle or lower levels. In the Soviet Union Khrushchev had attempted economic reforms from the top but they were sabotaged by middle-level bureaucrats in the CPSU who feared a loss of their own power. The same sort of resistance to Deng Xiaoping could develop even more easily in the CCP because "orthodox ideology" in China is to the left of Deng. His positions could too easily be called "the capitalist road." However, the longer Deng Xiaoping holds control, the more easily this ideological center can shift his way. The rectification purge of the party in the mid-1980s helped the changes in ideological emphasis go deeper into the middle and lower levels of the party. Time is a critical factor, however, because the current leaders are old. In 1985 some older leaders resigned in favor of younger people, but youth is no guarantee that Mao Zedong's more collectivist ideas are defeated. Market mechanisms do not seem sufficiently entrenched to withstand a strong central planning challenge. See John F. Burns, "China Appoints Five Newcomers to Ruling Politburo," *The New York Times* (September 25, 1985), p. 4, and Julian Baum, "China Anniversary: Festivity and Debate," *Christian Science Monitor* (October 1, 1985), p. 1, for further details.

26. Macherras, *Modern China*, pp. 606, 620.

27. Ibid., p. 634.

28. These statements, which appear to ignore the potential of new class antagonisms, easily affront someone loyal to Mao Zedong. Mao did not insist on poverty, but he correctly saw that spiritual factors were more important than material wealth. In the process of implementing this truth, however, neither the spiritual factors nor the wealth were being developed. Human intelligence has not yet solved the problem of the *necessary balance* between the spiritual and material factors that *limits* both. Consequently, one factor is normally pushed at the expense of the other, which penalizes individual serenity. Maoism was not deliberately antiwealth,

nor the Deng administration deliberately antispiritual. The battles each fought, however, required that only one be emphasized. In the process, balance was the victim.

29. Takashi Oka, "Chinese Find Seeds of Fortune in Industry," *Christian Science Monitor* (April 25, 1984), p. 10.

30. "Backdrop to the Turmoil," *The New York Times* (May 25, 1989), p. 6.

31. Leo Orleans, *China's Population Policies and Population Data: Review and Update*, prepared for the Committee on Foreign Affairs, U.S. House of Representatives (Washington D.C.: U.S. Government Printing Office, 1981), p. 8; cited in Kay Ann Johnson, *Women, the Family, and Peasant Revolution in China*, p. 226.

32. See Ann Scott Tyson, "Rebirth of Maoism in China," *Christian Science Monitor* (April 11, 1989), p. 1, and Nicholas D. Kristof, "Mao's Legacy Is Now Called 'a Historical Tragedy'," *The New York Times* (February 7, 1989), p. 5.

33. Summary in "The New Constitution," *Peking Review*, 22 (March 1979): 9. See also another summary contained in the Preamble to the State Constitution, reported in *Beijing Review* (December 27, 1982), pp. 10–12.

34. David E. Sanger, "Now Beijing Blames a Single Villian for All Its Ills," *The New York Times*, (September 6, 1989), p. 4.

35. Ann Scott Tyson, "China Clamps Down on Farmers," *Christian Science Monitor*, (February 5, 1990), p. 6, and "Hard-line Leaders Prefer Stability to Economic Reform," ibid., (March 1, 1990), p. 7. The need to justify the conservatism led to a spate of articles in volumes 32 and 33 of the *Beijing Review* in 1989 and 1990 praising Marxism-Leninism and describing why China opposed what it called bourgeois liberalization.

DISCUSSION QUESTIONS

1. Describe some specific ways that Western nations encouraged the crisis of modernization in China in the nineteenth century.

2. How was the 1921 formation of the CCP an echo of Lenin's theory of imperialism and the 1917 Bolshevik success?

3. How did Marxism fit into the Chinese tradition?

4. Briefly describe the Guomindang that the Chinese Red Army defeated in 1949. Who were two important leaders of that party?

5. What was the Cultural Revolution and how long did it last?

6. Why is the question "Was Mao Zedong a good Marxist?" so difficult to answer?

7. Why did the Sino-Soviet conflict openly erupt in the early 1960s? Why not earlier? Later?

8. How did the Great Leap Forward threaten Soviet hegemony of the socialist bloc?

9. What was Mao Zedong's solution to nearly every problem? Give examples.

10. Describe Mao's theory of contradictions.

11. What changes had Deng Xiaoping introduced in China? What threatens these changes?

12. Is contemporary China reforming or stagnating? Explain by operationalizing the terms.

13. Why might it be said that China needs a dramatic rise in political efficacy?

14. What happened in Tiananmen Square in May-June 1989?

15. Discuss the possibilities if the Tiananmen Square crisis had occurred in November-December 1989 instead of May-June.

16. How did China change in 1990? Why?

9

Minor Chords

Communism, or Marxism-Leninism, has been chosen as the ideology of many other countries in the world. This was especially noticeable in the heyday of national-liberation movements since 1945 in less-developed countries. Three reasons stand out as the basis for such a choice. First, the revolutionary national-liberation movements were ideologically anti-West because of the need to reject Western colonialism or imperialism. Second, the command economy in an authoritarian political system appealed to revolutionaries because it promised an indigenous construction of wealth in a fairly short time. Until the mid-1970s, the Soviet Union's economic growth rates were quite high, and there was no reason, at least until the 1980s, to understand the finite utility of the command economy. Third, Marxist-Leninist revolutionaries could anticipate necessary economic assistance from an anti-West Soviet bloc eager to have new friends.

However, when that aid from the Soviet bloc began to be more grudgingly given because the command economy's growth rates declined, the old anti-West attitudes could also lose much of the earlier fervor—at least in those countries where the hostility was not encouraged by America's own hostility to the communist regime. To illustrate these developments in communism, this chapter provides a brief overview of six countries: Ethiopia and Angola in Africa, Cuba and Nicaragua in Latin America, and Vietnam and Cambodia in Asia.[1]

AFRICA

The continent of Africa contains over fifty separate countries whose boundaries, for the most part, were drawn by colonial powers at the Berlin Conference of 1884/85. Ethiopia and Angola are but two African nations: black, poor, and troubled.

Ethiopia and Angola practice a form of Marxism-Leninism called *scientific socialism* to distinguish it from non-Marxist African Socialism or tradi-

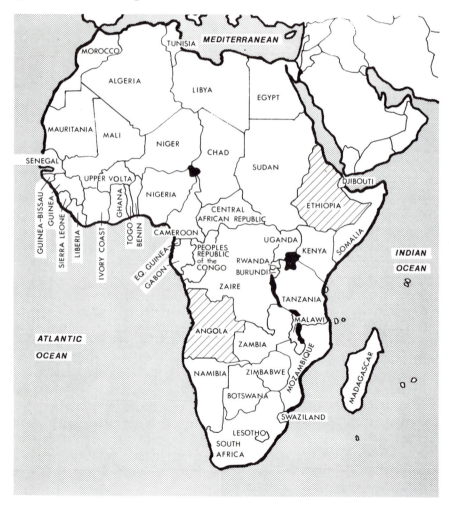

Map 7   Africa

tional African ways, which involve sharing within extended family networks, a personal wealth held in trust against social need, a rejection of divisions within society as violations of the social bond, and cooperative agriculture on commonly held land. Scientific socialism, on the other hand, pulls traditional African elements into the structured and industrial orientation of Marxism-Leninism; this includes the familiar context of class struggles and proletarian hegemony through the victory of Marxist-Leninist parties. This is the present position of Ethiopia and Angola, but in the face of difficulties the extent of the commitment to Marxism-Leninism has weakened.

Ethiopia

Haile Selassie, the former Ethiopian emperor, was eighty-two years old when he was deposed in 1974. He had been in power for forty-four years, and, as Ras Tafari, was crowned Haile Selassie ("Power of the Trinity") in 1930. His empire was based on a feudal system composed mainly of peasants living land-poor lives ruled by tradition and a relatively indifferent monarch. Despite the failure of the West in 1935 to protect Ethiopia from an invasion by fascist Italy, Haile Selassie remained pro-West throughout his long tenure as emperor. In 1974, when the army deposed the ailing monarch, the new group that replaced him, the Derg (Dergue), did not have a clear idea of what it would put in his place, but its members were united in opposing the Western powers that had supported the Emperor for so long. Their strong anti-West attitude caused the Derg to seek economic assistance from the Soviet Union even though Ethiopia was still receiving aid from the United States.

To the new leaders, a close friendship with the USSR would solve a number of problems. First, the Derg wanted to modernize Ethiopian society and to do so it needed technical and financial assistance. Additionally, the new government also faced two military threats: an already existing secessionist movement in the northern province of Eritrea, which was supported by the socialist bloc, and a potential territorial struggle with neighboring Somalia over an area called the Ogaden, which is situated between the two countries. In the early 1970s Somalia was an ally of the USSR and was receiving military aid from the Soviet Union. If Ethiopia and the USSR could become friendly then all of Ethiopia's problems would be easier to handle.

The timing was right for the new government to seek an alliance with the Soviet Union. Egyptian President Gamal Abdel Nasser had just forced Soviet advisers out of Egypt because of humiliating Egyptian defeats by the Israelis. Somalia too was a problem for Soviet leaders who were intensely reevaluating their policy toward northern Africa[2] when the anti-West military coup occurred in Ethiopia and an opportunity was created for the Soviets to balance the loss of Egypt with the gain of Ethiopia. This was too attractive for the Soviets to resist even though they had to abandon Somalia and the Eritrean independence movement. The Derg made the shift for the Soviets easier by creating a socialist context for their new Ethiopian government. In 1974, the Derg published the *Declaration of Socialism*, and, in 1975, the *Declaration on Economic Policy of Socialist Ethiopia*. As a result, Soviet leaders decided to back the new military government in Addis Ababa.

The socialist position adopted by Ethiopia was not all that radical at first; it sought to bridge Marxism-Leninism and African Socialism. National resources crucial for economic development or of indispensable service to the community were to be under government ownership or control. Economic activities that were not so amenable to government ownership were to be monitored closely but left in private hands.[3] Government involvement, it was believed, would prevent exploitation of the population while worker self-management would give people more power over their own lives. Education and health care were to be improved by both private foundations and government control.[4]

The declarations made Ethiopia sound socialistic, but the initial context had more to do with freedom than with authoritarianism. For example, along with the *Declaration of Socialism*, five fundamental principles were articulated: equality, self-reliance, the dignity of labor, the supremacy of the public good, and the indivisibility of Ethiopian unity.[5] Ethiopian socialism was a declaration of freedom as well as a mild form of Marxism-Leninism. But this moderate position did not last. When Mengistu Haile Mariam took power in 1977, he pulled Ethiopia away from moderation to a more rigid, Soviet-type socialism. Why? Because of confusion about goals and the military danger represented by Somalia.

The confusion about new directions was most visible in agriculture. After 1974, land redistribution was critically important for Ethiopian hopes of food self-sufficiency; however, the central government in Addis Ababa did not have the administrative staff or structure to supervise this redistribution. The task was therefore given to almost autonomous peasant associations, assisted by students sent out from the universities to teach literacy and help with the land reform. Confusion and misunderstanding created chaos in the vitally important agricultural sector. In their interpretations of what the government intended, the students were more radical than the peasants, most of whom believed that the proclamation on land reform gave ownership to those who tilled the soil. Most of the students and many Derg leaders thought that the proclamation meant some form of collectivization—at the least, cooperatives and a consolidation of small holdings. Peasants resisted student and government pressures that appeared to take precious land away instead of giving them access to more.[6] A stalemate developed on the redistribution interpretations. The critical need for food created pressure to decide quickly, and, because capitalized agriculture was ideologically repugnant, collectivized agriculture was imagined to be the answer, whether the farmers agreed or not.

Collectivization was supposed to occur in three stages. During the first stage, private plots could be retained while remaining land would be merged into a cooperative. Animals and equipment would be lent to the collective for a fee. The second stage would see the formation of state farms in which workers would receive wages for work performed. Private plots would still be permitted but all animals and equipment would be collectively owned. The third stage—communes—would occur, it was hoped, when productive capacity increased sufficiently.

The entire program faltered somewhere in the middle of the second stage. Peasants were forcibly moved from the north to work on state farms in the south, but those farms proved to be inefficient and expensive to operate. Even if the rains had come on time, the state farms would probably not have been sufficiently productive because of peasant opposition. But droughts came, and the parched soil could sustain neither grazing nor crops. Famine conditions and accompanying population migrations to better land or refugee centers postponed the collectivization campaign. Ethiopian food production continued to depend on individual farmers working plots assigned to them by the state. Because this was inadequate to feed the population, Ethiopia became dependent on food assistance from East *and* West in order to survive, and, at the same time, interfered with that food assistance for political and military reasons.

The second reason for increased authoritarianism was the worsening in 1977 of both the Somali and Eritrean military threats. The atmosphere in Addis Ababa became crisis-oriented, and the hard-line Marxist-Leninist Mengistu took charge. He quickly consolidated his power by establishing a countrywide Commission for Organizing the Working People of Ethiopia (COPWE) to act as his organization until a communist party could be created. Although Mengistu was endorsed as a "true revolutionary" by Cuba's Fidel Castro,[7] and the rhetoric of the Mengistu group highlighted freedom, equality, and prosperity,[8] Mengistu created a climate of terror in Ethiopia. His opponents were killed or imprisoned, and random, arbitrary cruelty seemed to characterize all sides of the political struggle. Revolutionary defense squads were created to combat a counterrevolution that had not existed before, and thousands of people were killed in the small country of 35 million. Fear and uncertainty created doubts even among Mengistu supporters, and people began to wonder if the government had become a new kind of fascism.[9]

The instability in Ethiopia encouraged Somalia to invade the Ogaden in the summer of 1977. By November the Ethiopian military situation was critical, and Mengistu asked Fidel Castro for help. By April 1978 about 17,000 Cuban troops were in Ethiopia fighting against the Somalis while the Soviet Union provided military equipment and some naval assistance against Eritrea. During seven weeks in 1978, the Cuban/Ethiopian forces pushed the Somalis back out of the Ogaden and reclaimed the area for Ethiopia.[10] Ethiopian troops then turned back to the long-standing Eritrean conflict in the north where Cuban forces, officially at least, did not wish to fight. Cuba had, after all, supported the Eritrean secessionists before Ethiopia joined the socialist side.[11] By 1984 most of the Cuban forces had left.

In September 1984, COPWE's organizational work culminated in the formal inauguration of the Communist party (the Workers' Party) as the only legal political party in Ethiopia. Mengistu became its first Secretary General. An 11-member Politburo, a 136-member Central Committee, and a 10-year economic plan were announced by the party convention. A flurry of rhetoric claimed that the new party marked a historic step in the transition from a feudal bourgeois regime in 1974 to a communist society. Through a referendum on February 1, 1987, the country became the People's Democratic Republic of Ethiopia, with the 50,000-member Workers' Party as the guiding force of the state. The applause, fanfare, and excitement of all this, however, could not disguise the insecurity of the Mengistu regime. It continued to face armed opposition in several Ethiopian areas besides Eritrea, and as Soviet aid declined from the $3.5 billion received in the period 1977 to 1987,[12] the possibility of ever attaining the affluence anticipated by Marxism seemed extremely remote.

What is visible is an ideological government committed to centralized decision making and authoritarian rule in one of the poorest and hungriest countries in the world. Although rapid increases in literacy and progress in vaccination programs can be credited to the authoritarian Ethiopian government, it has little else in its favor. Military reversals in 1989, the weakening of the Soviet resolve to underwrite continuing civil wars, continuing famine, as well as a massive refugee and resettlement problem, forced Mengistu to look to the West for assistance. Real solutions to Ethiopia's problems in the 1990s, as long as Mengistu remains in power, seem remote. The development of communism in such a context seems impossible.

Angola

Angola, located in southwest Africa, was a colony of Portugal until the 1970s. By the time independence was achieved in 1975, several different Angolan factions were competing against each other for control of the country. The new Angolan government that emerged from this pre-liberation struggle was the Popular Movement for the Liberation of Angola (MPLA in Portuguese) led by Agostinho Neto. The MPLA was mildly socialist and for some time had been receiving aid from the USSR and other socialist countries.

In 1962, the MPLA adopted a two-stage program. First, its minimum program sought an end to colonialism, sovereignty for Angola, and alliance with other progressive, anticolonial African forces. Second, its maximum program called for equality, unity of all African peoples, freedoms of speech, conscience, press, and assembly, and universal suffrage. Although the maximum program called for an end to the economic privileges of colonial times and an equitable redistribution of land, it also insisted that industry and *private* enterprise be protected. The 1962 program concluded with a wish to avoid alignment with either side in the superpower struggle.[13]

Holden Roberto, the leader of a second faction, the National Angolan Liberation Front (FNLA in Portuguese), backed for a time by the United States, considered the MPLA people "communists" because of their tilt toward socialism and the aid received from the Soviet Union. The United States' government agreed with Roberto and financially supported the FNLA in a struggle against the MPLA. American economic assistance to Roberto was especially visible in 1975 but stopped altogether a year later, during a brief period of U.S. isolationism after America's abrupt withdrawal from Vietnam.[14]

A third major group was the National Union for Total Independence of Angola (UNITA). This faction, led by Jonas Savimbi, who initially sounded socialistic, flirted with the Chinese, opposed the MPLA, but ended up being supported by the United States and the Republic of South Africa.[15] Savimbi's opposition to the Luanda government continued through the 1970s and 1980s.

In 1974 a military coup in Portugal overthrew the right-wing government of Antonio de Oliveira Salazar. The new leaders in Lisbon granted two of its African colonies, Angola and Mozambique, independence. The original Alvor agreement signed on January 15, 1975, formalizing the transfer of power from Portugal to Angola, called for a coalition government of the three nationalist guerrilla groups plus a contingent of Portuguese officials.[16] This transition government never materialized, however, because the three internal groups were fighting among themselves for Angola, and at least two of them had external support. In this context, the Alvor documents were irrelevant. The MPLA was uninterested in sharing power with others it considered enemies. The grafitti on Luanda walls, *A luta armada continua* ("The armed struggle continues") told the story.

This second war of liberation, fought mainly between the MPLA (supported by the Soviet Union) and UNITA (supported by the United States and South Africa), proceeded slowly until South Africa invaded Angola in 1975 and placed the popular MPLA in grave jeopardy. At this time some 400 Cubans were in Angola in various advising and helping capacities: military, medical, engineering, and teaching. The South African invasion caused President Neto to ask for Cuban military help, and in the last months of 1975 nearly 10,000 Cuban troops arrived. The South Africans were pushed back but the resulting instability and dependence on Soviet and Cuban assistance helped push the formerly mild MPLA socialism in the direction of a more rigid Soviet model. The MPLA was reconstituted a Workers' Party in 1977 and became known as the MPLA-PT.

Continuing invasions of Angola by South Africa caused the need for more Cuban troops, and a total of some 37,000 were in place by 1987, mainly used as rear-guard support. The ideological divisions remained in this civil war, which never seemed to end, but the lines of that division were confusing. While the United States certainly supported UNITA and Jonas Savimbi to the tune of $15 million per year, the United States also sent millions of dollars in food aid to Angolans living in MPLA territory through the U.N. Children's Fund and medical assistance through the Red Cross. Angola remained a most-favored nation in terms of trade with the United States, and Western oil companies, protected by Cuban troops, provided profits from Angolan oil that paid for the MPLA war effort. Clearly an anomaly in cold war terms, and even more so after the Angolan government sought to move away from a command economy toward free markets in late 1987.[17]

Efforts to end the civil struggle were difficult because the Luanda government would not negotiate with Savimbi and because of the complications arising from the presence of both Cuban and South African troops in Angola. The need for such a settlement was overwhelming, however, because the Angolan government had never had the opportunity to establish the stability it needed so that it could use its oil revenues for development purposes. If it could attain that stability, it could then proceed with the struggle for better food production and distribution, and the battle against illiteracy, inflation, and poor health care. Instead of development there is displacement of the population, famine and disrupted food distribution, and heavy casualties of both adults and children. As former education minister, Artur Lestana Pepetela, observed in 1984:

> We were plunged into the East-West conflict and now we don't even know who we are. Every aspect of our lives is imbued with alienation and contradiction— black market vs. official planning, proletarian ideology in a rural society, pro-Soviet rhetoric while doing business with the West. Only peace will allow us finally to realize who we are and where we want to go.[18]

Negotiations for peace took place in 1988 but without the participation of Savimbi's UNITA. As a result, the peace accords, called the Namibia Agreement, which were signed in December 1988 by Angola, Cuba, and South Africa, and which permitted the beginning of the withdrawal of some 50,000 Cuban troops in January 1989, did not bring peace.[19] UNITA controlled too much of the country. *A luta armada continua.* But an increasing Soviet unwillingness to spend billions of dollars in Angola made Luanda more receptive to negotiations with UNITA. A tenuous cease-fire in mid-1989 brought some hope, but within months the peace seemed as deadly as the war. Both UNITA and Luanda claimed violations of the truce by the other side. Negotiations continued in 1990. Both sides claim to want democracy, but evidently without the other side. Understandable but frustrating for people in Angola tired of the killing. Marxism-Leninism in Angola is being kept alive by the struggle; without it the ideology would moderate and fade.

* * *

Both Ethiopia and Angola thus represent two different types of Marxist-Leninist systems in Africa. The former regimes were oriented to the West, and so the goal of the liberating forces was liberation from the West as well as from the old regimes. Once the new governments made the choice to ally themselves with the Soviet Union, the Western powers became actively opposed to the new regimes, which deepened the earlier anti-West decision and perpetuated the Soviet connection.

Ethiopia, more so than Angola, was a dictatorship dedicated to the Soviet model. But even in Ethiopia, the cold war boundaries are sometimes hard to find. This is even more true of Angola. If both countries could be left alone, they might make decent progress with a combination of democracy and African socialism.

LATIN AMERICA

Cuba

Prior to the Bolshevik success in 1917, concepts of Marxism and socialism came to Latin America through books, immigrants, and travel, creating an intellectual leftism that fit into the emerging nationalism and anti-imperialism of the nineteenth century. In general, the socialist groups were simply more radical than the other liberal groups that arose, and often the radicalism had more to do with anarchism than Marxism.

Map 8 Central America

However, after the Bolshevik creation of the Third International, communist parties began to form in Latin America. In Havana, the Cuban Communist party was organized in 1925, a few years after communist parties formed in Mexico, Argentina, Chile, Brazil, and Uruguay. They were all small groups that were frequently divided on ideological questions, and they attempted to work in countries that had very small and uneducated labor forces. They were not very effective, therefore, and were often ignored by Moscow in favor of trade relations with Latin American governments.

The Soviet Union might ignore Latin American communist parties, but the United States did not, particularly after World War II when the United States became preoccupied with anticommunism. In Cuba, political leaders gained American support by repressing the Communist party. This tendency to repress opposition was carried to new heights in 1952 when Fulgencio Batista cancelled scheduled elections and seized power. He moved against all political parties, including the small group of communists. However, the threat to Batista's power did not come from the Cuban Communist party, but from a young lawyer who had been running for office in 1952 when Batista cancelled the elections. His name was Fidel Castro Ruz.

Castro was the son of a planter who had emigrated from Spain; he was a Roman Catholic, bourgeois young man who came out of a well-off Cuban economic group denied access to real power by the oligarchy of wealth and privilege organized around the sugar interests. When Batista seized power in 1952, Castro's opposition to Batista created a focal point for a liberal opposition that was weary of seeing its ideals betrayed by the forces of money, prestige, and power. The hero of the liberals was not Karl Marx, but José Martí, a man who symbolized Cuban independence from Spain and inspired dramatic change.

José Martí (1853–1895) was born in Havana, and, like Castro, the son of Spanish emigrants. He became a passionate advocate of Cuban independence from Spain; when he was only seventeen he was arrested and banished to Spain. There he received degrees in law, philosophy, and letters; travelled to France, Mexico, Guatemala, and then back to Cuba from which he was again banished in 1879 for political reasons. Martí lived for a time in the slums of New York City, supporting himself as an art critic for *The New York Sun* and privately working for Cuban independence.[20]

Romantic idealism and sympathy for the lower classes in society distinguished Martí's writings until the 1886 Haymarket riot in the United States caused him to identify more closely with the working class. Although he knew of Marx, and wrote an obituary tribute to him in 1883, Martí's identification with Marx was really through Marx's humanism and support of the European underdogs—the new industrial workers. Martí blended his understanding of Marx with his desires for Cuban independence and his hostility toward the United States. The United States had many attractive attributes, he thought, but it had risen to great power at the expense of its neighbors. He feared that the United States would not leave Cuba alone once Cuba gained independence from Spain. "I have lived in the bowels of the monster and I know it,"[21] Martí commented.

Independence from Spain came in 1898. Dominance by the United States followed, as Martí had feared, but so did oppressive Cuban governments. It was easy to link one with the other. Cuban governments were much longer on promises than on performance and were so tied to the United States that to be against one was to be against the other. Yankee domination was perceived by many as the chief evil facing Cuba.

Castro's opposition to Batista in 1952 began in this context of a liberal, anti-American ideology that followed the ideas of José Martí rather than Karl Marx or Lenin. On July 26, 1953, Castro's small force attacked the army barracks at Moncada; the attack gave them a name for their movement, the *26 Julio* movement, but little else. Their second attempt to establish a base in the mountains of Oriente Province from which to fight Batista was successful. The *26 Julio* movement was a force of about 300 guerrillas, often supported by local citizens.

In 1955 the group issued a manifesto calling for restoration of political democracy, social justice, a return to the 1940 constitution that Batista's 1952 coup had violated, and redistribution of land among the peasants. Their demands were actually *more* radical than the supposedly revolutionary aims of the Cuban Communist party, partly because the *26 Julio* people were willing to fight openly for their goals. The Soviet Union strongly discouraged insurrectionary violence by Latin American communists, and the Cuban party followed these instructions even though party members were anti-Batista and wished the Castro forces well. If Castro were successful in the liberal struggle against Batista, he might create opportunities for them to work for the proletarian revolution they were seeking as a maximum program.[22] The Cuban Communist party and Castro's *26 Julio* movement were going in separate directions even if they shared an antipathy for Batista and the United States.

In 1959, a decade after the Chinese communists were successful, the Castro forces were victorious over Batista; the new regime sought economic assistance from the United States, other Latin American countries, and also from the Soviet Union. In the beginning, the coup seemed like any other Latin American coup, including the initial confusion. Hardly anyone paid attention. As Castro himself said twenty-five years later: "No mention was made then of the Marxist-Leninist Party, of socialism and of internationalism; capitalism was not even mentioned by name. Indeed, very few would have understood its true meaning at the time."[23] Castro's dramatic announcement in December 1961 that he was Marxist-Leninist came as a great surprise.

Why the sudden change? Why adopt an ideology that would tie Cuba to Soviet directions? Four reasons appear significant in hindsight. First, Castro distrusted and feared the ability of the United States to interfere in and thwart the possibility of a social revolution in Cuba. Soviet Russia was, on the other hand, thousands of miles away. Second, he needed to rally popular support behind him, and the Cuban Communist party had the organizational skills to help him do this. Third, he had come to feel that his idea of a social revolution for Cuba—including improving literacy, health care, industrialization, and diversity in agriculture—fit what he understood

Fidel Castro   1927–

of communism.[24] Fourth, the U.S.-sponsored Bay of Pigs invasion in 1961 made America an *active* enemy and pushed him toward linkage with the "other" superpower, the USSR.

Although Castro can be faulted for not returning to the 1940 constitution as he had promised, very little else in the 1955 manifesto was threatened by Castro's switch to Marxism-Leninism. Indeed, relying on private enterprise to accomplish his social goals implied a reliance on the United States that had proven detrimental to *Cuban* development. By declaring himself a Marxist-Leninist, Castro could nationalize U.S.-owned enterprises as compensation to the Cuban people for past imperialist oppression and use the enterprises to benefit Cuba. This too had an appeal—particularly if the risks to Cuba were mitigated by reliance on the USSR.

After his abrupt change, Castro purged the Communist party of potential opponents and made the party a personal instrument through which he could control Cuba. His December 1961 decision caused moderates in the *26 Julio* movement to resign, thus giving him a freer hand. He combined the purged party and the remnant of the *26 Julio* movement into *his* party, and then carried that same *caudillo* independence into his foreign policy by attempting to push insurrections in other Latin American countries. If communist parties would not lead a Cuban-style armed revolt in Latin America, Castro would encourage more revolutionary splinter groups to develop.

His insurrectionary push annoyed Soviet leaders, who saw Latin America as within the U.S. sphere of influence and as a source of profitable trade relations for themselves. In the early 1960s, Cuban leaders diligently sought to export their particular version of the "revolution," just as the Comintern had earlier sought to export the Bolshevik version. Cuba wasn't any more successful than was the Comintern in exporting revolution—for a time Cuba's major export was people, as thousands of Cubans emigrated to escape Castro's authoritarian society. Cuba's adventurism ended shortly after the 1967 failure of the Bolivian insurrection in which Cuban revolutionary Che Guevara lost his life. Castro turned inward and began concentrating on internal problems while becoming a cooperative partner of Soviet international ambitions. Instead of the socialist world's independent maverick seeking *his* form of insurrection in other countries, Castro began aiding *other* people's insurrections in places such as Angola and Ethiopia. Because these other liberation movements were also supported by Moscow, Castro appeared to be a servant of Soviet rather than Cuban foreign policy. This impression of being a salesperson for Soviet interests was heightened by his efforts in 1979 to draw nonaligned nations into the Soviet orbit during a conference in Havana.[25]

What has Castro accomplished in Cuba? He heads an honest government in comparison to many other Latin nations. Medical care is about the best in Latin America, and Cuban doctors have been sent to other Third World countries to help set up medical programs. The massive attack on illiteracy has had a profound impact on the Cuban citizenry. Child labor has long been abolished as a regular part of the Cuban economy. Land was redistributed long ago, and rents for property were greatly reduced. Havana, which used to be the playground of the very rich, became a city of high moral character and has only recently seen a return of its old flair. An experiment with rapid industrialization was shelved in favor of a dependence on diversified agriculture. Sugar, however, was still the major crop, and the Soviet Union and Eastern Europe were the best customers. Some seventy percent of Cuban foreign trade was with the USSR.

There have been and still are political prisoners. Some people have been kept in prison long past their sentences. Charges by Amnesty International about mistreatment and occasional execution of political prisoners in Cuba have been substantiated by those occasionally released from jail.[26] In addition, Cuba has some juvenile delinquency, general crime, commodity hoarding, strict rationing, and frequent shortages of goods. World prices for sugar often fall below production costs and this, except for Soviet purchases at higher prices, damages the Cuban economy. All of the negative things that can be said of Cuba, however, including mistreated prisoners, were present before the revolution, usually in greater degree. The positive things were not.

In addition, the Cuba of 10 million people, for a time at least, became an active participant on the world stage, not only in the normal sense of trade and diplomatic relations, but also by sending troops to countries such as Ethiopia and Angola and professionals like doctors, nurses, and teachers to other Third World areas. Cuban soldiers appeared to be a proxy army for the Soviet international objectives, but the civilian involvement has earned Cuba respect in Third World quarters. As a result, Cuba was no longer an isolated country in Latin America. However, it has been a respect earned with Cuban sacrifice. In December 1989 Castro announced Cuban casualties in Africa over the previous fifteen years. According to his statement, some 400,000 soldiers and technical advisers were sent to Africa, and 2,289 were killed there. Over 2,000 of these died in Angola alone.[27]

To what extent were the civilian professional people sent to other countries distinct from the Cuban military? Were Castro's nurses and teachers just soldiers in disguise? Castro said that they were not. American leaders such as President Ronald Reagan did not believe him; hence, the American invasion of Grenada in 1983 because of the presence of Cuban contruction workers. This disbelief also explains the great difference in reported numbers of Cuban military personnel in Nicaragua during the 1980s; the United States claimed high numbers that include civilian personnel, and Castro reported much smaller totals that excluded civilians from the military. Regardless of one's perspective, however, Castro's methods have changed. His assistance was not so much to insurrectionary movements as it was to friendly *governments* trying to stay in power against Western-sponsored opposition. Perhaps the 1973 crushing of the Marxist government of Salvadore Allende in Chile stimulated the new approach: a Cuban revolutionary force of ideological mercenaries and missionaries; one set for military situations, and the other to help improve education, roads, businesses, and health care in Third World countries.

But all is not positive for Castro. First, the people of Cuba are not free. Despite Castro's genuine popularity, the sacrifice of liberty for equality has not been a happy one for everyone. Some dissent is visible, with more suspected beneath the surface, but it is carefully controlled. Second, Cuban debts to the USSR continue to mount. In late 1989 it was estimated that Soviet subsidies to Cuba amounted to a staggering total, some $11 million to 12 million per day, some of which must be repaid at some time. According to earlier projections the Cuban debt (not including military aid) to the Soviet Union stood at $22 billion, increasing by $3 billion annually.[28] Third, Castro has resisted and resented the democratic evolution in the Soviet Union and East Europe. His own *perestroika* occurred between 1980 and 1986 when farmers were allowed to sell surpluses, and material rather than ideological incentives were used to increase productivity. This experiment ceased in 1986 and Cuba returned to moral incentives and voluntary work. It is clear that Castro has not changed his mind. In 1989, for example, his attitude about the changes in European communism indicated very clearly that he was no longer the leftist he had been—he had become an example of the right wing against which he earlier fought. He banned several Soviet publications from sales in Cuba, calling the weekly *Moscow News* and the monthly *Spudnik* promoters of bourgeois democracy and the American way of life. An editorial in *Granma* complained that readers of those two Soviet publications could be led astray into believing that socialism has failed and that it was not historically inevitable.[29] On December 8, 1989, Castro bluntly rejected Gorbachev-style reforms: "If destiny assigns us the role of one day being among the last defenders of socialism in a world in which the Yankee empire has succeeded in embodying Hitler's dream of world domination, we will know how to defend this bulwark to the last drop of blood."[30] This apparent gamble that Gorbachev will fail makes Cuba's economic and political future look bleak. Harbingers of that future came in 1989 when factories in Eastern Europe raised prices on goods to be exported to Cuba, and in 1990 when the USSR announced an end to its subsidized trading by 1991. Fidel Castro unwisely feels that sustaining the important niche carved for Cuba in the Latin American and international scene needs the moral tones of the cold war. As relations between the United States and the Soviet Union improve, Castro's conservatism increasingly becomes an historical oddity, endangering not only Soviet subsidies but also Castro's rule in Cuba. Sometimes the penalty for swimming against the flow is drowning.

Although Cuba and Fidel Castro have come a long way since 1959, they do not appear to be advancing. Indeed, they sound like the Chinese leadership. In February 1990, Cuban Communist party leaders claimed that they could avoid the "mistakes" made elsewhere (like in Eastern Europe) and perfect a single Leninist party based on democratic centralism.[31] As communist leaders in Bulgaria, Czechoslovakia, Hungary, the German Democratic Republic, Poland, Romania, and, indeed, even in the Soviet Union have discovered, such mindless mouthing of discredited platitudes no longer works. All it takes is a modern-day Martin Luther willing to nail theses on a church door in Havana.

Nicaragua

Nicaragua is a small nation situated between Mexico and Colombia, part of the land bridge connecting North and South America. It is a mountainous and volatile area lying in a hurricane belt and subject to the wet or dry spells of monsoon-style rainfall.

This area was ruled by Spain for three centuries. Under Spanish rule the people native to the area were considered servants of the conquerors and had no place in the decision-making structure. Spain was mainly interested in control so that gold and silver could be easily extracted. In 1823, when Karl Marx was only five years old, countries in the area gained their independence from Spain. A United Provinces of Central America arose, composed of El Salvador, Honduras, Nicaragua, Guatemala, and Costa Rica, but the union lasted only until 1838. The tiny countries were again separate.

Characteristics inherited from their colonial past, like plantation agriculture and growing the same crop year after year, proved difficult to change. Land holdings tended to be large and in a few hands. Politically and economically the Central American societies were dominated by the landholding elites; their relative isolation seemed to encourage centralized, corrupt, and authoritarian political systems. The growing importance of world trade in the nineteenth century stimulated the emergence of a commercial class, but this group formed only a small middle class that aped the elites more than it mitigated between rich and poor. Military groups gradually consolidated within each country and formed powerful, nearly autonomous institutions.

In the twentieth century three sociopolitical trends were visible: the older, historically rooted authoritarian tradition, democratic tendencies that had difficulty taking root except in Costa Rica, and a socialism that blended anarchism, democratic socialism, and Marxism. By the 1970s, in the words of the Kissinger Report, the trend toward a more open political system, visible in some parts of Central America, had been reversed in Nicaragua, Guatemala, and El Salvador.

> In each of these three countries, resistance to change on the part of the dominant military and civilian groups became stronger as demands for a larger share of national income, increased social services and greater political participa-

tion spread from the middle class to the masses of the urban and rural poor. The armed forces tightened their control over the day-to-day activities of the government and more harshly repressed perceived challenges to their power from trade union or political movements.[32]

The historical situation in Nicaragua leading up to the present, briefly summarized, might begin with the familiar pattern of American marines landing in Nicaragua in 1924 to suppress the disorder that had followed elections. A guerrilla leader, Cesar Augusto Sandino, fought against the occupation from 1927 to 1933 when the American forces withdrew. In 1934 Sandino was assassinated by Anastasio Somoza, the American-trained head of the Nicaraguan National Guard. Somoza set up a military dictatorship, was assassinated himself in 1956, and his son Luis and trusted friends ruled the country until Luis died in 1967. At that point, Anastasio Somoza Debayle, another son, became President. The Kissinger Report described the rule of Anastasio Somoza Jr. as follows:

> His rule was characterized by greed and corruption so far beyond even the levels of the past that it might well be called a kleptocracy; it included a brazen reaping of immense private profits from international relief efforts following the devastating earthquake of 1972. And as opposition to his regime increased, repression became systemic and increasingly pervasive.[33]

In 1979 the Somoza government was overthrown. The group that replaced it, the Sandinistas—named after the earlier guerrilla leader—were a coalition of leftist groups including the old Nicaraguan Socialist party, which had been a pro-Soviet communist party. The various factions, however, including the communists, were not given much power. The small ruling group of intellectuals and four priests at the top was decidedly left of center, but their actual commitment to Marxism-Leninism seemed debatable. Initially, the Sandinistas promised elections, and they accepted American economic aid of approximately $117 million, but this "business as usual" orientation changed quickly. As though operating as a *reverse* image of the conservative swing in the United States' 1980 elections that brought President Ronald Reagan to the White House, the Sandinistas moved further to the left. Government Decree No. 67 adopted Marxism-Leninism as Nicaragua's ideology and made the Sandinista coalition the only political party in Nicaragua. The country tilted toward alliances and trade agreements with Cuba and the Soviet Union.

What had happened? Why the apparently sudden switch to Marxism-Leninism? Because, just as earlier in Cuba, the ruling group decided on the necessity of a clear choice between the politics-as-usual position that continued a domination by the United States and striking out in a different, leftist direction. This explanation, however, is too simple for Nicaragua. At least two other reasons need explication.

First, as with the liberation struggles in Ethiopia, Angola, and Cuba, the nature of the previous regime determined the ideology. Opposition to the right-wing Somoza government, which was supported by the United States, dictated an anti-American leftism. But it was more complicated than that. When a particular government changed in a country, the existing East or West orientation of that country in cold war terms was threatened or at least questioned. Both the United States and the Soviet Union required assurances that a former "pawn" was not being lost to the "other side." If those assurances were not strong enough, the superpowers often *assumed* that an ideological change had occurred and treated the new ruling group accordingly: as either a new friend or a new enemy. For example, Imre Nagy's 1956 idea of neutrality in the East-West struggle or the 1968 Action Program in Czechoslovakia was assumed by Soviet leaders as implying a tilt toward the West. Similarly, the American invasion of Grenada in 1983 assumed that the New Jewel Movement ruling that tiny island had become pro-East in its orientation. Military suppression of the new governments occurred in all three cases. In Nicaragua's case, Somoza's corrupt right-wing government supported by the United States evoked an anti-American leftism in its opposition, which in turn triggered concentrated opposition by the United States that pushed the Sandinistas *further* to the left. The alternative was capitulation to the old order.

Second, a considerable part of the moral thrust of the leftism in Nicaragua, and in many other Latin American countries, derives from the *liberation theology* practised by many Roman Catholic priests and nuns. The theology of liberation seeks to liberate people from perpetual poverty through the application of Christian principles. It therefore often finds itself in conflict with the established church, which has for centuries accepted a hierarchical class structure as normal. Some liberation theologians argue that Jesus Christ came to establish the Kingdom of God *on earth*. "Thy kingdom come, thy will be done, on earth as it is in heaven." These words from the Lord's Prayer are taken very seriously, as is the belief that the Kingdom of God was to be society of equal brothers and sisters living peaceful, harmonious lives in a democratic theocracy. Christ's goal, in this view, was frustrated by the early organization of a hierarchical church that became *part* of the very world it should have tried to change. A true Christian response to this state of affairs, it is argued, is *opposition to all forms of oppression that perpetuate socioeconomic, hierarchical divisions of the world into rich and poor classes.* In the minds of liberation theologians, the official Catholic Church headed by the Pope has long been on the side of oppressive governments. So has the United States. Therefore, because both the Church and the United States are wrong, the struggle for progressive reform leading to the earthly Kingdom of God sees both Church and U.S. opposition to liberation goals as *proof* that the rebellion is on the right moral track. Whatever supports the oppression of God's children is morally wrong, and whatever is against the oppressors must be right. Since Latin American communist rebels seem to be fighting the same "enemy" in the name of Marxism, the moral and communist rebels find sufficient ground to link their struggles together.[34] Liberation theology is passionately opposed to the perpetual poverty engendered by the sort of capitalism visible in Latin America, but it sees the solutions to that poverty as more complicated than it once did, and now is less attracted to Marxism even though it continues to work on the left in search of viable solutions compatible with its spiritual interests.

For these two reasons the Sandinista government moved to a clearer Marxism-Leninism, alliances with Cuba and the Soviet Union, and progressive reforms within Nicaragua against illiteracy, disease, and economic exploitation. Progress was made, but the United States would not leave this "shifted pawn" alone. A Marxist-Leninist Nicaragua seemed an alien presence in the U.S. sphere of influence. American support, some of it illegal, maintained viability in a rebel group called the "contras," which sought the destabilization of Nicaraguan society so as to unseat the Sandinistas. In 1984 the Central Intelligence Agency (CIA) mined the main Nicaraguan harbor at Corinto. In addition, the United States maintained a naval armada in both the Caribbean and in the Pacific Ocean off both coasts of Central America; five airfields in Honduras just to the west of Nicaragua; and radar stations, reconnaissance flights, and thousands of personnel—mainly because of Nicaragua. The threat to U.S. interests did not arise from Nicaragua, a country of 2.5 million people with approximately eight-tenths of an acre per person, but from the expansion of Soviet-Cuban influence in the Caribbean, seen in cold war terms long after the cold war has faded from view in other areas of the world.

For most of its brief history, therefore, Nicaragua fought the contras with Cuban and Soviet assistance, while the opposition used American equipment, private and official American financing, and U.S. advisers. This war for survival made both liberty and equality impossible. Some land reform occurred, and both medical care and literacy rates improved, but the decade of struggle turned Nicaragua into a battleground of ideas: support for the Sandinistas or the contras, and support of the official church versus liberation theology. Over 30,000 Nicaraguans were killed.

In 1987 President Oscar Arias Sanchez of Costa Rica devised a peace plan for Central America, which the United States government seemed to dislike, but which was eventually accepted by the Sandinistas, calling for a ceasefire, negotiations, concessions to the opposition, and eventual democratic elections. Nicaragua complied with the plan, not perfectly, but better than the American-supported governments in El Salvador, Guatemala, and Honduras.[35]

However, millions of dollars continued to be spent by the United States on support for the contras, while economic and military aid continued to flow into Nicaragua from the Soviet Union, the East European bloc, and

Cuba. Despite these unsettled conditions, in February 1989 the five Central American presidents agreed on a peace plan that involved disarming the contras and moving them out of Honduras where they were camped. In exchange Nicaragua agreed that the opposition could take part in pre-election campaigning. But neither the United States nor Cuba could leave the country alone, the United States with money to support both the contras and the political opposition to the Sandinistas, and the Cubans with military assistance to Managua and through Nicaragua to the leftist guerrillas in El Salvador.

Tiny Nicaragua, already the scene of political and theological power struggles, economically deteriorated as a result of continual fighting, the U.S. boycott, dwindling Soviet supplies, and prospects of peace that seem jinxed first by one thing and then another. Nicaragua confronted a simultaneous North-South (rich vs. poor), East-West, and Vatican-liberation theology struggle, which had to be an ideological whirlpool with few handholds. Whether the understandably authoritarian Sandinistas could have engineered a worthwhile transformation of Nicaraguan society under such circumstances was doubtful.

The possibility became academic in February 1990. In free elections, the opposition group led by Violeta Barrios de Chamorro, the National Opposition Union, overwhelmingly won the election, and she was installed as Nicaragua's new president in April 1990. President Chamorro had been a member of the Sandinista junta in July 1979, but she left in April 1980 to become a sharp critic of Sandinista authoritarianism. Her husband, Pedro Joaquin Chamorro, editor of the newspaper *La Prensa*, had been assassinated in 1978 during the Somoza regime. After she left the Sandinistas, Mrs. Chamorro became editor of the newspaper and the most visible critic of the government for the next ten years. Her victory in 1990 was a vindication of her struggle.

The voters in Nicaragua, therefore, repudiated the Marxist-Leninist government in favor of Violeta Chamorro and the National Opposition Union—a coalition of fourteen parties. No one would have been surprised if the Sandinista government had rejected the election results and declared martial law, as right- or left-wing authoritarian governments in the past have repeatedly done. To the credit of the Sandinistas, that option was not chosen, and Nicaraguan citizens had an opportunity to try a different path.

*   *   *

Cuba and Nicaragua represent two small Latin American nations that have reacted to U.S. domination and right-wing, corrupt governments by establishing Marxist-Leninist governments. Opposition pressure from the United States has been intense, in part because of lost "pawns" but also because these two countries are in the Caribbean area very close to American shores. Cuba has had a longer history in this context and provides a model that Nicaragua tried to follow.

Recent events in both countries revealed marked differences, however. In Cuba there is an increased ideological rigidity that resembles China's fear of change and suggests Cuban isolation in a world of dramatically altered communism. In Nicaragua, free elections defeated the Sandinista government in favor of a coalition led by Violeta Chamorro. Marxism-Leninism was reinforced in Cuba, but defeated in Nicaragua.

ASIA

Vietnam

In Asia, communist power was also born of colonialism, imperialism, and war. Korea, for example, had been a colony of Japan and, after Japan's defeat in World War II, was divided at the 38th parallel to allow the United States to administer the area south of that line and the USSR the area to the north. This dual administration was to last for a period of five years (1945–1950) to allow time for Korean elections to be held. Each of the superpowers installed its own regime in its own area. When the United Nations Commission arrived in 1947 to set up the elections, it was denied permission to enter the Soviet-administered North. Elections, held only in the South, established the anticommunist government of Syngman Rhee. Shortly after, the Soviets installed the communist government of Kim Il Sung in the North.

Dividing a country to resolve American-Soviet competition over an area was popular after World War II and difficult to dismantle once in place. This kind of division, previously effected in Germany and Korea, was also applied to Vietnam, in Southeast Asia.

By 1945 Vietnam's struggle for independence had already been a long one. According to Stanley Karnow, the battle had been going on for nearly 500 years and had involved at various times the United States, Japan, France, Portugal, and China.[36] Appeals by Vietnam for American assistance date back over 100 years! In 1861 when the Vietnamese emperor was forced to surrender to the French, he appealed to President Abraham Lincoln for assistance. In 1919, when President Woodrow Wilson was in Paris, Ho Chi Minh (1890–1969) sought an appointment to present his case for Vietnamese independence to Wilson. In both cases the American presidents were preoccupied: President Lincoln with a Civil War, and President Wilson with the Versailles Treaty to end World War I.[37] No help was given.

France's long occupation of Vietnam was interrupted at the beginning of World War II when the French in Vietnam surrendered to the Japanese. In May 1941 the Eighth Plenum of the Indochinese Communist Party (ICP), up until that time an insignificant part of the Comintern, founded the Vietminh, or Vietnam Independence League. Ho Chi Minh, still in southern

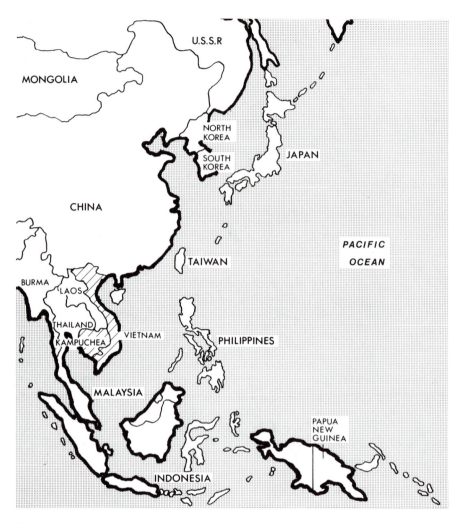

Map 9 Southeast Asia

France, saw this new development as a vehicle for utilizing the confusion of the war and the capitulation of the French to the Japanese in order to achieve independence under communist rule. His appeal to the Vietnamese people did not, however, mention socialism or communism, but rather appealed to tradition and heritage.[38]

The American president, Franklin D. Roosevelt, emphatically did not want the French to resume their colonization of Vietnam after World War II. Assistant Secretary of State Adolf Berle brought up the question as early as 1943: "...whether, in the Far East, we are reestablishing the western colonial empires or whether we are letting the East liberate itself if it can do so. I feel that the matter should be discussed on a high level with the

President for his decision."[39] The matter was discussed, and President Roosevelt was determined that the French, for whom he had little respect, should not be permitted to recolonize Indochina. He favored an international trusteeship for the area and Stalin agreed.

After the defeat of Japan in 1945, however, there was a good deal of confusion about postwar goals for Asia, a confusion made worse by President Roosevelt's death in April 1945. Aided by the British, the French were able to resume control in southern Vietnam, but not in the North where Ho Chi Minh and the Vietminh were already in control. The French then tried to retake the North, and an armed struggle ensued in which the United States, increasingly driven by an anticommunist ideology, gradually assumed the major role against the Vietminh. The defeat of the U.S.-supported French in 1954 brought peace resolutions that divided Vietnam at the 19th parallel until unifying elections could take place. But the American-dominated South feared it would lose an election to the popular Ho Chi Minh and would not permit the elections to take place. Naturally, hostilities gradually resumed, but this time the Vietminh were pitted first against American advisers to southern forces, and then after 1965 against American military units, assisted by contingents from New Zealand, Australia, and South Vietnam.

In his 1981 book, *Vietnam: The Revolutionary Path*, Thomas Hodgkin observed:

> If left to themselves the Vietnamese would have set about the reconstruction of their society, distorted by eighty-seven years of colonial rule, in accordance with the ICP's general theory of national-democratic, followed by socialist, revolution. They, both people and party, would have made mistakes and experienced setbacks, but there is no doubt about the general direction they would have travelled. But the forces of great power intervention did not permit this kind of peaceful, progressive development. . . . [C]learly the character of the Vietnamese revolution was such as to present a particularly serious threat to the structure of Western imperialism.[40]

Ten years later, in 1975, the Vietminh, or Vietcong, were victorious and quickly absorbed the South into the structure and organization of an enlarged Vietnamese Communist party. Unification of the 54 million Vietnamese proceeded on the basis of plans already drawn up in the North prior to the victory in 1975, and no time was permitted for a negotiated, phased integration.

The rapid imposition of excessively ideological policies in the South created more problems than necessary in a country already beset with difficulties. Re-education (concentration) camps were established in every province except one to imprison former and suspected enemies.[41] Directives from Hanoi interfered with food production in the South, and severe malnutrition resulted. Private enterprise was initially throttled and economic growth stagnated. The decision to invade Cambodia (Kampuchea) in

December 1978 created the need to keep nearly 150,000 troops in Cambodia as well as nearly 60,000 in Laos, severely straining an already tight economic situation.

No one believed that pulling Vietnam together after all those decades of fighting would be easy, and it has not been. Growing crops was difficult at first because farmland often contained unexploded bombs or had been poisoned by over 300 pounds of dioxin (1 part per billion is a health risk) in defoliants sprayed during the war. Droughts and typhoons didn't help either. Organizing peasants into cooperatives and collective farms was less difficult in the central areas, but quite difficult in the rich Mekong Delta in the south. Central planners in Hanoi were slow to see the differences among the northern, central, and southern areas.[42] In the first few years after the victory in 1975 they applied too much ideology too quickly to the south. By the end of 1979 in the southern Mekong areas the collectivization policy had been reversed and peasants were encouraged to grow crops for their own use and sale, even on government-owned land. Small private-sector businesses were also permitted after 1979 in an effort to stimulate a nearly stagnant economy.[43]

Such liberalizations, however, did not solve Vietnamese problems. The economic performance grew, but not as fast as inflation.[44] In April 1988 Vietnam, a former rice exporter, felt compelled to seek food aid from its former enemies. Half of its troop force in Laos was cut. Vietnamese leaders could not understand why they received so much international attention between 1945 and 1975 and so little afterwards. Even attempts at democracy were tried in early 1989, before models existed in other communist countries.

In terms of foreign policy, Vietnam aligned itself with the Soviet Union in the Sino-Soviet conflict because it has historically disliked neighboring China. Vietnam's dependence on Soviet assistance, however, was extensive, and costly for the Soviet Union as well. To help defray the approximately $1 billion per year in assistance received from the Soviet Union, Vietnamese labor battalions are sent to work in the USSR where they receive very low pay.

Hanoi's pro-Soviet position affected ethnic Chinese in Vietnam: They were expelled and their property was confiscated. Their treatment contributed to an already large number of Vietnamese "boat people" fleeing the country, as well as increasing the acrimony between China and Vietnam. Raids and frequent artillery fire across the borders became common events for both China and Vietnam. From the Soviet Union' perspective, such activity kept China preoccupied with its *southern* borders, reducing its military strength along northern borders with the USSR.

The pro-Soviet direction of Vietnam benefited Moscow in two other ways. The Soviet Union acquired naval bases in the South China Sea that can support Soviet shipping needs. In addition, the Vietnamese military was available for use as proxy forces in neighboring Cambodia, assisting the Soviet Union in its competition with China. The 1978 Vietnamese invasion of Cambodia occurred a month after Vietnamese leaders signed a twenty-five-year treaty with the Soviet Union, suggesting that the invasion was part of the treaty discussion. True, the Pol Pot regime in Cambodia was anti-Vietnam, but a stronger reason for the invasion was Moscow's unhappiness with the linkage between Cambodia and China, and a fear that the horrible events between 1975 and 1978 in Cambodia would bring yet another Western intervention in Southeast Asia. (See next section.) Unseating the Pol Pot government was a way of slapping at China as well as preserving Soviet naval power in the area. For Vietnam, however, the invasion and occupation of Cambodia deepened the already existing hostility with China, and resulted in a seventeen-day attack on Vietnam by China in early 1979 to punish Hanoi for its occupation of Cambodia.

Tensions began to relax in 1988 and especially 1989 as Vietnam indicated a willingness to negotiate a withdrawal from Cambodia, improved its relations with China, further relaxed the ideological control of the economy, and revealed less affection for Soviet influence. The continuing need for Soviet assistance, however, prevented any real independence from emerging. By September 1989 Vietnam claimed to have withdrawn entirely from Cambodia, but this claim was immediately challenged by China.

Vietnam in 1990 was a confused mixture of partial reforms and ideological restraints on further liberalization. The younger leaders appear eager to emulate the evolution of communism elsewhere, but older leaders are restrained by memories of the long struggle to get where they are. To them, Marxism-Leninism is still very much alive.[45]

Cambodia

Cambodia, the final example of a contemporary minor chord, is both interesting and different. Sometimes called Kampuchea, Cambodia is a poor country that became entangled in the long Vietnam conflict. Its political system had been a constitutional monarchy, headed by Prince Norodom Sihanouk, assisted by a parliament. For years it remained neutral during the long wars in Vietnam, but by 1970 that neutrality was irretrievably shattered, and a period of great suffering began.

Vietnamese communists had used areas of Cambodia adjacent to Vietnam as supply centers and as part of the supply trail leading from the North to the battles in the South. In 1970, American forces invaded Cambodia and swiftly destroyed the Vietnamese supplies and infrastructure. This invasion was followed by prolonged American bombing that reduced an already poor society to extremely primitive conditions. The tonnage of bombs dropped by American planes on Cambodia in just six months of 1973 exceeded by half the entire tonnage dropped on Japan in World War II. The bombs dropped were blockbusters, percussion bombs, napalm, and chemical defoliants.[46] This scale of warfare killed or wounded at least a million people, a sixth of the entire population, and created 3 million refugees. A former exporter of rice, Cambodia now had difficulty growing enough for its own population. The country became almost completely dependent on external American sources of food, medical supplies, and equipment.

To complicate the matter further, in 1970 the Sihanouk government was ousted in a coup by a right-wing military leader, General Lon Nol; it was Lon Nol's government the United States tried to uphold from 1970 to 1975. Meanwhile, in the jungles, opposition led by Red Khmer, or the Khmer Rouge, a group of Cambodian intellectuals who had become communists while studying in France, was greatly aided by the American invasion of 1970. The U.S. incursion forced Vietnamese communists deeper into the country-side where they seized control from the Lon Nol forces and thus made these areas easier for the Khmer Rouge to take over after the Viet forces had left.

Prince Sihanouk, in exile in China, decided to form a coalition group of all those Cambodians who were anti-Lon Nol, including the communists. The fact that the Khmer Rouge were in opposition to his enemy, Lon Nol, made it appear more respectable. Rapidly the Khmer took control of the coalition and led the fight against Lon Nol. Some Soviet and Chinese help was given, but American arms were easy to confiscate from retreating or defecting Lon Nol troops. The Khmer Rouge soon became the dominant force in the country. When Lon Nol fled the country in 1975, he left behind a political vacuum, devastation, and suffering caused by years of a one-sided war.

The problem was particularly acute in the capital city of Phnom Penh. In April 1975, a report filed by Americans departing from Phnom Penh contained this paragraph:

> Therefore, without large-scale external food and equipment assistance there will be widespread starvation between now and next February. . . . Slave labor and starvation rations for over half the nation's people. . .will be a cruel necessity for this year, and general deprivation and suffering will stretch over the next two to three years before Cambodia can get back to rice self-sufficiency.[47]

Phnom Penh had become swollen with refugees. Its population had gone from about 600,000 to over 3 million. The city could not be fed or sup-plied. No food or supplies of that magnitude existed anywhere in the coun-try. The abrupt departure of the Americans suggested to the Khmer Rouge that the Americans were cynically hoping that the desperate people left within Phnom Penh would, within a matter of months, demand the return of a pro-Western, noncommunist government.

The cities of Cambodia, Phnom Penh included, were, therefore, evacuated by Khmer forces. Abruptly, and at gun point if necessary. Transportation for the old, sick, or handicapped was insufficient. Food sup-plies along the way to resettlement centers were inadequate. The numbers of internal refugees created by the evacuation overwhelmed Khmer leaders. Many thousands of people died, perhaps as many as 2 million. Some were executed. According to refugees some of the executions were deliberate and carried out against putative enemies of the new regime, such as former Lon Nol army officers. Other executions appear to have been arbitrary and directed against anyone who irritated a guard—whether the source of annoyance was a woman, a child, or an old man.

The Khmer goal apparently was to get people back on the land to grow food, but the abrupt manner of accomplishing this purpose was an ideological rejection of all *dependent* urbanization and industrialization. Both the genocidal evacuation and arbitrary agricultural resettlement were costly efforts to achieve self-sufficiency at a point when crops still had to be planted, when irrigation schemes to provide a three-crop year were only planned, not implemented. In retrospect it was most unwise, but the alternative was to let the cities starve. Evacuation, planned to be temporary, was chosen instead. In 1977 the cities began to be repopulated, after extensive refurbishing, with the intention of reestablishing industrialization on a much lower, more "people-oriented" level.[48]

During the first few years following the 1975 Khmer takeover, there seems to have been no mention of Marxism-Leninism. The Communist party was simply known as the *Angkar* (Organization) or *Angkar Loeu* (Organization on High), or even *Angkar Padevat* (Red Organization). The secrecy, the absence of politics, and the clear identification with the lower classes of the society made the Khmer Rouge appear to be merciless, deeply revolutionary, and profoundly egalitarian. In September 1977 the people were told that the revolution was being led by the Communist party and that its Secretary General was a man named Pol Pot (b. 1928).

The Cambodian society had been organized into agricultural cooperatives based on the old village-unit system. Rapid collectivization, begun in the early months of 1976, was so abrupt and arbitrary that it was more like punishment than economic reorganization. Peasant homes and temples were destroyed, property was confiscated or destroyed, and very simple housing was constructed. Families worked separately in work teams and only slept together. Schooling for the young was minimal. Long work days were common, as was hunger. By 1978 the harshness of the situation was beginning to ease, but refugee reports indicated that random cruelty, killings, and beatings had continued.[49]

The Vietnamese invaded in December 1978 and were in control of Cambodia, including Phnom Penh and most of the cities, for the next eleven years. About 150,000 Vietnamese troops were stationed in Cambodia in the beginning. Allegations that the Vietnamese were trying to colonize Cambodia were denied by the new government, called the Cambodian Peoples' Revolutionary Party (PRK). The denial was not believed, however, since it was a government that had been installed and supported by Vietnam, and the ruling party, the PRK, was loyal to both Vietnamese and Soviet interests.

The Chinese continued to support the old Khmer party, which was now called the Party of Democratic Cambodia (PDK), in a coalition with two noncommunist resistance groups sometimes headed by Prince Sihanouk. The United States aided the allegedly noncommunist part of the resistance to the PRK, even though the coalition contained the Khmer Rouge. This coalition of three forces held little of the country but was a continuing problem for Vietnamese troops. The stalemate, punctuated with occasional military clashes, continued until 1987 when peace negotiations were begun but failed to bring about a resolution. Hopes for peace were contaminated by hostility, distrust, and by fears of a Khmer resurgence. Even the Vietnamese withdrawal in 1989 failed to bring peace because of Chinese and American hostility to the PRK and the real possibility of a return of the Khmer Rouge. Peace in Phnom Penh remained tenuous and uncertain.

In the meantime, Cambodia has moved from severe shortages of nearly everything important to improved harvests beginning in 1987 and modest successes in the private sector, especially in the cities. The PRK government, particularly as communist governments elsewhere increasingly show signs of reform and need for popular support, may be the best solution for Cambodia in the 1990s. The Khmer Rouge may have reformed, as some allege, but has never acknowledged the crimes committed between 1975 and 1978, and the Pol Pot leadership is only older, not necessarily changed. Trusting the Khmer Rouge seems an unnecessary risk. If major powers, including China and Vietnam, could leave Cambodia alone, the country might regain some of its past glory. In an era when pawns seem less important, such a hope does not seem utopian. The possibilities for Cambodia, under such a scenario, would not be communism, but a viable democratic socialism of the sort being sought in many other countries. If Cambodia is not left alone, the senseless civil war will continue, and only the most primitive sort of socialism will be possible for the estimated 6 million people of Cambodia.[50]

* * *

Vietnam and Cambodia represent very different examples of the implementation of Marxism-Leninism. Vietnam's case resembles China's in that an old communist party from the early Comintern days fought a long civil struggle before final victory (in 1975) but differs in that Vietnam also had to fight the French and the Americans for that victory. Mistakes made between 1975 and 1978—the application of too rigid an ideology and excessively punitive measures against former enemies—have retarded Vietnamese recovery. Since 1978, progress has been steadier, but Vietnam's recovery requires greater independence from the Soviet Union, a less ideological society, and less involvement in the affairs of either Cambodia or Laos. Political and economic viability might then finally be the reward for this country's protracted struggle for independence.

Marxism-Leninism in Cambodia resulted from United States and Vietcong violations of Cambodian neutrality during the prolonged Vietnam war.

The invasion by the United States in 1970, subsequent bombings, and the Western-backed Lon Nol government from 1970 to 1975 all left a country to the Khmer Rouge that was devasted, hungry, and impoverished. The Khmer or Pol Pot period saw a genocidal application of a most rigid ideology that ended only with the Vietnamese invasion in 1978. Until 1989 Cambodia was an occupied country with sporadic outbursts of a continuing civil war financed by outside nations. The new decade holds promise for Cambodia only if those external powers stop interfering.

AFTERWORD

The sketches in this chapter reveal both the continuing appeal of Marxism-Leninism and the importance of understanding that appeal in the context of international relations, especially between the Soviet Union and the United States. Since the 1960s and particularly since the 1970s, China must also be regarded in the international equation.

What good does it do to know all this information about communism? Communism might be the ideology of over one-third of the world's population, but isn't it dying? The final chapter tries to answer that question.

NOTES

1. Many modern articles and books provide general and specific information on these countries. Other consulted sources appear in the Bibliography.

2. The intense Soviet reevaluation of its policies in Africa was motivated by a desire to decrease both American and Chinese influence on the continent by aiding and supporting liberation movements that had some socialist aspirations even in countries that were very backward ecomomically. This policy change began when Portugal withdrew from its former American possessions. See David Albright, "The Middle East and Africa in Recent Soviet Policy," in *Soviet Foreign Policy in the 1980s*, ed. Roger E. Kanet (New York: Praeger 1982), pp. 288–303.

3. Pamphlet, *Declaration on Economic Policy of Socialist Ethiopia*, Addis Ababa, 1975.

4. Ibid.

5. "Declaration of the Provisional Government of Socialist Ethiopia," December 20, 1974, p. 8.

6. Harold Nelson and Irving Kaplan, eds., *Ethiopia: A Country Study* (Washington, D.C.: U.S. Army, 1981), pp. 153–155.

7. Fidel Castro, Interview with Simon Malley, *Afrique-Asie*, May 16, 1977, p. 16; cited in Fred Halliday and Maxine Molyneux, *The Ethiopian Revolution* (London: Verso Editions and NLB, 1981), p. 254.

8. Nelson and Kaplan, *Ethiopia*, p. 208. See also Halliday and Molyneux, *Ethiopian Revolution*, p. 137.

9. John Markakis and Nega Ayele, *Class and Revolution in Ethiopia* (Nottingham: Spokesman, The Russell Press, Ltd., 1978), pp. 163–169. Also see Halliday and Molyneux, *Ethiopian Revolution*, pp. 122–127, especially p. 123.

10. Haggai Erlich, *The Struggle Over Eritrea, 1962–1978* (Stanford, Calif.: Hoover Institute Press, 1983), p. 112.

11.   John Duggan, in an unpublished manuscript, May 1980, entitled "International Aspects of the War in Eritrea," argued that Cubans defended Asmara (in Eritrea) in early 1978, that Cuban advisers helped with Ethiopian artillery, and with a few air strikes. This, however, was denied by Havanna officials. Cited in Halliday and Molyneux, *Ethiopian Revolution*, p. 254, n. 49. The Eritreans were an Italian colony when captured by the British in 1941. In 1952 the United Nations made Eritrea a federated part of Haile Selassie's Ethiopia. In 1962 Ethiopia ended the federation and seized Eritrea. The Marxist government, therefore, continued an existing military drive against Eritrean separatism to maintain Ethiopian access to the Red Sea.

12.   "Ethiopians Officially Joining Ranks of Communist Nations," *The New York Times* (February 23, 1987), p. 4, and James Brooke, "In Ethiopia, Rulers Seem Widely Resented," *The New York Times* (March 15, 1987), p. 6.

13.   Jennifer Davis, George Houser, Susan Rogers, and Herb Shore, *No One Can Stop the Rain* (New York: The Africa Fund, 1976), p. 24.

14.   Ole Gjerstand, *The People in Power* (Richmond, B.C., Canada: Liberation Support Movement Information Center, 1977), pp. 9, 10. See also Davis and others, *No One Can Stop the Rain*, p. 38.

15.   Ole Gjerstand, *People in Power*, p. 10. Also see Gerald Bender, "Angola: Left, Right, and Wrong," *Foreign Politics*, 43 (Summer 1981): 53–69. See p. 56 especially for the varied backing that Angolan groups received. UNITA and FNLA were supported in 1975/76 by China, the United States, Zaire, North Korea, Romania, and India. The UNITA-FNLA coalition was labeled pro-West. The MPLA was adopted by the Soviet Union, Cuba, Yugoslavia, Sweden, Denmark, and Nigeria. It was labelled pro-Soviet. "We-Them" eyeglasses make the world seem much simpler than it is.

16.   See *Angola: The Independence Agreement* (Luanda: Ministry of Mass Communication, 1975).

17.   James Brooke, "Adam Smith Crowds Marx in Angola," *The New York Times* (December 29, 1987), p. 4.

18.   Artur Lestana Pepetela, quoted in Piero Benetazzo, "Angola Paradox: Nation Both Loves, Hates Its East-West Patrons," *Christian Science Monitor* (January 20, 1984), p. 12.

19.   The withdrawal of Cuban troops was temporarily suspended in January 1990. At that point some 31,000 of the 50,000 troops had already departed, indicating a withdrawal pace ahead of scheduled completion in 1991.

20.   Ramon Eduardo Ruiz, *Cuba: The Making of a Revolution* (Amherst: University of Massachusetts Press, 1968), p. 62.

21.   Ibid., p. 73. See also pp. 68–71.

22.   Jacques Arnault, *Cuba and Marxism*, trans. in excerpts by U.S. Commerce Department, Washington, D.C., from a French-language essay on the Cuban Revolution by Jacques Arnault, Chapters 4 through Conclusion, which appeared in the monthly French Communist Party review *La nouvelle critique*, 139, Paris (September-October 1962), pp. 82–206. Excerpt cited is p. 5 of the translation.

23.   Fidel Castro, "Cuba Cannot Export Revolution, Nor Can the United States Prevent It," Speech, Santiago de Cuba, January 1, 1984 (La Habana, Editora Politica, 1984), p. 6.

24.   Ramon Eduardo Ruiz, *Cuba: The Making of a Revolution*, p. 116.

25.   Arlene Idol Broadhurst, "Foreign Policy and Internationalism: The Case of Cuba," in Lawrence Whetten, *The Present State of Communist Internationalism* (Lexington, Mass.: D.C. Heath, 1983), pp. 160–162.

26.   Fox Butterfield, "Life as a Political Prisoner in Cuba: Beatings and Secret Prayer," *The New York Times* (July 14, 1984), p. 5.

27.   Larry Rohter, "Castro Says He'll Resist Changes Like Those Sweeping Bloc," *The New York Times* (December 9, 1989), p. 7.

28.   Broadhurst, "Foreign Policy and Internationalism," p. 112.

29.   "Soviet Journals Banned By Cuba as Bourgeois," *The New York Times* (August 5, 1989), p. 2.

30.   Rohter, "Castro Says He'll Resist Changes."

31. "Cubans Outline Plan to 'Perfect' Communist Rule," *The New York Times*, February 18, 1990, p. 9.

32. Draft, *Report of the National Bipartisan Commission on Central America*, January 11, 1984, p. 21. The *Report* is also available from Macmillan in New York in paperback.

33. Ibid., pp. 21–22.

34. The *moral* Christian or liberation theology side of the Sandinista struggle is why so many U.S. Christians were involved in active support of the Nicaraguan government even though the official American attitude is very much the opposite. An extensive literature on liberation theology exists and is growing. A representative sample would include the following: Richard Batey, *Jesus and the Poor* (New York: Harper & Row, 1972), Rosemary Radford Reuther, *To Change the World: Christology and Cultural Criticism* (New York: Crossroad, 1981), Gustavo Gutierrez, *A Theology of Liberation: History, Politics, and Salvation*, Sister Caridad Inda trans. and John Eagleson, ed. (Maryknoll, N.Y.: Orbis Books, 1973), Father Camilo Torris, *Revolutionary Writings* (New York: Harper Colophon Book, 1972), Rosemary Radford Reuther, *The Radical Kingdom: The Western Experience of Messianic Hope* (New York: Harper & Row, 1970), and Ernesto Cardenal, *The Gospel in Solentiname* (Maryknoll, N.Y.: Orbis Books, 1982).

35. Editorial, "Who's Living Up to the Arias Plan?," *The New York Times* (March 11, 1988), p. 26.

36. Stanley Karnow, *Vietnam: A History* (New York: Viking Press, 1983), reviewed in Colin Leinster, "Vietnam's 500-Year War," *Business Week* (October 24, 1983), pp. 12–14.

37. Ibid.

38. Ho Chi Minh, "Letter by Ho Chi Minh from Abroad, June 6, 1941," in Gareth Porter, ed., *Vietnam: The Definitive Documentation of Human Decisions* (Stanfordville, N.Y.: Earl Coleman Enterprises, Inc., Publishers, 1979), p. 1.

39. "Memorandum of Conversation by the Assistant Secretary of State, Adolf Berle, October 21, 1943," in ibid., p. 9.

40. Thomas Hodgkin, *Vietnam: The Revolutionary Path* (New York: St. Martin's Press, 1981), p. 334.

41. Nguyen Van Canh, *Vietnamese Communism, 1975–1982* (Stanford, Calif.: Hoover Institute Press, 1983), pp. 189–205.

42. The differences in northern, central, and southern Vietnam appear to have been created by the nature of French occupation in the nineteenth and twentieth centuries. The north was least accepting of French ways, the south the most accepting, while the central area was somewhere in between. The differences were strong, and the Hanoi government should have been aware of them.

43. Hodgkin, *Vietnam: The Revolutionary Path*, p. 24. See also Clayton Jones, "Line between socialism and capitalism blurs in Vietnam," *Christian Science Monitor* (November 18, 1987), p. 7.

44. For details see William J. Duiker, "Vietnam: The Challenge of Reform," *Current History*, 88 (April 1989): 177.

45. See Douglas Pike, "Change and Continuity in Vietnam," *Current History*, Vol. 89, ibid 545, March 1990, pp. 117ff.

46. Gavan McCormack, "The Cambodian Revolution, 1975–1978: The Problem of Knowing the Truth," *Journal of Contemporary Asia*, 10 (1980): 77.

47. Ibid.

48. Ibid., p. 79.

49. Ibid., pp. 95ff. The actual scale of arbitrary cruelty is impossible to determine, but that a great deal did occur is attested to by too many different people to ignore or pass off as a manipulation of the refugee interview or a distortion by the Western news media.

50. For background on this issue see Barbara Crossette, "Bargaining to Keep Pol Pot Away from Phnom Penh," *The New York Times* (July 17, 1988), p. 3E; Steven Erlanger, "The Return of the Khmer Rouge," *The New York Times Magazine* (March 5, 1989), pp. 24ff; "The Choices in Cambodia," *Washington Post National Weekly Edition* (December 4–10, 1989), p. 27; "Ignored: A Path to Peace in Cambodia," *The New York Times*, (May 7, 1990), p. 14; and "Big Aims, Small Means on Cambodia," *The New York Times*, (July 2, 1990), p. 12.

DISCUSSION QUESTIONS

1. Why were some countries divided in half after World War II? Name three countries where this occurred.
2. Why could Fidel Castro's success *in 1959* hardly be called a communist victory?
3. Were the Sandinistas already Marxist-Leninist when they were victorious over Somoza in 1979? Explain what happened.
4. What factors contributed to the deepening of Marxist-Leninist beliefs in Cuba, Ethiopia, Nicaragua, and Angola in the late 1970s and 1980s?
5. What event in 1990 made Nicaragua unique among the six countries described in this chapter?
6. What different alliances and problems have affected Vietnam and Cambodia?
7. Why did Fidel Castro choose Marxism-Leninism in 1961?
8. How was Nicaragua caught in three simultaneous international conflicts? Was Vietnam as well? Explain.
9. Where have Cuban forces been decisive in determining outcomes of Third World conflicts? Are these Cuban forces exclusively military?
10. Why did the Khmer Rouge evacuate the cities of Cambodia?
11. What do the words "Thy Kingdom Come" from the Lord's Prayer have to do with Marxism-Leninism, liberation theology, and the Roman Catholic Church?
12. What mistake did Vietnam make during 1975 to 1978? Did Ethiopia make a similar mistake?
13. Are (were) there circumstances when American anticommunism makes sense? Explain.
14. In what ways has the adoption of Marxism-Leninism been beneficial and in what ways harmful to the six countries described in this chapter?

10

The Future of Communism

The story of communism indicates that much of the twentieth century was affected by Marxism and Marxism-Leninism. Events in 1989/90, however, demonstrated that one of those tides in history had occurred. Communism seemed to be disappearing or in retreat. Even in Benin, a small country of some 4.5 million people located west of Nigeria, the fifteen-year communist experiment appeared over. Mozambique's Marxism underwent significant reforms, as it did also in the Congo. On the other side of the world in Malaysia, communist rebels ended a forty-one-year insurgency that had cost thousands of lives by agreeing to a cease-fire and pledging to respect the laws of Malaysia and Thailand. Mongolia ended the dominant role of its Communist party, permitted opposition parties, and called for extensive economic liberalization. In the Soviet Union the constitutional monopoly of the CPSU was repealed and power was gradually shifted to the new, mostly elected institutions of government: the presidency, Congress of People's Deputies, and Supreme Soviet. Opposition parties in the Soviet Union and Eastern Europe bested communist candidates in many local and national elections in 1990. Clearly, the tide of history moved against what had come to be known as communism, and some began to speak of it in the past tense. Indeed, some implied, the slow recognition of the end of communism suggested stupidity: The specter that haunted Europe in 1848 now haunted only those too slow-footed to jump clear of the wreck.[1] It would seem a reasonable precaution, therefore, to alert the undertaker that a funeral for communism was not far off.

The difficulty still present, however, is to understand *what* has died. First, are we talking about the totalitarian monolith? Totalitarianism was always a bad model and a world-wide monolith never existed. Second, are we talking about revolutionary communist groups around the world? Those are still very much alive even though "world communism" was weakened considerably by events in Eastern Europe and the Soviet Union. Third, are we imagining the death of communism because the command economy and the authoritarian ideology are being reformed? This would mean moving away from the Marxism-Leninism that came to be associated with the Soviet Union and the Third International. Is this what is happening in the Soviet Union? If so, is it being replaced by something non-Marxist or by something that can still be called socialism/communism? A thoughtful individual might want to reflect on each of these possibilities before coming to a conclusion.

DID THE "TOTALITARIAN" MONOLITH RECENTLY FRACTURE?

Communism for a long time was viewed as a monolith directed from deep inside the Kremlin—that on the world stage all communist parties were puppets manipulated from Moscow. Communism was a cancerous growth spreading from the Kremlin according to some mysterious timetable for world domination. This view of communism was very widely held, and all attempts at reform or evidences of diversity were tricks designed to fool the unwary.

The difficulty with this view of communism is that such a monolith never existed. There was heterodoxy rather than unity right from the beginning. It was covered up for a while, but it was always there. All ideologies, including Marxism, are subtly altered when implemented, and, over time, become even more different unless forcibly constrained as was the case for decades in Eastern Europe. Holding together an ideological movement over time is nearly impossible as many non-Marxists have found, and organizations and institutions to hold international communism together have been lacking for decades. Differences between systems and parties (both ruling and nonruling) grew in the past fifty years well beyond the point where reversal was possible.

Why then did so many people act as though it were a monolith? Because the diversity was either not believed or recognized, because the language of communism obscured differences, and because people feared it. Communism was identified with the power of the Soviet Union so much that one observer in 1989 went as far as to claim that communism was born in 1917!² The frequently overstated threat of Soviet weapons was taken as the threat of communism against the "free world."

The veil of secrecy surrounding almost everything in the Soviet Union in the days before *glasnost* helped to perpetuate both the distance and the fear. Phrases like "the iron curtain" helped to solidify the sense of "otherness" in communism that helped to maintain the distance. An entire generation was brought up to believe that there were only two sides: a "we" and a "they," and *both* sides energetically maintained an artificial gulf between the two systems. Like tribal people taught to fear and hate the "others" across the river, children and adults in both camps were indoctrinated and frightened into complying with these tribal sanctions. In America, "soft on communism" became a very powerful weapon to use against intellectuals or political opponents, and to avoid that charge people often made careers based on their opposition to a communism they usually did not understand. Oppressive foreign governments that alleged a similar anticommunism were given economic and military aid by the United States even though those governments were cruelly authoritarian systems that cynically denied their people even a minimum of liberty. This became very confusing because the United States would often support in an anticommunist system (think of El Salvador) what it would otherwise condemn as tyranny in a communist government. Is it any wonder that so many people thought that this evil thing known as communism was a unified system manipulated from deep inside the Kremlin?

The facts tell a different story. For a time the Communist International (1919–1943) imperfectly held parties together and expelled dissidents as though they were heretics. Then the Communist Information Bureau (1947–1956) tried to maintain a sort of European orthodoxy by expelling Yugoslavia and coordinating events in Eastern Europe. But after 1957 no regularly meeting international body acted as a homeostatic mechanism for the communist movement, and unity became hard to find. The only agency creating institutionalized unity between 1958 and 1990 was the *World Marxist Review*, with fifty-two national parties on its editorial council and fourteen on its editorial board. However, some 287 other Marxist-Leninist parties throughout the world were not represented on either the council or the board.³

International All-Party Conferences maintained an illusion of unity until 1960, but it took nine years to call another—so great was the polarization of communist parties over the USSR–China struggle. The Soviet Union wanted unity to condemn China, but it could not get it. Too many parties disagreed. Polycentrism was no longer hidden, and proletarian internationalism disappeared. Disputes hardened into strong differences. A clear example of this change occurred in 1966 in North Korea where Kim Il Sung argued that his "juche" ideology, as he called it, meant a rejection of foreign models and a specifically *Korean* revolutionary practice. Twenty-three years before the dramatic events of 1989, Kim declared that independence un-equivocally. "Communists," he stated, "accept no 'hub' or 'centre' whatsoever in the international communist movement. . . ."[4]

European communist parties also moved away from monocentrism, and the momentum carried polycentrism well beyond the major power con-tenders to the smaller nonruling parties whose needs differed from those of the major communist powers. The Italian Communist Party (PCI), for example, sought power in Italian *elections* rather than through a proletarian revolution. Still calling themselves communists at that time, party members tried to etch out a different path from the one provided by the USSR, a path more reformist than revolutionary.

When an All-Party Conference was finally held in June 1969, cohesion seemed attainable only because China was temporarily unpopular. China had refused to cooperate with the Soviet Union in aiding North Vietnam against the U.S. military, and the ongoing cultural revolution in China dismayed other parties. The timing looked auspicious for a conference con-demnation of China, but the new diversity had made delegates suspicious of *any* agreement with Moscow. Instead of affirming unity, the conference approved diversity and the right of dissent within world communism and strongly affirmed individual party autonomy within the framework of an international fraternity. The concluding document contained some aston-ishing passages two decades before 1989. The following sentence is the clearest: "As there is no leading center of the international communist move-ment, voluntary co-ordination of the actions of Parties in order effectively to carry out the tasks before them acquires increased importance."[5]

Subsequent attempts by Moscow to hold conferences in 1976, 1977, and 1980 were frustrated by the growing diversity. The one clause, "As there is no leading center. . . ," said it very effectively. Polycentrism was definitely and permanently present, but the diversity did not stop there. The unwill-ingness to be dominated by the Soviet Union quietly slipped over into an unwillingness to accept any part of the old proletarian internationalism. Thus, well before Mikhail Gorbachev came to power in March 1985, the old unity was gone. Evolution had already occurred in communism, even though covered up by Soviet leaders and ignored by "totalitarians" who refused to see it.

The major division in the movement for a long time lay between cen-trists loyal to Moscow in the old way, and autonomists who increasingly stressed independence from Moscow and a commitment to pluralist democ-racy and reformism. The Soviet Union, compliant East European parties, Vietnam, and Cuba were in the first group. The second, led by the PCI, in-cluded the Spanish (PCE), British, Swedish, Belgian, Norwegian, Dutch, and Icelandic parties, as well as a brief involvement of the French Communist Party, and about sixteen others. A label developed around these autonomous parties, particularly the more vocal PCE and PCI. The label was "Eurocommunism," a different road to socialism that adapted Marxism-Leninism to the traditions of West European societies and claimed an independence from the Soviet Union that had not previously been thought possible. Euro-communism was an exciting but temporary innovation. Its peak period lasted only two years (1975–1977). Even though in some ways Eurocommunism prefigured later developments, it now seems only historically interesting because its brief strength came solely from the PCI.

Gradually other divisions in world communism became clear, and it may be surprising to realize how many different groupings there were. (See Table 10.1.)

Not even the continuing existence of the Warsaw Treaty Organization maintained unity because the flow of international dialogue depended far more on arms reduction momentum and far less on antiquated defensive alliances. Within communism itself there was an increasing de-ideologizing both within and between countries, and a greater toleration of ambiguity in how others applied or described the Marxist-Leninist heritage. This was particularly true in European communism.

Hence the problem: When one talks about the future of communism is one speaking of some sort of monolithic, unreformable "whole" that never existed and has been quite diverse for decades? If not a "whole," whose communism does one mean? The evolution of communism is not the same thing as a terminal illness. Only people who accepted the totalitarian model could argue this way because the model stated that communism could not reform itself—the only way it could change was to get worse, not better.

Once the notion of disunity is accepted and the possibility of reforming communism is granted, the discussion can move to a firmer plane. Clearly, for example, where communism was imposed by military force, as in most

TABLE 10.1   Major Categories of Marxist-Leninist Parties*

Pro-Soviet parties	110
Eurocommunist parties (mainly 1975–1977)	28
Pro-Chinese	45
Pro-Mao (loyal to Mao but not the Chinese CP)	17
Pro-Albania	22
Pro-Castro	7
Trotskyist parties in the Fourth International	25
Other Trotskyist parties	51

Source: Charles Hobday, *Communist and Marxist Parties of the World* (Essex: Longman Group Ltd., 1986), pp. 395–410.

*Some of the above are factions within parties, so the total number of categories will exceed the total number of parties. Not included: Marxist parties that are not Marxist-Leninist, those that make up the World Socialist Movement, nor the 75 groups conducting guerrilla or terrorist operations across the world with varying degrees of loyalty to Marxism-Leninism or to Marx.

of Eastern Europe, the changes that occurred in 1989/90 spelled the end of communism in that area. Even social democracy will have a difficult time, at least until associations with previous communist administrations are forgotten or forgiven. Additionally, Gorbachev's reduction in militancy around the world encouraged changes in those areas formerly dependent on Soviet military and economic aid, such as Ethiopia, Laos, Angola, Vietnam, and Cuba. The expected drying up of Soviet aid in the 1990s will remove any benefit from opposing necessary democratic and economic reforms. Thus, the future of communism in its present form in these areas is doubtful. In the Soviet Union itself, however, the future of communism is less clear. The Leninist variant of Marxism will decline in significance, but nonauthoritarian socialism/communism will endure for some time. This may also be true in other areas of the world such as China where the old ideology cannot be indefinitely maintained without a military dictatorship.

*   *   *

What one can see in the present is a disappearance of communism in some areas, an altered and declining communism in other areas, and a stubbornly held orthodoxy in still others. The ideology has lost much of its luster and appeal; it is in serious decline, but it has not disappeared.

The lack of unity exhibited by communism for the past few decades means that the rapid evolution of political and economic systems in 1989/90 should not be taken as the demise of communism, but instead as a more open evolution and change. Talking about the end of the whole because of the death of the part is simplistic.

HAS REVOLUTIONARY COMMUNISM DIED?
THE SHINING PATH IN PERU

Substantial changes in communism have occurred in both the Soviet Union and Eastern Europe, from which scholars derive most of their data. It is therefore understandable that scholarly opinion so often incorrectly places communism in the obituary column. But Europe is not the only perspective. Revolutionary communism still exists in the world, and for *those* parts of the world the continued relevance of Marxism-Leninism is not a disappearing phenomenon. The scholar or diplomat entrenched in the latest data from Eastern Europe may shrug off such continued revolutionary activity as unimportant, but, for instance, to the people in Peru the Shining Path guerrillas are highly significant.

Communism as ideological justifier for revolutionary activity may have faded but it is still present. There are approximately seventy-five terrorist or revolutionary groups in the world that are still attempting to implement their particular blend of anti-West, anticapitalist, antiestablishment ideas. Only some of these will be influenced by changes in the Soviet Union and Eastern Europe. Their ideology may not be easily recognizable as Marxism or Marxism-Leninism, and the ideology might seem harsh, but the revolutionary justification dimension of Marx's legacy continues to be quite visible. The Shining Path guerrilla movement in Peru is one example of such a group. Its Marxism-Leninism-Maoist ideology has been altered, as it has been elsewhere, to fit a particular place, and particular circumstances—in this case Peru.

The Shining Path began in 1970 in the department of Ayacucho southeast of Lima, Peru, a region high atop the Andes. The group's full name is the Peruvian Communist Party in the Shining Path of José Carlos Mariategui, and it came to be known simply as *Sendero Luminoso*, or Shining Path. The founder of this party, Abimael Guzman Reynoso (b. 1934), a former professor of philosophy at the University of Huamanga in Ayacucho, received his Ph.D. and a second degree in law from the San Agustin National University in Arequipa.[6]

Abimael Guzman was one of the members of the Communist Party of Peru who broke away in 1964 to form a pro-Chinese faction to protest the "revisionist" Moscow path of a peaceful road to socialism. Guzman found even this pro-China group insufficiently oriented to the peasants, however, and in 1970 he began the Shining Path movement, using his university position as personnel director to recruit radical faculty and students. Guzman's wife, Augusta La Torre, is an important ideologue of the movement, and many members of the Shining Path are women. (In 1982, Edith Lagos was one of the first members to be killed by the Peruvian army.) The 1970s was a decade of building an organization that surfaced in May 1980 during the presidential election in Peru.[7]

The Shining Path is a radical Maoist organization dedicated to the notion of revolution by and for the countryside against all that is represented by the cities. Ideologically, it ties Maoism to its interpretation of the ideas of the founder of Peruvian socialism, José Carlos Mariategui (1894–1930), who believed that the original basis for Peruvian socialism lay in the pre-Columbian peasant community destroyed by Spanish conquerers centuries before. The descendants of this proud people, the Quechua-speaking peasants of today, live in other areas besides Peru, and because of this the Shining Path group can be said to have transnational aspirations that include Argentina, Bolivia, Chile, Ecuador, and perhaps Columbia.

Abimael Guzman became known as the "Fourth Sword of Marxism" following Marx, Lenin, Mao, but most of the thrust of his ideology is derived from Mao's orientation of communism to the peasantry of China. Guzman seeks to destroy the national market economy, industry, the banking system, foreign trade, currency, and the ownership of land beyond a two hectare (4.9 acres) limit. In place of all this would be communal villages and barter exchanges oriented to peasant needs.

The method chosen by Guzman to reach this vague goal is violence directed against the cities (blowing up power lines, bridges, etc.) and against government officials, village administrators, and large landowners (assassinations). Its weapons are dynamite stolen from Peruvian mines and rifles stolen from the police. It receives no outside support and finances itself by bank robberies, taxes on peasants, and a tariff on the distribution of coca—the base of cocaine—partly grown in one of the areas it controls.[8]

The size of the Shining Path movement is not known, but in recent years it established several front organizations, including a newspaper. In one sense it is a cult that treats Guzman as a guru, and in another sense it resembles a racial war between the darker-hued peasants and the fairer-skinned city dwellers. The existence of the group and both army and police action against it resulted in over 17,500 deaths during the 1980s, costing Peru about $15 billion. In 1989, while European communism was altering dramatically, political violence in Peru took the lives of 3,198 people and cost the government some $3.2 billion. The number of reported deaths either for the decade or for 1989 did not include those who have "disappeared" after being arrested by security police.[9] This violent, terroristic atmosphere worsened in 1990. The Shining Path is not a minor phenomenon, and, although it might have difficulty surviving the death of its founder, it is growing rather than shrinking.

Nor is it a local phenomenon within Peru. Sendero is strongest in its base area of Ayacucho and the five mountain states of Peru, but it has virtual control in many other areas. In some localities Sendero appears to operate a parallel state as did the Vietcong from 1965 to 1975 in Vietnam. In Lima, the capital city, Sendero is popular among university students. The walls of the buildings at San Marcos University shout "Long Live the Peoples' War" and various pearls of Guzman's thought.[10]

The Shining Path is not a local phenomenon in another sense. On April 7, 1990, United States civilian pilots flew UH-1H Huey gunships so that Peruvian gunners could fire M-60 machine guns at Shining Path positions in the Upper Huallaga Valley in northcentral Peru. The American presence? Part of the war against drugs: Drug Enforcement Administration agents, pilots and mechanics from the National Air Transport, Inc., and helicopters from the U.S. State Department on loan to the Peruvian national police.[11] The United States also plans to spend some $35 million to finance the construction of a new military training base in the Upper Huallaga Valley where American Green Berets or Special Forces will train and equip six battalions, provide river patrol boats, and refurbish twenty ground-attack jets. Some drug experts on the scene predict a second base for 1991.[12] This prompted Tom Wicker to write his "This Is Where I Came In" column referring to the way in which Americans became ever more thoroughly drawn into the Vietnamese civil war.[13]

This proposed military base is not directed against the extremely wealthy drug lords but against the Shining Path guerrillas in Peru. Do not misunderstand; the point is not to make Sendero an object of sympathy or to choose sides between the Shining Path and the Peruvian Army. The point is that the suggested American base is not directed against drugs as much as it is against the Sendero communism. If the United States wants to stop peasants from coca growing, American aid can build a 350-mile railroad from Lima into the highlands so that Peruvian peasants can profit from food crops the way they now do from coca. Unfortunately, it is easier to send troops.

Revolutionary communists demand their own future, and they probably will as long as the governments they oppose are locked into their own ideological rigidity. In situations of wide gaps between rich and poor and governments interested only in maintaining an oppressive status quo, revolution and its ideological justification will seem the only answer. The Marxist-Leninist-Maoism of the Shining Path guerrillas seems quite distant from original Marxism, but it also indicates continuing flexibility in interpretation and an enduring relevance of revolutionary Marxism. The seventy-four other guerrilla and terrorist organizations around the world also differ widely in their interpretations of Marxism, size, potential for success, and prospects of evolution to less ideological parties, but their existence in the 1990s testifies to the continuing significance of Marx's rejection of the oppressive ruling class and his affirmation of the liberating potential of the oppressed masses. Communism in this understanding of the word remains a specter that still haunts with a vengeance.

*   *   *

Revolutionary communism will continue into the future. These movements that use Marxism or a variety of Marxism to justify wars of liberation show few signs of ending. The Shining Path in Peru is a useful example of such revolutionary activity because it is not affected by changes in European communism or whether Chinese or Cuban communism begins to reform. Its isolation and the difficulty of its struggle protect it from such influences.

THE CHARACTER OF REFORMING SOVIET COMMUNISM: HAS THE DREAM DISAPPEARED?

Marx's dream of a world of equals, as described in Chapter 4, was a nineteenth-century variant of a very old longing for the return of the golden age wherein hierarchies have disappeared. "When Adam delved and Eve

Mikhail S. Gorbachev 1931–

span, who was then the gentleman?" were words that moved peasants to revolt in the fourteenth century and the dream of equality these words represented inspired Thomas More, Thomas Münzer, Gerrard Winstanley, Joachim of Fiora, Francis of Assisi, and many others like Karl Marx. Marx's ideas, however, were the only ones to receive the severe test of prolonged implementation and practice. That practice did *not* demonstrate the full utility of egalitarian ideas. The question asked, therefore, is to the point: Have the failures of various implementations of Marxism caused the dream to disappear? Is the best that Soviet reformers can hope for some sort of convergence with Western politics and economics? Will Soviet reforms end Soviet socialism/communism?

Many people think so. Non-Marxists gloat at the evident failure of authoritarian communism in the Soviet Union while Marxists who have mistakenly accepted the command economy as part of their ideology are alarmed at what seem to be ideological heresies in the USSR.[14] The decline of significance of the CPSU makes what Gorbachev is trying to accomplish seem very different from any sort of Leninist orthodoxy.

Part of the difficulty in comprehending and interpreting events in the USSR is the radical evolution of Gorbachev's ideas. During an initial period from 1985 to 1987 he seemed to feel that comprehensive economic reform was a matter of making speeches. Then he began to make drastic changes that did not stop the economic decline. The democratic reforms that began after the 19th Party Conference in mid-1988 and the constitutional amendments in December 1988 were followed by the implementation of these changes in 1989. Democratic elections created a new government, and in March 1990 Gorbachev as president was given sufficient power to rule the USSR without the CPSU. Political efficacy gradually rose even though the economy continued to deteriorate. The slow pace of economic reform up to this point, however, allowed time for an opposition to economic reform to develop sufficient strength to gut *perestroika* of any real substance.

This curious confusion was abetted by the fact that Gorbachev, even in 1989, reflected a dangerous ambivalence about *perestroika* and his goal. It was clear that he wanted to leave the mistakes (authoritarianism) behind and creatively adapt Marxism to people's present-day needs, but his idea of *perestroika* remained fuzzy enough to make the path to that goal unclear as well.

> Some people reproach us that we have no clear-cut, detailed plan to realize the concept of perestroika. One can hardly agree with the way the question is put. I believe that we would have made a theoretical error if we began to impose ready-made schemes on society again, or tried to squeeze actual life into schemes. This was the characteristic feature of Stalinism with which we have parted ways. . . .
>
> The founders of Marxism never engaged in inventing specific forms and mechanisms for the development of a new society. They developed the socialist

idea, relying on actual social life and the practice of the revolutionary working-class movement of their time.

We now take a wider, deeper and more realistic view of socialism than in the recent past. We view it as a world process in which, along with socialist countries with different stages of socioeconomic and political development, there are also various currents of socialist thought in the rest of the world and some social movements different in their composition and motivation. . . .

Notions of a new aspect of socialism form naturally in the process of identifying and theoretically comprehending the basic requirements and interests of people nowadays. On this basis, it is possible to work out goals and programs adequate to the present-day reality but at the same time oriented toward the future.[15]

Gorbachev's complicated answer essentially stated that socialism should not be written off because some forms of socialism are being discarded, nor because the pre-1985 Soviet form has not worked. Gorbachev argued that not only were these forms not specifically Marxist but they were mistakes that the CPSU was trying to correct. World socialism to Gorbachev, including inputs from the Swedish model of socialism, was seen as a world process moving toward what he called *humane socialism;* which is an orientation toward scientific and technological progress based on people's creative endeavors and the development of democracy.[16]

This would be a difficult-to-implement, nondogmatic Marxism, which very much needs clear, comprehensive economic reforms that turn around the Soviet economy before it reaches absolute chaos. However, in mid-1990, when firm resolve was needed to impose something like the Polish model of rapid reform, Soviet leaders bowed to public opinion and again postponed the stringent measures that are apparently necessary to get the economy moving again.

A certain amount of groping in the dark is not only understandable but commendable. What Gorbachev is attempting to do has never been done before. In a sense it is like turning a large liner at sea—it takes time and much space before the turn is completed. It would certainly help the person at the helm, Gorbachev, to have a clearer idea of the end point of the turn, but he knows far better what he wants to turn away from than he knows where he wants to end up.

In the discussion of the draft platform for the 28th Party Congress, Gorbachev stated that the proposed platform was dedicated to accomplishing the short-term and strategic tasks of Soviet society along lines of the renewal of socialism.[17] What did "renewal of socialism" mean? It meant seeking socialist goals by methods that have worked in other countries and cultures.

We remain committed to the choice made in October 1917, to the socialist idea, but we are moving away from a dogmatic understanding of that idea, refusing to sacrifice people's real interests to schematic constructs. We are setting the task of realizing the principle of social justice step by step, without the slightest illusions or expectations of a quick miracle. We intend to do this by rejecting the prejudices of the past and various ideological taboos and by using everything valuable that exists in other societies, in their economies and social sphere, political life, organization of production and everyday life, science and technology, culture, and spiritual and intellectual creativity. . . .[18]

Soviet communism does not appear to be fading into some kind of convergence with Western economic and political models, but intends to use parts of those models to achieve *socialist* ends. But the words "moving away from a dogmatic understanding of that idea," spoken in 1990 by Gorbachev, meant a move *away* from communism because since 1919 "communism" has been tied to the Leninist, dogmatic version of Marxism. In pulling away from that version, Gorbachev turned away from Lenin and what came to be known as Marxism-Leninism.

In 1918 Lenin changed the name of the Bolsheviks to the Communist Party, and in 1919 he caused the formation of the Third or Communist International, demanding that adhering parties rename themselves "communist." Those decisions separated the two words "socialism" and "communism" more completely than when they stood for different phases of the future society. In rejecting the authoritarian past in the Soviet Union, Gorbachev appeared to be leaping over this separation of the words back to a period when they were more or less interchangeable, allowing the disintegration of the Communist Party of the Soviet Union in order to lead the country to a renewed vision of social democracy. He has already been partially successful.[19]

In presiding over this ideological reformation, Gorbachev simultaneously played the roles of both Pope Leo X and Martin Luther; and just as Martin Luther became a different kind of Christian rather than a new kind of Roman Catholic, so Gorbachev became a different kind of Marxist rather than a new kind of communist. He tried, as Roy Medvedev argued in *Kommunist*, to maintain a Marxism cleansed of Stalinist deformations, rather than reject the whole of Marxism as some of his advisers wanted to do.[20] What confused the issue was that he remained in charge of the Communist party (CPSU).

In part because of Gorbachev's understandable lack of clarity about the extent of his ideological change, public opinion in the USSR became pessimistic and Western observers perplexed. Jeanne J. Kirkpatrick expressed this confusion at a conference in November 1989 when she said that it was difficult to know whether Gorbachev was seeking an end to authoritarian communism (Stalinism and the command economy) or whether he sought the end of socialism itself. Was Gorbachev trying to start where Lenin left off, she asked, or where Alexander Kerensky left off?[21]

Kirkpatrick's way of putting the question did not go far enough on one hand and went too far on the other—outside of the Marxist framework. She made the either/or link between Lenin and the anti-Bolshevik Kerensky, but that was not the issue. Gorbachev could have drawn inspiration from the liberal Bukharin in the late 1920s, which would have had the advantage of maintaining Lenin's position as the revolutionary hero. But what Gorbachev intended was deeper: rejecting the Leninist variant of socialism and aligning himself with a socialism that works, one associated with the man Lenin believed to be socialism's greatest enemy at the turn of the century, Eduard Bernstein, who sought to revise Marxism to fit the needs of the democratically inclined and reformist SPD, discussed in Chapter 5.

Just as Martin Luther found ideological support in St. Augustine, so Gorbachev can find ideological rootage in the Revisionism of Bernstein, in part picked up by the Mensheviks in prerevolutionary Russia. Bernstein (and many Mensheviks) were spokespeople for a form of democratic socialism in which the egalitarian dream was fundamentally conditioned by democratic liberties. Marx and Engels, Gorbachev argued above, did not create specific forms and mechanisms for the development of a new society, and that meant that there weren't any. In rejecting Stalinism, a code word for authoritarian communism, Gorbachev rejected most of Lenin as well, even if he did not want to say so for a while. The division in socialism/communism, prefigured by the split in the Second International between Bernstein and Lenin, was a division between very different interpretations of Marx to support either democratic or authoritarian methods of attaining the socialist future. The Leninist, authoritarian attempt to create that society, however, even though attractive at the time, could not survive the long haul. It placed a revolutionary party in power but gave it little incentive to find nonauthoritarian methods of achieving socialism/communism. In fact, it did not work. The goal was submerged by the method of reaching it. The hope of a world of shared abundance, produced without exploitation and greed, a world without fear with harmoniously working parts, a world of cooperative brothers and sisters at peace with each other was never realized. Instead, after initial progress, authoritarian systems threatened rather than encouraged the development of that new world.

But why didn't it work? Because the command economy, on which far too much reliance was placed, stopped delivering. That threatened the whole ideology and party because, unwisely, the authoritarian ideology and party had identified with the command economy. This was a possibility that had worried Nikita Khrushchev many decades before. Khrushchev believed that competition with capitalism was only possible if the Soviets changed priorities and organization so as to supply food and consumer goods to the public. If capitalism does this better than we do, Khrushchev argued, it will be very difficult to maintain our point of view, and we would, eventually, risk the possibility of a bankrupt ideology.[22] What Khruschev feared had come to pass.

Gorbachev, like Bernstein, seeks a route to the future that works in the present—a market socialism. He wants a route where nonideological egalitarianism balances with liberty—a path that rejects counterproductive authoritarian measures. He still has faith in the egalitarian dream, but reached by a very different method: political pluralism, private property at lower levels of the economy, a free market with flexible prices, and far less state interference in the economy. Some argued that this was no longer Marxism, but as Marxism itself is so riddled with ambiguity it is difficult to specify its boundaries. Bernstein felt that he was still a Marxist, and so does Gorbachev. The humanism in Marxism that Marx himself did not always acknowledge gives the dream continued life despite the fact that new economic methods have to be found. Thus the holders of the dream grope for answers and hope that, this time, they will get it right. As long as this attitude lasts, socialism/communism has a future, even if the CPSU and the old ideology disappear. The vision of the future will no longer dominate the present. Instead, a pragmatic present will create its own future.

*   *   *

The egalitarian dream continues as does the faith in creatively applied Marxism as the vehicle for that dream. In the Soviet Union, however, those vague aspirations for the future are sought through democratic and free-market methods. This means the end of the authoritarian variant of Marxism in the Soviet Union—the end of communism as it has come to be understood since 1919. But these enormous changes do not diminish the importance of the egalitarian dream. Although it is certainly possible in the next decade for the dream to be once again absorbed by the method, it is still distinct at present. In any event, the ideology that was once narrowed to one man once again has a widened focus.

AFTERWORD

If these interpretations are proven correct, the future will reveal remnants of the old authoritarian communism, such as the Shining Path, while the creative force behind the dream increasingly becomes identified with the socialism rejected by both Lenin and the Third International in 1920. In this sense the future should see the end of Leninism and the emergence of a less ideological socialism/communism compatible with coalition politics, environmental protection, democratic governments, and relatively free markets on a global scale.

The nonauthoritarian path would increasingly invite a blend of Adam Smith and Karl Marx: liberty balanced with egalitarianism in a workable social democracy where ideological authoritarianism has given way to pragmatism and flexibility. The goal will then become not a future aspiration but a present achievement.

NOTES

1. David C. Unger, "European Marxism, 1848–1989," *The New York Times* (December 4, 1989), p. 26.

2. Andre Chambraud, *L'Evenement du Jeudi*, reprinted and translated from the Paris leftist weekly as "Testing Time for Both Socialism and Communism," *World Press Review*, 36, no. 12 (December 1989):12.

3. Charles Hobday, compiler, *Communist and Marxist Parties of the World*, a Keesing's Reference Publication (Essex: Longman Group Ltd, 1986), pp. 395–407.

4. Kim Il Sung, "The Present Situation and the Tasks of Our Party," October 5, 1966, *On Juche in Our Revolution*, vol. 1 (Pyongyang: Foreign Languages Publishing House, 1975), excerpted from pp. 559–561.

5. *Documents Adopted by the International Conference of Communist and Workers' Parties, 5–17 June 1969* (Moscow: Novosti Press Agency Publishing House, n.d.), p. 63.

6. Some details derived from Gordon H. McCormick, "The Shining Path and Peruvian Terrorism," a Rand Corporation paper published in January 1987.

7. Ibid., pp. 2, 5, 9.

8. Ibid.; also Kathryn Leger, "Peru's Maoist rebels target ruling party," *Christian Science Monitor* (October 15, 1987), p. 11; Alan Riding, "Peruvian Guerrillas Emerge as an Urban Political Force," *The New York Times* (July 17, 1988), p. 1; Clara Germani, "Peru's Guerrilla War Hits Higher Pitch," *Christian Science Monitor* (August 17, 1988), p. 7; Kathryn Leger, "Peru's Rebels Flourish in Drug Zone," *Christian Science Monitor* (May 12, 1989), p. 3. "Peru Holds 15,000 in Killing of Ex-Defense Chief," *The New York Times* (January 11, 1990), p. 8; and James Brooke, "Terror Attacks in Peru Drive Foreigners Out of Hinterland, *The New York Times* (January 15, 1990), p. 5.

9. James Brooke, "Ex-Defense Chief of Peru is Killed," *The New York Times*, January 10, 1990, p. 1.

10. Tina Rosenberg, "To the Victor Will Go the Spoiled in Peru," *The Washington Post Weekly Edition* (April 30–May 6, 1990), p. 23.

11. James Brooke, "Anti-Drug Pilots in Peru Battle Guerrillas," *The New York Times* (April 12, 1990), p. 1.

12. James Brooke, "U.S. Will Arm Peru To Fight Leftists in New Drug Push," *The New York Times* (April 22, 1990), p. 1.

13. Tom Wicker, "This Is Where I Came In," *The New York Times* (April 22, 1990), p. 19.

14. Sam Marcy, *Perestroika: A Marxist Critique* (New York: WW Publishers, 1990), p. x.

15. Taken from "Excerpts from Pravda Article by Gorbachev," *The New York Times* (November 27, 1989), p. 8.

16. Mikhail Gorbachev, *Perestroika* (New York: Harper & Row, 1987), p. 170.

17. Mikhail Gorbachev, *Pravda* (February 6, 1990), pp. 1–2, condensed translation by *Current Digest of the Soviet Press*, 42:6, (March 14, 1990):4.

18. Ibid.

19. Because the media understandably concentrate on conflict situations, news of successful political developments in the Soviet Union tends to be underreported. See Randy Kritkausky, *"The Perestroika TV Doesn't See,"* *Christian Science Monitor* (November 15, 1989), p. 19.

20. Roy Medvedev, *Kommunist* No. 7, 1990, cited in Vera Tolz and Elizabeth Teague, "Tsipko Urges Ridding Soviet Society of Marxist Ideology," *Report on the USSR* Radio Liberty vol 2, [June 8, 1990] p. 5. Also see Elizabeth Teague, "Gorbachev Aide Jettisons Communism, Cuts Marx Down to Size," *ibid.,* p. 1.

21. Jeanne J. Kirkpatrick, "The End of a Utopian Vision," *The Failure of Communism: The Western Response* (Munich: Radio Free Europe/Radio Liberty Fund, Inc., 1989), p. 36.

22. Strobe Talbott, trans. and ed., *Khrushchev Remembers: The Last Testament* (Boston: Little Brown & Co., 1974), p. 146.

DISCUSSION QUESTIONS

1. Why is it so difficult to determine whether or not communism is dying? Is it a matter of semantics? Explain.
2. Has capitalism evolved in the twentienth century the way communism has? Give examples.
3. Describe the ideology of the Shining Path. Why would these ideas either appeal to or not appeal to someone living in Peru?
4. Name six major groupings of Marxist-Leninist parties in 1986.
5. Has the egalitarian dream of communism died? Why or why not?
6. What specifically does it mean to suggest that Gorbachev is a latter-day Eduard Bernstein?
7. What is the danger involved in the American presence in Peru?
8. Why would a railroad be a better idea in Peru than the Special Forces?

Glossary

1. **Alienation**   An old word that has had a variety of meanings in its long history. The Latin version refers to the legal transfer of property, or, in a medical sense, a mental disorder. However, alienation in the modern context was first used in philosophy, specifically German Idealism, in the sense of an unnatural separation between entities that belonged together. In particular, alienation referred to the unaware externalizing of self or reason. Hegel used the concept to describe the unnecessary gap between the created world of cultural institutions and the self, which was not aware of that world as an encompassing self-creation. Hegel's philosophy was based on this notion of historical alienation; human history was the arena in which that alienation was overcome. Ludwig Feuerbach placed alienation in a religious context by describing God as an externalization of human essence, whose perceived distance from the human measured the depth of alienation. The human essence had to be pulled back to overcome the problem. Feuerbach also argued that Hegelianism itself contributed to alienation by abstracting human reason and then acting as though it were a living thing. This was true, Feuerbach thought, even though all activity of Hegel's World Reason took place in the consciousness of real people.

   Marx accepted the Feuerbachian analysis and went beyond it to describe alienation in a materialistic sense, as found particularly in human labor, symbolized by the proletariat. The creative force of a person's life, Marx felt, stood apart from that person as an external, alien object, confronting humans as a nonhuman other. The proletarian revolution would overcome this alienation by abolishing classes and by socializing the means of production.

   The term can be generalized to refer to a human sense of lostness in the complex urban environment of industrial societies. It can also be used as a Marxist critique of existing communist societies as not having overcome alienation. Leaders of these regimes have not welcomed such criticism.

2. **Anarchism**   Translating the word loosely from the Greek, it is the denial of the *arche*, the overriding principle of organization, and thus denial of the state. Anarchists in the late eighteenth and nineteenth centuries demanded a natural form of social organization and sought revolution as a method of ridding society of unnatural forms of human organization, such as the state or any organization requiring coercion for its continued existence. Liberty, equality, and fraternity could not exist simultaneously with the state. The anarchists formed a part, frequently an unstable part, of the socialist movement in the nineteenth century.

Some anarchists stressed individualism, for example, William Godwin (1756–1836), Pierre Joseph Proudhon (1809–1865), and Max Stirner (1806–1856). Others were known more for their collectivist variants, such as Mikhail Bakunin (1814–1876) and Pyotr Kropotkin (1842–1921). However, the distinction should not be taken too seriously. Proudhon, for example, advocated a mutualism of economic interchange that was not too far from Kropotkin's idea of mutual aid. In addition, anarchists varied on the need for violence. Bakunin was in favor of violence as the means to gain the stateless future, while Godwin and Leo Tolstoy (1828–1920) stressed a nonviolent, ethical variant.

Marxism and anarchism have much in common, but the firmly voiced need for an authoritative dictatorship of the proletariat after the revolution separated the two groups. They often fought with each other while at the same time admiring each other. Disputes between Bakunin and Marx allegedly broke up the First International.

Anarchists stressed individual liberties so much that they had a difficult task forming any sort of unified movement. Anarchism was, nonetheless, very influential in Italy and Spain, as well as in France. Frustrated anarchists sometimes became assassins, and this terrorist label was applied to the whole movement. The cartoon figure of an evil man ready to throw a bomb came to symbolize the whole of anarchism.

3. **Babeuf, François Noel** (1760–1797)   One of the leaders of the Conspiracy of Equals who failed to overthrow the conservative French government in 1796. Babeuf, or Graccus, stood for an agricultural communism that was achieved by destroying private property rather than equalizing it. He is sometimes called the father of European communism because of his emphasis on the abolition of property, and he deserves the title for having moved beyond the vague ideas of equality in the French revolutionary period to the position that equality of consumption could occur only if regulated by the community as a whole. This regulation would require a temporary dictatorship after power had been seized in order to bring about the primitive equality for the whole society.

After Babeuf's death, his ideas were changed from agricultural to industrial communism and transmitted to other early nineteenth century radicals by Philippe Michel Buonarrotti (1761–1837), an Italian born, naturalized French citizen who had been a Babeuf disciple. Babeuf's roots had lain in the Jacobin movement and in the philosophy of Jean Jacques Rousseau, and Buonarrotti helped to bring this tradition forward to such people as Louis Auguste Blanqui, a contemporary of Marx.

4. **Blanqui, Louis Auguste** (1805–1881)   A French radical in the Babeuvist tradition, Blanqui was influential on the French left and spent half of his life in prison because of his revolutionary activities. Some consider him the originator of the concept of the dictatorship of the proletariat but there are reasons to think that he may have picked this up from the Babeuvists. In any case there is suffi-

cient ambiguity about his notion of *proletariat* to argue that a debate about who thought of what first is moot. Blanqui equated proletarian with *toiler*, somewhat like modern uses of the term do, and toilers to Blanqui included peasants, then a majority of the French population. He advocated first gaining the dictatorship and then appealing to the more conservative French peasants, which sounded like a minority dictatorship in the name of the majority. This latter position is the one normally attributed to Blanqui, usually pejoratively, linking Blanqui with other authoritarian radicals in a Jacobin-Babeuvist-Blanquist tradition of armed seizure of power by a minority, a tradition to which Lenin's name would later be added. Blanqui's influence was much stronger than Marx's in the Paris Commune of 1871.

5. **Bourgeoisie** (n.), **bourgeois** (adj.)   A term used by Marxists to denote the ruling class in a capitalist mode of production. It is, however, a fairly loose term that is sometimes used as a synonym for the middle class. In theory, the bourgeoisie was the agent class of the earlier revolution that broke the feudalist mode of production and opened the way for capitalism's full development. The bourgeoisie was, therefore, the ruling class of the capitalist era; it owned the means of production and needed the proletariat in order to produce. The ideology of the bourgeoisie is classical liberalism, an ideology discarded at the first sign of a threat to bourgeois power. Lurking below the surface of the liberalism and progressive character of bourgeois society, in other words, lay a reactionary proclivity to an authoritarian defense of privilege.

As a synonym for *enemy*, the term becomes more difficult when the owners of the means of production include small stockholders who themselves work for a living and do not just use capital to make more money, as in Marx's version. Partly for this reason, Bernstein's Revisionism appeared at the end of the nineteenth century.

6. **Bukharin, Nikolai Ivanovich** (1888–1938)   A Russian Bolshevik of considerable reputation and influence. He became a Bolshevik in 1906, experienced several arrests and exiles, participated in socialist groups in Europe, and emigrated to the United States in 1916, where he edited a Russian-language newspaper in New York with Trotsky. He returned to Russia in 1917 and led the Moscow uprising, but, unlike Stalin, Bukharin did not always follow the official line of the party set by Lenin or, later, by Stalin. He was to the left of Lenin in 1917 and 1918, supporting the workers' opposition, for example. In 1921, he fully approved the New Economic Policy, as well as the emphasis on socialism in one country that helped Stalin against Trotsky. In 1928, he did not want to relinquish the NEP in favor of Stalin's rapid industrialization plans and fell out of favor with the dictator. Bukharin disappeared from public view, was arrested in 1937, and executed in 1938. He had made substantial contributions to Lenin's theoretical development and was an old Bolshevik with stature, both of which Stalin had difficulty tolerating.

7. **Cadres**   A framework or organization principle that was used in the 1790s by the French revolutionary government when it needed to incorporate many new and raw recruits into its military, without the old aristocracy, to form an officer corps. The term came to mean the skilled leadership of inexperienced people. Later, in countries administered by a minority party, cadre was used to refer to the skilled group leading the rest in some local situation. The need to take great care in cadre selection caused the development of the *nomenklatura* system described below.

8. **Class**   A word that became quite important in the late eighteenth and early nineteenth centuries when it denoted one's role in the production process rather

than simply a rank or position within society. Saint-Simon, Babeuf, and Lorenz von Stein, among others, described nineteenth-century society as a two-class milieu, to which Marx and others added the idea of conflict between the two classes as the motor of history. The result was a dynamic social system wherein class antagonism was the expression of conflict arising out of the mode of production, resulting from the divisions of classes into owners and nonowners of property (or the means of production). Marx was aware that there were classes other than the two major ones, but he paid them scant attention. Examples of the other classes would be the petite bourgeoisie (small business people) and the lumpenproletariat (the dregs of the working class).

9. **Class consciousness**   An awareness of one's class position in society coupled with a desire to end oppression by the eradication of class stratification. To Marx and Engels, class consciousness connoted revolutionary readiness in the proletariat, but Lenin determined that working-class consciousness would plateau at the trade union level, far short of revolutionary attitudes. The term evolved along with the word *proletariat* to apply in preindustrial societies to desires of oppressed peoples, expressed by the cadre party, to overthrow the conditions of their dependence.

10. **Collectivization of agriculture**   Marx believed that agriculure in the postrevolutionary society would operate in the same way as factories—by collective, coordinated labor. In actual practice, however, Marxism was applied to societies where capitalism had yet to be developed, and the collectivization of agriculture became a means of rural *control*, allowing food surpluses to be extracted and exported to pay for industrialization. Collectivization normally is a coercive combining of formerly private farms into a single entity that is assigned heavy production quotas by the state and that suffers from a lack of agricultural investment during periods of intensive industrialization.

11. **Cominform**   A shorthand way of writing Communism Information Bureau, an organization founded in September 1947 in Poland as a regional international group composed of delegates from the USSR, Yugoslavia, Hungary, Poland, Czechoslovakia, Bulgaria, and Romania, as well as from the Italian and French Communist parties. It was formally dissolved in April of 1956. Its headquarters in the beginning were in Belgrade, before Tito's Yugoslavia was ousted in 1948.

    Each country's central committee sent two delegates to the organization, which sought an exchange of information between countries and a continuation of contacts between lower-level leaders. A journal was published that expressed Moscow's version of events, permitting an official line to be promulgated in the absence of any other organization.

    The ouster of Yugoslavia resulted from Stalin's displeasure with Tito and caused the headquarters to be moved to Bucharest, Romania. The Cominform organization was dissolved in 1956 in an atmosphere of détente with the West, pro-Tito sentiment by Khrushchev, and a sense that it had outlived its purpose.

12. **Commodity production**   The word *commodity* in Marxist parlance refers to a product of human labor that embodies a particular social relation, depending on the mode of production of that specific stage of human history. A commodity can be produced for use or for exchange. Since early history, however, commodity production for exchange has led to an increasing gap between producer and goods produced, making commodity production, particularly in capitalism, synonymous with alienation. The embodiment of human labor, the product, confronts one as an alien object rather than as something one has produced oneself. The term is used most frequently with reference to capitalism and is often used pejoratively to express alienating relations of property.

13. **Cooperative**   A voluntary or involuntary association of persons for the sake of jointly conducting specific affairs. Normally the gains of the activity are enhanced by the cooperative effort and this is the motivation for the organization. It can be a producer or consumer cooperative or even a group set up to fight fires in a local area. Marx felt that the cooperative principle was too general to overcome capitalism, and in authoritarian communist systems the rural cooperative is sometimes seen as a preliminary step toward full collectivization. Voluntary cooperatives often have the flavor of grass-roots democracy, whereas involuntary ones find themselves at the bottom of a chain of centralized commands.

14. **Cult of the personality**   A phrase normally used with reference to either Stalin or Mao Zedong. In a more generalized form, the expression stands for a dictatorship in which the autocrat receives adulation well beyond the limits of common sense. The personality cult violates the principle of collegial rule which is supposed to operate and normally does. The principle of collegiality does not prevent a centralization or focus of power in one person, but it does mean that decisions are collective ones. The limitations on Khrushchev, for example, visible in the changes he tried to make in the USSR, or the later constraints on Brezhnev, visible in the preliminary period before the invasion of Czechoslovakia, reflect this collegiality that operates even though both Khrushchev and Brezhnev appeared to be dictators. Hero worship allows a person to rule *without* the party apparatus. This was evidently by choice for Stalin, but for Mao Zedong a necessity considering the opposition he had within the CCP.

15. **Democratic centralism**   A principle of organization applied to all communist parties modelled after Lenin's Bolsheviks. Basically the concept sought to combine democracy and centralism by permitting debates to occur on various issues prior to a decision by party leaders, but not afterward. Once the decision was made, a party member's only response was obedience. The chance to disagree or debate the issue was foreclosed by the decision.

    Like all ideas, this worked imperfectly in practice. Democracy was too easily overshadowed by centralism, particularly during crisis times when decisions had to be made quickly, and a military kind of discipline resulted that was later reinforced by the Stalin economic model. In theory, lower levels of the party elect representatives to meet in higher-level groups, all the way up to the top. But, in practice, the top has selected delegates for the lower levels to choose. This trend away from democracy and toward centralism was facilitated by the Tenth Party Congress decision against factionalism in 1921.

16. **Dialectics**   The dialectic began as a device by which a philosopher could lead a person in the search for truth by arousing mental conflict between one's perceptions and a challenging reality. The goal was the discovery of truth, and the method became a balancing of opposites needing resolution. With Aristotle, the concept became formalized and a part of logic. When Hegel hypostatized that logic, the dialectic became the manner in which the universe itself evolved. Conflict between positions, ideas, forces, and people *demanded* resolution, and this pushed history forward. Marx moved the dialectic into the material world as description of the resolution of antagonistic conflict between the owners and nonowners of the means of production. Sometimes this is described as Thesis meeting Antithesis resulting in Synthesis. Although overly simplified, this triadic formulation is a useful way of understanding the underlying process.

17. **Dialectical materialism**   Friedrich Engels in particular expanded the understanding of the dialectic process from history into the world of nature and science as an objective law of evolutionary development. In the world of nature the human is not surrounded by "things" so much as by "processes," and those

processes develop dialectically through the resolution of conflict into higher forms, continually and inevitably. Such an expansion of inevitability affected historical materialism because it seemed to increase determinism at the expense of human voluntarism. Dialectical materialism underscored the inevitable progress of the dialectical, historical process and gave an aura of "science" to socialism—a sense of inevitable triumph of the socialist cause as events and forces worked out their internal destiny. Scientific socialism as a concept arose from this kind of thinking.

18. **Fetish**   An inanimate object that is accorded animate, usually human powers. Marx used the word to refer to inanimate things to which humans gave powers from themselves. These objects then confronted the human as powerful others, contributing to alienation. Examples are money, treated as though it has power in its own right, and commodity production, which creates objects confronting the laborer as other when in fact they were created by human labor. A thought-provoking example might well be communism itself, often treated by the West as an evil force having supernatural powers.

19. **Finance capitalism**   An important prerequisite for monopoly capitalism. The phrase was useful in the description of the mechanics of imperialism as Lenin developed his ideas around 1916. It refers to that part of the expansion of capitalism where central banking interests play a very important role in financing capitalist expansion and coordinating the formerly loose character of capitalist production.

20. **Fourth International**   An anti-Stalinist international organization formed by Trotsky and his disciples, called Trotskyists, in September 1938. The organization was crippled almost immediately by the outbreak of World War II and by the assassination of Trotsky in 1940. The Fourth International never became numerically or politically significant except in very local situations.

21. *Glasnost*   The root of this Russian word (glas) is eye, the organ of sight. Combinations of the root with various suffixes could mean eyelash, eye glasses, etc. A frequent connotation of the root word is doing something in the sight of someone else, and thus *glasnost* means publicity or openness. The word's prominence began with the emergence of Mikhail Gorbachev in 1985, and implied a greater freedom to express diverse opinions in public. The concept was off to a slow start, however, until the impossibility and danger of suppressing news of the 1986 Chernobyl nuclear accident made it possible to publicize information unflattering to the Soviet Union's image of itself, such as disasters or civil unrest. After 1986, *glasnost* expanded to become an integral part of *perestroika*. Investigative jounalism and far greater information sharing by the Soviet government has led to public opinion polling that is taken quite seriously by authorities. Even *Pravda*, a formerly boring CPSU newspaper that was usually used as toilet paper, is now eagerly read for news. Public and special interest groups, and ethnic rivalry have all increased due to *glasnost.*

22. **Humanism**   A much misunderstood word, *humanism* can refer to classical Greek and Roman studies as a variant of the word *humanities* found in most university catalogs. More often, however, it refers to an emphasis on humans and specifically human solutions to problems that can be either a seeking of the deity's goals through work that benefits the human condition or an insistence on humans solving their own problems without reference to any outside agency such as a transcendental deity.

Nothing intrinsic to the word humanism, therefore, indicates atheism. A Christian or Moslem humanism is quite possible. With Feuerbach and Marx, however, a return to the human of the essence earlier given to the deity meant that religion had to be abolished *in order that a truly human existence could occur.*

This meant that atheism was the other side of the humanist coin—one could not be conceived without the other, but it was the humanism that was emphasized. Those opposed to Marxism emphasize the atheism and ignore the humanism.

23. **Idealism**   A philosophic position of long historical significance that seeks to locate reality in idea rather than in matter. Idealism understands the world of things as an approximation of ideas or as a particular manifestation of a universal apprehended only in the mind. Philosophical idealism is not a romantic, utopian kind of thinking, but rather is a statement about where basic reality is located—in spirit or idea rather than in matter. Plato and Hegel were prominent idealists.

24. **Marxism-Leninism**   Marxism as understood and applied by Lenin. The success of the Bolsheviks in seizing and holding onto power in Russia created a patina of correctness over Marxism-Leninism that was then reinforced by expected conformity within the Communist International. Marxism-Leninism came to mean the applicability of Marxism to less-developed societies, an antiimperialist force, and a means of organizing liberation movements. Its chief impact, therefore, has been in the underdeveloped world where the concept of revolution led by a party in the name of the proletariat through a violent insurrection has had great appeal. Marxism–Leninism was the official ideology of the Soviet Union.

25. **Materialism**   Like idealism, materialism is a philosophical position that seeks to locate basic reality. Unlike idealism, however, materialism finds reality in physical matter. Ideas reflect material reality rather than the other way around. Marx's materialism de-idealized Hegelianism. The advantage of materialism is that it describes measurable phenomena rather than abstractions, although it can become an abstraction in itself.

26. **Means of production**   The productive forces of any society. Laborers and instruments of production, such as simple or complex machinery and tools, constitute the means of producing the wherewithal of social survival. Obviously, owning the means of production gives great power to the owning class.

27. **Mode of production**   The way the means of production are organized or coordinated in a given period. The mode of production determines the relationships within the production process. The components of the relationship are labor, workers, products, tools, techniques, and ownership. A given mode of production expresses definite relationships between and among these elements. For instance, a product may be collectively or privately owned, produced by individual artisans working alone or by collective labor in a factory system, and produced for exchange or for use, that is, for the satisfaction of needs without the intervening market. Marx wrote that the organization of productive forces has traditionally been characterized by a basic division of labor that separates the owners and nonowners of the means of production into two antagonistic classes. The mode of production periodically undergoes a transformation through changes in commodity exchange and technology, laying the basis for social revolution.

28. **Monopoly capitalism**   The stage in capitalism's historical development where ruthless competition reduces the number of capitalists and concentrates capital in the hands of the few who own most of the productive forces. When finance capitalism is added, monopoly capitalism becomes a major component of late capitalism in its imperialist phase—so characterizing the entire economy that the developed nation stands over the underdeveloped nation as the bourgeoisie does to the proletariat. In the absence of imperialism, or as a result of the breakdown of imperialism, monopoly capitalism is part of the death throes

of the capitalist mode of production. Its efficient economy of scale has increasingly made human labor superfluous, thus decreasing the rate of profit, increasing both the size of the industrial reserve army and the potential gravity of inevitable crises because unemployed workers make very poor consumers.

29. **Negation (of the negation)**   A philosophical concept older than Hegel but used by him particularly to mean denying the denier, or negating the negator—the completion of the dialectical drive involving as well a return to the beginning of the process. Marx used the concept to refer to the abolition of private property in the proletarian revolution, or the expropriating of the expropriator. Private property in this sense negates human life by artificially alienating it. Abolishing private property thus denies the negator. Since Marx derived the idea from Hegel, it is fair to ask whether Marx also intended the negation of the negation to represent a return to the beginning. There is a reluctance in Marxism to admit this, but historical materialism does seem to suggest that all of history represents a departure from and a return to primitive communism *plus* the technological achievements of the intervening centuries. Later, Engels extended the concept in dialectical materialism to the world of nature and science. Lenin and other Soviet philosophers have sought to continue this tradition.

30. *Nomenklatura*   A list of high party and state offices organized in terms of which level of the Communist party is responsible for appointing people to them. The word is shorthand for appointment from the top down by administrative bodies that are at some distance from the activity represented. For example, the party Central Committee normally has a long list of positions that it must fill, including heads of Central Committee departments, editors of party newspapers, first secretaries of regional party organizations, high state officials, and high military personnel. Regional party levels will also have responsibility for high appointments in their areas, as will district and city party organizations. Nomenklatura is a method of maintaining tight control over both party and state officials who have any real responsibility in the society. It can also be the vehicle for patronage and nepotism.

31. **Paris Commune of 1871**   A revolutionary socialist organization in Paris that formed immediately after French forces surrendered to the Prussians in the Franco-Prussian War. The Commune attempted to extend federations of autonomous communities throughout France. Some interpreted it as the final outcome of the French Revolution of 1789; others saw it as the precursor of proletarian revolutionary activity, a preliminary step that culminated in the 1917 October Revolution in Russia.

   However it was interpreted, its ideological impact on socialism was profound for generations. The Commune began in March of 1871 out of the determination of Paris not to surrender to the Prussians. Radical sentiments were exacerbated by food shortages, and patriotism was stimulated by the weakness of Adolphe Thiers and the French National Assembly. The Commune was dominated by Jacobin and Blanquist influences and received strong initial support from the population. Part of the fascinating story of the Commune is the internal struggle between socialist radical democracy and the more centrist Jacobinism, with the latter eventually triumphing. Nearly twenty thousand people died before the central Versailles government reasserted its control in May 1871. The bloody suppression of the communards created martyrs and gave the Commune extended ideological life.

   Marxism was not a major influence in the Commune. Besides Jacobinism and Blanquism, the ideas of Proudhon and Saint-Simon were more in evidence than the ideas of Marx. Some of the radicals, however, were members or delegates to the First International of which Marx was a principal leader. Many of the communards were not from the working class, and this fact marks an early indication of elasticity in the word *proletariat.*

32. ***Perestroika***   A Russian word normally translated as restructuring, redoing, or reforming. Its vagueness promises more than is normally deliverable, and its overuse by Soviet leaders has led to cynicism in the general public. Normally, *perestroika* refers to a comprehensive restructuring of the command economy, but the word has also been used to describe political and social reforms such as occurred in 1989 and 1990. Both *perestroika* and the word *glasnost* became key words in the Gorbachev era.

33. **Private property**   In the Marxist sense private property is property that separates people from their natural essence as humans. Private property is the result of already existing alienation, and, once it is introduced, it becomes a profound exacerbator of that alienation. Private property ultimately results in the externalization of the human essence in material commodities. One's life becomes a race to acquire, like an addict seeking that which destroys the self, and one's comparative personal worth is measured by those acquisitions. In a sense, communism can be defined as the abolition of this kind of separating, alienating, harming private property. The goal of that abolition is the reacquisition of the social human essence. Because such private property is particularly visible in the productive process, socialization of the means of production is necessary.

34. **Proletariat**   This word refers particularly to the working class in an industrial society. In Marx's analysis, however, that working class represented more than a class in society. Thus, proletariat also stood for nonowners of the means of production in the capitalist division of labor and, therefore, was also a symbol of the "oppressed." The proletariat represented alienation in the earthly sphere as religion did for Marx in the heavenly sphere. To end its class oppression, the proletariat must end its class existence, and in so doing it would end alienation for all people. The word stood for a great deal more than simply "industrial working class," which helps to explain how it could be so expandable in post-Marx revolutionary situations.

35. **State capitalism**   Although this term refers to a capitalist society in which the government plays an important role in the economy, it is normally used as a pejorative description of allegedly socialist societies. Although the means of production have been socialized, the poverty of the country and the authoritarianism of the revolutionary party combine to create rapid economic growth controlled by the state. This economic growth seeks capital formation just as Western capitalism does, but by a different means. Thus, many socialist countries give every appearance of being capitalist, with the state's bureaucrats functioning as entrepreneurs. Although this sounds deplorable to a Marxist, it has an appeal to underdeveloped countries that wish to "catch up" with the industrialized world without sharing power with a new bourgeoisie.

36. **Superstructure**   In a Marxist sense, the term refers to the forms of society constructed on the economic foundation. In this view, the institutions of any society such as law, religion, morality, marriage, property, and so forth reflect the economic base in a given period. Even the consciousness of people in that period—how one thinks of oneself and of others—is conditioned by that economic foundation. Changes in the economic foundation cause changes in the superstructure even though the causative arrows do not simply go one way. Superstructure could influence economic base, but the predominant direction of influence is from economic foundation to superstructure.

37. **Surplus value**   The notion of surplus value was an important part of Marx's

analysis of capitalism. According to the labor theory of value, the monetary value of any article is a reflection of the amount of socially necessary labor time expended in its manufacture. Supply and demand pressures are understood as creating fluctuations from the average value determined by labor time. Something that took four hours of socially necessary labor time to make is worth twice the value of an article taking only two hours.

Costs to a capitalist factory owner are both fixed and variable. Fixed costs include raw materials and machinery; variable costs refer to wages. By not paying the worker for some of the daily toil, the capitalist has a commodity with value that in part cost nothing to produce. Selling it, therefore, brings profits. Surplus value refers particularly to that unremunerated labor time in which the values created by the worker are "surplus" in the sense that payment for them was not made. Thus, profits are indeed theft from the workers, but without them capitalism could not perform its necessary historical function.

38. **Totalitarianism** A term popularized by Carl Friedrich and Zbigniew Brzezinski in their book, *Totalitarian Dictatorship and Autocracy*, first published in 1956 by Harvard University Press. Although they sought to provide a purely descriptive model of communist and fascist systems, the term they used for this model could not, at the same time, avoid taking on a pejorative connotation. The authors felt that communist and fascist societies represented something quite new in human history. They were characterized by six elements: (1) an officially adopted, elaborate ideology focused on a perfected future; (2) a single mass party consisting of a small minority of the population and led by a dictator; (3) a technologically modern system of terroristic rule through party and secret police; (4) a near-complete control of all forms of mass communication; (5) a near-complete monopoly of effective weapons of armed combat; and (6) a bureaucratically organized and centrally controlled economy.

Thousands of words were written in support of or in opposition to this model and much of the discussion really revolved around the pejorativeness of the model rather than its specific components. In general, the model describes the Stalinist period in the USSR quite well, but is a weaker characterization of both fascist systems and subsequent Soviet leadership. For a time, however, to be for or against the totalitarian model was a litmus test of one's left or right ideological position.

39. **Trotsky, Leon** (Lev Davidovich Bronstein; 1879–1940) One of the most influential people in the Bolshevik Revolution and the decade that followed. He was already an active revolutionary in 1903 when the Bolsheviks and Menshiviks split. Trotsky was against Lenin during that discussion and, for a time, sought to mediate between the two groups. He became an active Bolshevik during the 1917 radical period after the March Revolution, and he came in as a leader. He was resented by most other top Bolsheviks for at least two reasons. First, he was a success. His skills as a speaker helped bring about the Bolshevik seizure of power, and his organizing ability created and inspired the new Red Army that defeated the White forces in the civil wars from 1918 and 1921. Second, Trotsky was an arrogant person, according to reports, who let others know that he considered them inferior. He was unwilling to take the position that Lenin wanted him to have, a sort of vice-presidential position to be shared with two others, that would have given him an institutional status for assuming power when Lenin became ill and died. He was absent from Moscow when Lenin died in January 1924, and his absence, his lack of institutional position other than as army commander, and the resentments of other leaders allowed Stalin to slip into a leadership vacuum that Trotsky himself helped create.

After Stalin forced him out, Trotsky became a rallying point for a pro-Lenin but anti-Stalin Bolshevism, began the Fourth International, and wrote extensively. He was murdered in Mexico City in 1940.

40. **Utopian socialism**   A variant of socialism that Marx disliked. He shied away from it for two reasons: first, it usually spelled out the precise detail of the future, thus locking the future into the image of the futurist; and, second, it failed to tie socialism into the necessary flow of historical development. These two tendencies made it a socialism of the imagination. The capacity of utopian socialist, however, to stimulate revolutionary attitudes among the working class was undeniable. Marx may not have liked them but they were extremely influential.

41. **War communism**   The type of government evident in the 1918–1921 Soviet period when the introduction of socialist and antisocialist measures through governmental decrees established a rigid control of the society made necessary by the need to fight a war of survival. Under war communism one sees a weakening of the socialist aspects and a strengthening of the authoritarian aspects of the society. Such periods, which normally follow the seizure of power, are marked by censorship of news media, abolition of opposition parties, and active counterrevolutionary effort. The major problem of war communism is the difficulty one has later in dismantling the antiliberal authoritarianism once it is in place.

42. **Warsaw Pact**   A military grouping of the European socialist bloc in the Warsaw Treaty Organization. Founded in 1955, the Warsaw Pact is a mutual defense organization useful both in confronting NATO and in subduing rebellious communists as in Czechoslovakia in 1968. It is frequently described as understrength and riddled with problems, but this is a common description of armies in peacetime. It began to disintegrate in 1989/90.

43. **Workers' councils**   Mechanisms for worker management of industrial operations. They are economic democracy in action, organized on the principle that factories and enterprises belong to the workers who labor in them. The amount of power actually possessed by workers' councils varies from country to country and from time to time. In Yugoslavia, they have traditionally had the power to determine factory operations, set wages and profits, determine working conditions, and hire and fire the manager. Workers' councils, not surprisingly, perform best when workers are active and interested, and become hollow shells when the workers are inactive and uninterested. In the absence of effective unions, workers' councils are a high-priority goal. Even with effective unions, these councils are sometimes desired as a means of gaining more labor control of the workplace.

Bibliography

ABRAMSKY, CHIMEN, and HENRY COLLINS, *Karl Marx and the British Labour Movement: Years of the First International.* London: Macmillan, 1965.

ADAMIC, LOUIS, *Dynamite: The Story of Class Violence in America.* New York: Viking Press, 1931.

ANDERSON, EVELYN, *Hammer or Anvil: The Story of the German Working-Class Movement.* London: Victor Gollancz, 1945.

Angola, the Independence Agreement. Launda: Ministry of Mass Communication, 1975.

ARTHUR, PAMELA ANN, "The Ethiopian Revolution: A Revolution from Above and Its Outcomes," Ph.D. dissertation, Northwestern University, 1982. Available on microfilm from University Microfilms International, Ann Arbor, Michigan.

AVINERI, SHLOMO, *Varieties of Marxism.* The Hague: Martinus Nijhoff, 1977.

BAHRO, RUDOLF, *The Alternative in Eastern Europe.* Oxford, England: New Left Books, 1978.

BAILER, SEWERYN, ed., *Inside Gorbachev's Russia.* Boulder, Colo.: Westview Press, 1989.

BAILEY, GLEN, *An Analysis of the Ethiopian Revolution,* Papers in International Studies, Africa Series No. 40. Athens, Ohio: Ohio University Center for International Studies, Africa Program, 1980.

BARGHORN, FREDERICK, *Politics in the USSR.* Boston: Little, Brown, 1966.

BARNETT, A. DOAK, *China after Mao.* Princeton, N.J.: Princeton University Press, 1967.

BASS, R., and E. MARBURY, eds., *The Soviet Yugoslav Controversy, 1948–1958: A Documentary Record.* New York: Prospect Books, 1959.

BATEY, RICHARD, *Jesus and the Poor.* New York: Harper & Row, 1972.

BAYLIS, THOMAS A., *Governing by Committee.* Albany: State University of New York Press, 1989.

BEREND, IVAN T., and GYORGY RANKI, *Underdevelopment and Economic Growth: Studies in Hungarian Social and Economic History.* Budapest: Akademiai, 1979.

BERNSTEIN, EDUARD, *Evolutionary Socialism.* New York: Schocken Books, 1961.

BLACKWELL, WILLIAM, *The Industrialization of Russia—An Historical Perspective.* New York: Thomas Y. Crowell, 1970.

BOETTKE, PETER, *The Political Economy of Soviet Socialism: The Formative Years, 1918–1928.* Boston: Kluwer Academic Publishers, 1990.

BOOTH, JOHN, *The End and the Beginning, The Nicaraguan Revolution* (Boulder, Colo.: Westview Press, 1982.

BORKENAU, FRANZ, *European Communism.* New York: Harper & Bros., 1953.

BROWN, ARCHIE, and JACK GRAY, eds., *Political Culture and Political Change in Communist States.* New York: Holmes & Meier, Publishers, 1977.

BRUCE, ROBERT V., *1877: Year of Violence.* New York: New Bobbs Merrill Co., 1959.

BRZEZINSKI, ZBIGNIEW, *The Soviet Bloc.* Cambridge, Mass.: Harvard University Press, 1967.

BULL, HEDLEY, *The Control of the Arms Race.* New York: Praeger, 1961.

BURG, STEVEN, *Conflict and Cohesion in Socialist Yugoslavia.* Princeton, N.J.: Princeton University Press, 1983.

BYRNES, ROBERT, *After Brezhnev.* Bloomington: Indiana University Press, 1983.

CAMPBELL, ROBERT W., *Soviet Economic Power: Organization, Growth, and Challenge.* Cambridge, Mass.: Houghton Mifflin, 1960.

CARRILLO, SANTIAGO, *Eurocommunism and the State.* London: Lawrence & Weshart, 1977.

CARSTEN, F. L., *Revolution in Central Europe, 1918–1919.* Berkely: University of California Press, 1972.

CARVER, TERRELL, *Marx and Engels: The Intellectual Relationship.* Bloomington: Indiana University Press, 1983.

CAUTE, DAVID, *The Left in Europe Since 1789.* New York: McGraw-Hill, 1966.

CHEN, THEODORE, *The Chinese Communist Regime, Documents and Commentary.* New York: Praeger, 1967.

CHERNYSHEVSKY, N. G., *Selected Philosophical Essays.* Moscow: Foreign Languages Publishing House, 1953.

CLUBB, O. EDMUND, *Twentieth Century China.* New York: Columbia University Press, 1972.

COHEN, LENARD, and JANE SHAPIRO, *Communist Systems in Comparative Perspective,* Garden City, N.Y.: Doubleday Anchor, 1974.

COLE, G. D. H., *A History of Socialist Thought,* vols. 1–4. London: Macmillan, 1953–1960.

_____, *A Short History of the British Working-Class Movement 1789–1947.* London: George Allen & Unwin, 1947.

CONQUEST, ROBERT, *Stalin and the Kirov Murder.* New York: Oxford University Press, 1989.

_____, *The Harvest of Sorrow.* New York: Oxford University Press, 1986.

CORNFORD, FRANCIS M., trans., *The Republic of Plato.* London: Oxford University Press, 1945.

D'AGOSTINO, ANTHONY, *Soviet Succession Struggles.* Boston: Allen & Unwin, 1988.

DANIELS, ROBERT V., *A Documentary History of Communism,* vol. I, *Communism in Russia;* vol. II, *Communism and the world.* Hanover, N.H.: University Press of New England, 1984.

_____, *The Conscience of the Revolution.* New York: Simon & Schuster, 1969.

Davis, Jennifer, George Houser, Susan Rogers, and Herb Shore, *No One Can Stop the Rain.* New York: The Africa Fund, 1976.

DAWSON, PERCY M., *Soviet Samples: Diary of an American Physiologist.* Ann Arbor, Mich.: Edwards Bros., 1938.

DEBRAY, REGIS, *Revolution in the Revolution,* trans. Bobbye Ortiz. New York: Grove Press, 1967.

DEUTSCHER, ISAAC, *Stalin.* New York: Random House, 1949.

_____, *The Unfinished Revolution—Russia 1917–1967.* New York: Oxford University Press, 1967.

Documents Adopted by the International Conference of Communist and Workers' Parties, 5–17 June 1969. Moscow: Novosti Press Agency Publishing House, n.d.

DURANT, WILL, *Caesar and Christ,* vol. 2, *The Age of Faith, vol. 4,* and *The Reformation,* vol. 6 of *The Story of Civilization.* New York: Simon & Schuster, 1944–1957.

EAGLESON, JOHN, ed., *Christians and Socialism, Documentation of the Christians for Socialism Movement in Latin America,* trans. John Drury. Maryknoll, N.Y.: Orbis Books, 1975.

EASTON, LOYD, and KURT GUDDAT, eds., *Writings of Young Marx on Philosophy and Society.* Garden City, N.Y.: Doubleday Anchor, 1967.

ELLUL, JACQUES, *The Political Illusion,* trans. Konrad Kellen. New York: Random Vintage Edition, 1972.

ENGELS, FRIEDRICH, *Herr Eugene Dühring's Revolution in Science.* New York: International Publishers, 1939.

_____, *The Condition of the Working Class in England,* trans. W. O. Henderson and W. H. Chaloner. Stanford, Calif.: Stanford University Press, 1968.

_____, *The Housing Question*. New York: International Publishers, n.d.
ERLICH, HAGGAI, *The Struggle over Eritrea 1962–1978*. Stanford, Calif.: Hoover Institution Press, 1983.
FAIRBANK, JOHN K., *The United States and China*. Cambridge, Mass.: Harvard University Press, 1959.
FAIRBANK, JOHN KING, *The Great Chinese Revolution, 1800–1985*. New York: Harper & Row, 1986.
FARER, TOM, *War Clouds on the Horn of Africa: The Widening Storm*, 2nd ed. New York: Carnegie Endowment for International Peace, 1979.
FEUER, LEWIS S., *Marx and Engels: Basic Writings on Politics and Philosophy*. Garden City, N.Y.: Doubleday, 1959.
_____, *Marx and the Intellectuals*. New York: Anchor Books, 1969.
FEUERBACH, LUDWIG, *The Essence of Christianity*. New York: Harper & Row, 1957.
FISCHER, LOUIS, *The Life of Lenin*. New York: Harper & Row, 1964.
FLERON, FREDERIC, JR., *Technology and Communist Culture: The Socio-Cultural Impact of Technology under Socialism*. New York: Praeger, 1977.
FRANKLAND, MARK, *The Sixth Continent: Mikhail Gorbachev and the Soviet Union*. New York: Harper & Row, 1987.
FRANKLIN, BRUCE, *The Essential Stalin*. Garden City, N.Y.: Doubleday Anchor, 1972.
FRIED, ALBERT, and RONALD SANDERS, eds., *Socialist Thought: A Documentary History*. Garden City, N.J.: Doubleday, 1964.
FRIEDRICH, CARL, ed., *The Philosophy of Hegel*. New York: Random House, 1954.
GADDIS, JOHN L., *The United States and the Origins of the Cold War, 1941–1947*. New York: Columbia University Press, 1972.
GARAUDY, ROGER, *From Anathema to Dialogue: A Marxist Challenge to the Christian Churches*, trans. Luke O'Neill. New York: Herder & Herder, 1966.
GEOGHEGAN, VINCENT, *Utopianism & Marxism*. London: Methuen, 1987.
GERASSI, JOHN, *Venceremos: Speeches and Writings of Che Guevara*. New York: Simon & Schuster, 1968.
GJERSTAD, OLE, *The People in Power*. Richmond, B.C., Canada: Liberation Support Movement Information Center, 1977.
GOLAN, GALIA, *The Czechoslovak Reform Movement: Communism in Crisis, 1962–1968*. Cambridge, England: Cambridge University Press, 1971.
_____, *Reform Rule in Czechoslovakia: The Dubcek Era, 1968–1969*. Cambridge, England: Cambridge University Press, 1973.
GOLDMAN, MARSHALL, *USSR in Crisis*. New York: W. W. Norton & Co., 1983.
GORBACHEV, MIKHAIL, *Perestroika*. New York: Harper & Row, 1987.
_____, *Toward a Better World*. New York: Richardson & Steirman 1987.
GOREN, ROBERTA, *The Soviet Union and Terrorism*. London: George Allen & Unwin, 1984.
GUTIERREZ, GUSTAVO, *A Theology of Liberation: History, Politics, and Salvation*, trans. Sister Caridad Inda, ed. John Eagleson. Maryknoll, N.Y.: Orbis Books, 1973.
HALLIDAY, FRED, and MAXINE MOLYNEUX, *The Ethiopian Revolution*. London: Verso Editions and NLB, 1981.
HARE, PAUL, HUGO RADICE, and NIGEL SWAIN, eds., *Hungary: A Decade of Economic Reform*. London: George Allen & Unwin, 1981.
HARRINGTON, MICHAEL, *Socialism*. New York: Saturday Review Press, 1970.
_____, *The Vast Majority—A Journey to the World's Poor*. New York: Simon & Schuster, 1977.
HARSCH, ERNEST, and TONY THOMAS, *Angola, The Hidden History of Washington's War*. New York: Pathfinder Press, Inc., 1976.
HEDGES, CHRIS, Why Father Poncel Joined El Salvador's Guerrilla Movement," *Christian Science Monitor*, January 5, 1984, p. 9.
HELLER, MIKHAIL, and ALEKSANDR M. NEKRICH, *Utopia in Power: The History of the Soviet Union from 1917 to the Present*, trans. Phyllis B. Carlos. New York: Summit Books, 1986.
HENDEL, SAMUEL, ed., *The Soviet Crucible: the Soviet System in Theory and Practice*. Princeton, N.J.: Van Nostrand, 1963.
HENRY, MICHEL, *Marx: A Philosophy of Human Reality*, trans. Kathleen McLaughlin, Bloomington: Indiana University Press, 1983.
HEWETT, ED A., *Reforming the Soviet Economy*. Washington, D.C.: Brookings Institution, 1988.
HILL, CHRISTOPHER, *The World Turned Upside Down: Radical Ideas During the English Revolution*. New York: Viking Press, 1972.
HILL, RONALD J., and PETER FRANK, *The Soviet Communist Party*, 3rd ed. Boston: Allen & Unwin, 1986.

HIMMELFARB, GERTRUDE, *The Idea of Poverty: England in the Early Industrial Age.* New York: Alfred A. Knopf, 1984.

HINTON, HAROLD C., *Communist China in World Politics.* Boston: Houghton Mifflin, 1966.

HOBDAY, CHARLES, compiler, *Communist and Marxist Parties of the World.* Santa Barbara, Calif.: ABC-CLIO, 1986.

HOBSBAWM, ERIC J., *The History of Marxism, vol. 1: Marxism in Marx's Day.* Bloomington: Indiana University Press, 1982.

HODGKIN, THOMAS, *Vietnam: The Revolutionary Path.* New York: St. Martin's Press, 1981.

HODGKINSON, HARRY, *The Language of Communism.* New York: Pitman Publishers, 1954.

HOLLANDER, PAUL, *Political Pilgrims: Travels of Western Intellectuals to the Soviet Union, China, and Cuba, 1928–1978.* New York: Oxford University Press, 1981.

HOROWITZ, IRVING, *Cuban Communism,* 5th ed. New Brunswick, N.J.: Transaction, 1984.

————, ed., *The Anarchists.* New York: Dell, 1964.

HOUGH, JERRY and MERLE FAINSOD, *How the Soviet System is Governed.* Cambridge, Mass.: Harvard University Press, 1980.

HOWE, IRVING, *Leon Trotsky.* New York: Viking Press, 1978.

HSIUNG, JAMES CHIEH, *Ideology and Practice, The Evolution of Chinese Communism.* New York: Praeger, 1970.

HUXLEY, ALDOUS, *Collected Essays.* New York: Harper & Bros., 1959.

IONESCU, GHITA, *The Politics of East European Societies.* New York: Praeger, 1967.

JOHNSON, KAY ANN, *Women, the Family, and Peasant Revolution in China.* Chicago: University of Chicago Press, 1983.

KADAR, JANOS, *Socialist Reconstruction in Hungary.* Budapest: Corvina Press, 1962.

KARNOW, STANLEY, *Vietnam: A History.* New York: Viking Press, 1983.

KEE, ALISTAIR, *Constantine versus Christ: The Triumph of Ideology.* London: SCM Press, Ltd., 1982.

KENNAN, GEORGE F., "The Sources of Soviet Conduct," *Foreign Affairs,* 25 (July 1947): 566–582.

KIM IL SUNG, *On Juche in Our Revolution,* vol. 1. Pyongyang: Foreign Languages Publishing House, 1975.

KOVRIG, BENNETT, *Communism in Hungary: From Kun to Kadar.* Stanford, Calif.: Hoover Institution Press, 1979.

KUSIN, VLADIMIR V., *The Czechoslovak Reform Movement, 1968.* London: International Research Documents, 1973.

LAQUEUR, W., and T. LABEDZ, eds., *The Future of the Communist Society.* New York: Praeger, 1962.

LEGUM, COLIN, *Ethiopia, The Fall of Haile Selassie's Empire.* New York: Africana Publishing Co., 1975.

LENIN, VLADIMIR, *State and Revolution.* New York: Vanguard, 1929.

————, Collected Works, vols. 1–45. Moscow: Foreign Languages Publishing House, 1963–1970.

LENDVAI, PAUL, *Eagles in Cobwebs, Nationalism and Communism in the Balkans.* Garden City, N.Y.: Doubleday, 1969.

LERNER, MICHAEL P., *The New Socialist Revolution.* New York: Dell, 1973.

LETTIS, RICHARD, and WILLIAM MORRIS, *The Hungarian Revolt.* New York: Scribner's, 1961.

LEWIN, MOSHE, *The Gorbachev Phenomenon.* Berkeley: University of California Press, 1988.

LICHTHEIM, GEORGE, *The Origins of Socialism.* New York: Praeger, 1969.

————, *A Short History of Socialism.* New York: Praeger, 1970.

LITVAN, GYORGY, and JANOS M. BAK, eds, *Socialism and Social Science: Selected Writings of Ervin Szabo.* London: Routledge & Kegan Paul, 1982.

LIU, ALAN P. L., *Political Culture and Group Confict in Communist China.* Santa Barbara, Calif.: Clio Books, 1976.

————, *How China Is Ruled,* Englewood Cliffs, N.J.: Prentice-Hall, 1986.

LLERENA, MARIO, *The Unsuspected Revolution: The Birth and Rise of Castroism.* Ithaca, N.Y.: Cornell University Press, 1978.

MACHERRAS, COLIN, *Modern China: A Chronology from 1842 to the Present.* San Francisco: W. H. Freeman, 1982.

MACSHANE, DENIS, *Solidarity.* Nottingham, England: Spokesman, 1981.

MANCALL, MARK, *China At The Center.* New York: Macmillan, The Free Press, 1984.

MANDEL, ERNEST, and BRIAN PEARCE, *Marxist Economic Theory.* New York: Monthly Review Press, 1968.

MANUEL, FRANK, and FRITZIE MANUEL, *Utopian Thought in the Western World.* Cambridge, Mass.: Harvard University Press, 1979.

MAO ZEDONG, *Selected Works.* Beijing: Foreign Languages Press, 1967.

MARCUSE, HERBERT, *One Dimensional Man.* Boston: Beacon Press, 1964.
MARITAIN, JACQUES, *Integral Humanism: Temporal and Spiritual Problems of a New Chistendom*, trans. Joseph W. Evans. South Bend, Ind.: University of Notre Dame Press, 1973.
MARKAKIS, JOHN, and NEGA AYELE, *Class and Revolution in Ethiopia.* Nottingham, England: Spokesman, The Russell Press, Ltd., 1978.
MARX, KARL, *The Poverty of Philosophy.* Moscow: Foreign Languages Publishing House, n.d.
————, and FRIEDRICH ENGELS, *Selected Correspondence.* Moscow: Foreign Languages Publishing House, n.d.
————, *Selected Works*, vols. 1–3. Moscow: Progress Publishers, 1970.
MATTHEWS, HERBERT, *Fidel Castro.* New York: Simon & Schuster, 1970.
MCCARNEY, JOE, *The Real World of Ideology.* Sussex, England: Harvester Press, Ltd., 1980.
MCCORMACK, GAVAN, *"The Kampuchean Revolution 1975–1978: The Problem of Knowing the Truth," Journal of Contemporary Asia*, 10 (1980): 77ff.
MCLELLAN, DAVID, *Marx before Marxism.* New York: Harper & Row, 1970.
————, *Karl Marx, His Life and Thought.* New York: Harper & Row, 1973.
————, *Friedrich Engels.* New York: Viking Press, 1977.
————, *Marxism after Marx.* New York: Harper & Row, 1979.
————, trans., *The Grundrisee.* New York: Harper & Row, 1971.
MEDISH, FADIM, *The Soviet Union*, 3rd ed. Englewood Cliffs, N.J.: Prentice-Hall, Inc., 1987.
MEDVEDEV, ROY, *The October Revolution.* New York: Columbia University Press, 1979.
MEEK, RONALD L., ed., *Marx and Engels on the Population Bomb.* Berkeley, Calif.: Ramparts Press, 1971.
MEHARENNA, SELEMON, "The Ethiopian Way to Socialism, The Role of Politico-Institutional Factors in Modernizing the Ethiopian Political System." Excerpta ex dissertatione ad Doctoratum in Facultate Scientiarum Socialium, Pontificiae Universitatis Gregorianae, Roma, 1980.
MEISNER, MAURICE, *Mao's China.* New York: The Free Press, 1977.
MENDELSOHN, EZRA, *Class Struggle in the Pale: The Formative Years of the Jewish Workers' Movement in Tsarist Russia.* New York: Cambridge University Press, 1970.
MEYER, ALFRED G., *Leninsism.* New York: Praeger, 1962.
————, *Marxism: Unity of Thought and Practice.* Cambridge, Mass.: Harvard University Press, 1964.
————, *Communism* 4th ed. New York: Random House, 1984.
MIRANDA, JOSÉ PORFIRIO, *Marx and the Bible: A Critique of the Philosophy of Oppression*, trans. John Eagleson. Maryknoll, N.Y.: Orbis Books, 1974.
"National Convergence of Angola," pamphlet produced by the National Convergence of Angola, a political movement opposed to the government, 1984.
NELSON, HAROLD, and IRVING KAPLAN, eds., *Ethiopia: A Country Study.* (Washington, D.C.: U.S. Army, 1981.
NETTL, J. P., *The Soviet Achievement.* New York: Harcourt, Brace & World, 1967.
NETTL, PETER, *Rosa Luxemburg.* London: Oxford University Press, 1969.
NOVE, ALEC, *An Economic History of the U.S.S.R.* Harmondsworth, Middlesex, England: Penguin Books, 1969.
NWAFOR, AZINNA, *Revolution and Socialism in Ethiopia.* Rowsbury, Mass.: Omenana, 1981.
O'MALLEY, JOSEPH, ed., *Karl Marx—Critique of Hegel's Philosophy of Right* Cambridge, England: Cambridge University Press, 1970.
O'NEILL, WILLIAM, *A Better World—The Great Schism, Stalinism and the Intellectuals.* New York: Simon & Schuster, 1982.
OZINGA, JAMES R., "The Relevance of Marx and Lenin to the Soviet Transition to Communism," Ph.D. dissertation, Michigan State University, 1968, Alfred G. Meyer director. Available on microfilm from the University of Michigan collection at Ann Arbor.
————, *Communism: A Tarnished Promise.* Columbus, Ohio: Charles E. Merrill, 1975.
————, *The Prodigal Human.* Jefferson, N.C.: McFarland, 1985.
———— *The Rapacki Plan for the Denuclearization of Central Europe.* Jefferson, N.C.: McFarland & Co., 1989.
PADOVER, SAUL, ed., *Karl Marx Library on Revolution.* New York: McGraw-Hill, 1971.
————, and trans., *The Letters of Karl Marx.* Englewood Cliffs, N.J.: Prentice-Hall, Inc. 1979.
PAYNTON, CLIFFORD, and ROBERT BLACKEY, eds., *Why Revolution?* Cambridge, Mass.: Schenkman, 1971.
PERSKY, STAN, and HENRY FLAM, eds., *The Solidarity Sourcebook.* Vancouver: New Star Books, 1982.

PORTER, GARETH, eds., *Vietnam: The Definitive Documentation of Human Decisions*. Standfordville, N.Y.: Earl M. Coleman Enterprises, Inc., Publishers, 1979.

RAKOWSKA-HARMSTONE, TERESA, and ANDRE GYORKY, eds., *Communism in Eastern Europe*. Bloomington: Indiana University Press, 1981.

REIMAN, JEFFREY, *The Rich Get Richer and the Poor Get Prison*. New York: John Wiley & Sons, 1979.

REIQUAM, STEVE W., ed., *Solidarity and Poland*. Washington, D.C.: Wilson Center Press, 1988.

REUTHER, ROSEMARY RADFORD, *The Radical Kingdom: The Western Experience of Messianic Hope*. New York: Harper & Row, 1970.

————, *To Change the World: Christology and Cultural Criticism*. New York: Crossroad, 1981.

REVEL, JEAN-FRANÇOIS, *Without Marx or Jesus: The New American Revolution Has Begun*. New York: Dell, 1971.

ROTHSCHILD, JOSEPH, *Communist East Europe*. New York: Walker & Co., 1964.

RUBINSTEIN, ALVIN, *Soviet Foreign Policy Since World War II*. Cambridge, Mass.: Winthrop, 1981.

RUIZ, RAMON EDUARDO, *Cuba: The Making of Revolution*. Amherst: University of Massachusetts Press, 1968.

RUSINOW, DENNISON, *Yugoslavia, A Fractured Federalism*. Washington, D.C.: Wilson Center Press, 1988.

SABINE, GEORGE, *The Works of Gerrard Winstanley*. New York: Russell & Russell, 1965.

SCHAPIRO, LEONARD, *The Communist Party of the Soviet Union*. New York: Random House, Vintage Books, 1971.

————, *The Origin of the Communist Autocracy*. New York: Praeger, 1955.

————, *The USSR and the Future*. New York: Praeger, 1963.

SCHRAM, STUART, *The Political Thought of Mao Tse-Tung*. New York: Praeger, 1969.

SCHWARTZ, HARRY, *Prague's 200 Days*. New York: Praeger, 1969.

SHARLET, ROBERT, *The New Soviet Constitution of 1977*. Brunswick, Ohio: King's Court Communications, Inc., 1978.

SHUB, DAVID, *Lenin*. Baltimore: Penguin Books, 1966.

SIBLEY, MULFORD, *Political Ideas and Ideologies*. New York: Harper & Row, 1970.

SILBER, IRWIN, ed., *Voices of National Liberation*. New York: Central Book Co., 1970.

SINGER, DANIEL, *The Road to Gdansk, Poland and the USSR*. New York: Monthly Review Press, 1981.

SIVARD, RUTH LEGER, *World Military and Social Expenditures, 1983*. Washington D.C.: World Priorities, 1983.

SKILLING, H. GORDON, *Czechoslovakia's Interrupted Revolution*. Princeton, N.J.: Princeton University Press, 1976.

SLUSSER, ROBERT M., *Stalin in October*. Baltimore: Johns Hopkins University Press, 1987.

SMART, NINIAN, *Beyond Ideology: Religion and the Future of Western Civilization*. San Francisco: Harper & Row, 1981.

SOROKIN, PITIRIM, *The Sociology of Revolution*. New York: Howard Fertig, 1967.

SPAULDING, WALLACE, "Checklist of the 'National Liberation Movement,'" *Problems of Communism*, 31, no. 2 (March-April 1982): 77–82.

————, "International Communist Organizations," in *International Yearbook of Communist Activity, 1984*, ed. Richard Starr. Stanford, Calif.: Hoover Institution Press, 1984.

STACE, W. T., *The Philosophy of Hegel*. London: Dover Publications, 1955.

STANLEY, MANFRED, *The Technological Conscience: Survival and Dignity in an Age of Expertise*. New York: The Free Press, 1978.

STARR, RICHARD, *Communist Regimes in East Europe*, 4th ed. Stanford, Calif.: Hoover Institution Press, 1982.

STEELE, JONATHON, *World Power*. London: Michael Joseph, Ltd., 1983.

STOJANOVIC, SVETOZAR, *Between Ideals and Reality: A Critique of Socialism and Its Future*, trans. Gerson Sher. New York: Oxford University Press, 1973.

SUMNER, COLIN, *Reading Ideologies: An Investigation into the Marxist Theory of Ideology and Law*. London: Academic Press, 1979.

SZABO, ERVIN, "Marx," in *Socialism and Social Science: Selected Writings of Ervin Szabo, 1877–1918*, ed. Gyorgy Litvan and Janos Bak. London: Routledge & Kegan Paul, 1982.

TATU, MICHAEL, *Power in the Kremlin: From Khrushchev to Kosygin*. New York: Viking Press, 1970.

TAYLOR, CHARLES, *Hegel*. Cambridge, England: Cambridge University Press, 1975.

TAYLOR, JAY, *China and Southeast Asia*. New York: Praeger, 1976.

THOMAS, S. BERNARD, *Labor and the Chinese Revolution: Class Strategies and Contradictions of Chinese Communism 1928–1948*. Ann Arbor: Center for Chinese Studies, University of Michigan, 1983.

THOMPSON, E. P., *The Making of the English Working Class*. New York: Pantheon Books, 1964.

TOKES, RUDOLF, ed., *Eurocommunism and Détente*. New York: New York University Press, 1978.

TOMA, PETER, and IVAN VOLGYES, *Politics in Hungary*. San Francisco: W. W. Freeman & Co., 1977.

TOPORNIN, BORIS, *The New Constitution of the USSR*. Moscow: Progress Publishers, 1980.

TORRES, FATHER CAMILO, *Revolutionary Writings*. New York: Harper Colophon Books, 1972.

TOURAINE, ALAIN, FRANCOIS DUBET, MICHEL WIEVIORKA, and JAN STRZELECKI, *Solidarity*. Cambridge, England: Cambridge University Press, 1983.

TUCKER, ROBERT, *The Soviet Political Mind*. New York: W. W. Norton & Co., 1971.

_____, ed., *Stalinism*. New York: W. W. Norton & Co., 1977.

TURIN, S. P., *From Peter the Great to Lenin*. New York: Augustus M. Kelly Reprint, 1968.

UTECHIN, S. V., *Russian Political Thought*. New York: Praeger, 1964.

VALENTA, JIRI, *Soviet Intervention in Czechoslovakia, 1968*. Baltimore: Johns Hopkins Univeristy Press, 1979.

VALENTINOV, NIKOLAI, *The Early Years of Lenin*. Ann Arbor: University of Michigan Press, 1969.

VAN CANH, NGUYEN, *Vietnam under Communism 1975–1982*. Stanford, Calif.: Hoover Institution Press, 1983.

VENTURI, F., *Roots of Revolution*. London: Weidenfeld & Nicolson, 1960.

VOLGYES, IVAN, *Politics in Eastern Europe*. Chicago: Dorsey Press, 1986.

VON RAUCH, GEORG, *A History of Soviet Russia*. New York: Praeger, 1964.

WALLER, MICHAEL, *The Language of Communism*. London: The Bodley Head, 1972.

WANG, JAMES C. F., *Contemporary Chinese Politics*. 3rd ed. (Englewood Cliffs, N.J.: Prentice-Hall, Inc. 1989.

WECHSLER, LAWRENCE, *Solidarity: Poland in the Season of its Passion*. New York: Simon & Schuster Fireside Book, 1981.

WEI, YUNG, ed., *Communist China: A System-Functional Reader*. Columbus, Ohio: Charles E. Merrill, 1972.

WESSON, ROBERT, *Communism and Communist Systems*. Englewood Cliffs, N.J.: Prentice-Hall, Inc., 1978.

WESTOBY, ADAM, *The Evolution of Communism*. New York: The Free Press, 1989.

WHETTEN, LAWRENCE L., ed., *The Present State of Communist Internationalism*. Lexington, Mass.: D. C. Heath & Co., 1983.

WILDMAN, ALLAN K., *The Making of a Workers' Revolution*. Chicago: University of Chicago Press, 1967.

WILSON, EDMUND, *To the Finland Station*. Garden City, N.Y.: Doubleday, 1953.

WRIGHT, ERIK OLIN, *Class, Crisis and the State*. London: Verso, 1979.

WYDEN, PETER, *Bay of Pigs: The Untold Story*. New York: Simon & Schuster, 1979.

YERGIN, DANIEL, *Shattered Peace*. Boston: Houghton Mifflin, 1977.

ZAGORIA, DONALD, *The Sino-Soviet Conflict*. New York: Atheneum, 1973.

_____, ed., *National Communism and Popular Revolt in Eastern Europe: A Selection of Documents on Events in Poland and Hungary, February-November 1956*. New York: Columbia University Press, 1956.

ZINNER, PAUL, *Revolution in Hungary*. New York: Columbia University Press, 1962.

Index